Re-enchanting Humanity

Re-enchanting Humanity

A Defense of the Human Spirit
Against Antihumanism, Misanthropy,
Mysticism, and Primitivism

Murray Bookchin

CASSELL

Cassell
Wellington House
125 Strand
London WC2R 0BB

215 Park Avenue South
New York
NY 10003

First published 1995

A catalogue record for this book is available from the British Library

ISBN 0–304–32843–X (hardback)
      0–304–32839–1 (paperback)

Design and typesetting Ben Cracknell

Printed and bound in Great Britain by Biddles Limited,
Guildford and King's Lynn

Contents

For my dear friend of fifty years, David Eisen

A caveat to the reader

Today, when environmentalism is under assault by Republican reactionaries in the United States, Tory reactionaries in Britain, and apologists for corporate interests everywhere, I wish to reiterate my emphatic support for *all* environmentalist tendencies that seek to preserve biotic diversity, clean air and water, chemically untainted foods, and wilderness areas. Much of my life – some forty years as a writer, lecturer, and activist in various movements – has been and remains assiduously committed to these environmental goals. It would be gross demagoguery for antihumanists, misanthropes, and primivitists – who in my view are seriously damaging the environmental cause – to identify their own regressive ideas with ecology *as such* and to challenge any criticism of them as an endeavor to subvert the ecology movement.

I find it necessary to make this statement to the reader because some years ago, a leading light in the deep ecology tendency scandalously accused me in *The Progressive* of capitulating to reactionaries in the United States after I criticized *his* ecomystical views as deleterious to the environmental movement. Nor is he the only one who has done so over the years in one way or another.

I have encountered such cynical behavior only once before in my lifetime – during the 1930s, when devotees of Stalin's version of Communism designated all of their critics as 'fascists' and worse for daring to challenge their policies. Such behavior should be severely reproved as cynical and demagogic if environmentalists are not to surrender the moral integrity that they claim for themselves and their ideas. What is at stake in such rhetorical charges is whether dissenting views within the ecology movement (which should be encouraged if the movement is to advance) are even possible or whether criticisms that concern the welfare of that movement can be intelligently explored on their own terms.

Having expressed this concern, it would be foolhardy to ignore the tendency of antihumanism (particularly trends like sociobiology,

Malthusianism, and deep ecology) to feed into the politically charged social Darwinism that is very much abroad today. The animalization of humanity that I believe these trends foster, their regressive absorption of major social concerns into biology – be they expressed in terms of genetics, demographics, or biocentrism – is now being stridently echoed by reactionary legislators who use zoological reductionism as an ideological weapon for waging war on the poor, the underprivileged, and the helpless. Thus in debates in the US Congress on reducing welfare benefits to the needy, a legislator from Florida who opposes such aid is reported to have held up a sign that said 'Do Not Feed the Alligators' and noted, 'We post these warnings because unnatural [sic!] feeding and artificial [sic!] care creates dependency'. A legislator from Wyoming is reported to have drawn 'a similar parallel with wolves' (Robin Toner, Resolved: no more bleeding hearts, *New York Times*, 'Week in Review' section, July 16, 1995).

In my view, this kind of 'natural law' mentality, directed overwhelmingly against the poor and underprivileged who desperately need material assistance, can very easily be derived from ideologiews that reduce human attibutes to the interplay of genes, to a demographics based on the behaviour of fruit flies, and to a biocentrism that renders human beings interchangable with alligators and wolves in terms of their 'intrinsic worth'. How precariously close these variants of antihumanism are to the lethal social ideologies that swept through Europe and America in the 1920s and 1930s, I shall leave it to the informed reader to judge.

MURRAY BOOKCHIN
May 1995

Acknowledgments

I cannot sufficiently thank my companion and colleague, Janet Biehl, for her scrupulous reading and copyediting of this book, as well as for her advice at every point in its preparation and her assistance in researching material for certain chapters. Her own unfinished book on deep ecology was one of the major sources for material on which I relied in writing my chapter on ecomysticism. To my editor, Steve Cook of Cassell, I owe a genuine debt for encouraging me throughout the preparation of the manuscript and for his patience in delays that were caused by ill health. I would also like to thank Steven Best and Richard Wolin for reading and advising me on my chapter on postmodernism. Their own work in this area has been immensely stimulating and deserves the widest reading public.

For the rest, the views I express in the following pages are entirely my own, and I alone must claim responsibility for any defects the book may contain. These views have been in the making for years and reflect changing polemical emphases in my writings that have emerged over time.

Prologue

This book deals with one of the most troubling conditions that afflicts society at the present time: a sweeping failure of nerve. I am speaking of a deep-seated cultural malaise that reflects a waning belief in our species' creative abilities. In a very real sense, we seem to be afraid of ourselves – of our uniquely human attributes. We seem to be suffering from a decline in human self-confidence and in our ability to create ethically meaningful lives that enrich humanity and the non-human world.

This decline in human self-confidence, to be sure, is not new. The ancient Mediterranean world fell into a period of declining moral stamina and self-worth that contributed to the onset of the so-called 'Dark Ages' in Europe. Medieval Europe, particularly in the fourteenth century and after, was torn apart spiritually and materially by dislocations so formidable that, as François Villon, France's greatest poet, lamented, roaming wolves from the countryside 'ate wind' in the dangerous and famine-stricken streets of Paris.

Yet in both of these periods, a sense of hope still lingered on in the human spirit, a belief in the moral and social redemption of humanity. Leprous as the human condition seemed to men and women in those demoralizing times, they shared a belief that our species was capable of achieving a better moral and social dispensation. Early Christianity, as it emerged from the dying ancient world, proclaimed the ultimate power of human virtue to achieve an earthly paradise and affirmed the existence of a providential design to guide errant souls. The Protestant Reformation that took form as early as the fourteenth century advanced a new message of individuality, self-certainty, and, in its more radical forms, the aspiration toward a sharing communistic society free of hierarchy.

In contrast to these earlier times, our own era, as the third millennium comes into view, proclaims a very different spiritual and social message. Even as technological advances offer the possibility of unprecedented material security, free time, physical well-being, and a reharmonization of our relationships with the natural world, a growing number of writers and speakers tell us that our very ingenuity in technology is really evidence of a chilling failure – resulting from our 'innate hubris' – to integrate our lives with the natural world. Indeed, we are asked to regard our remarkable human abilities for thought and innovation as attributes destructive of our very selves as well as the natural world. We are being taught to mistrust our abilities as human beings, to constrain our 'preening arrogance', presumably because we have set ourselves up as a species against the rest of the world of life. Such writers often personify our various institutional and technological achievements as demonic extensions of our own anthropocentric impulses and indifference to other living beings. Amidst a farrago of essentially misanthropic proclamations, we are hard put to know whether our own achievements are our 'friends' or 'foes'.

Yet in a certain sense some forces are demonic indeed – particularly giant corporations and nation-states. These very forces act oppressively upon own lives, effacing our faith in freedom and community by their commanding influence and complexity. The more intimate social life that existed in villages, towns, and neighborhoods only a century ago has yielded to an overpowering institutional gigantism that determines all aspects of our lives, from the ordinary affairs of everyday life to great social upheavals on a worldwide scale.

Hence it is not surprising that social life appears to unfold like an inexplicable mystery, beyond our ordinary understanding and control. Whether we see ourselves as villains or victims, we feel ourselves sinking into a morass of commanding social forces, ideological as well as institutional, that define our behavior and drain our very ability for self-determination in personal and public affairs. Helplessly at the disposal of vast socio-economic cross-currents, we are manipulated by a Kafkaesque world too cryptic to fathom. Our domestic politics are becoming too national in scope to allow for local forms of intervention, even as our international politics are becoming too worldwide in scope to be comprehended amidst the rhetoric of 'global markets' and 'global dependencies'.

Our lives include even more grim realities, such as the proliferation of nuclear weapons and materials, the socially induced famines that plague the so-called 'Third World', the almost unimpeded destruction of aboriginal cultures and the biosphere, the spread of tyranny over much of the planet even as world leaders smugly extol new advances in personal and social freedom. The list of contemporary malfeasances at every level of life could be extended endlessly, from the implosion of the inner cities to the destruction of the ozone layer. Hence the loss of self-certainty that marked popular attitudes only two generations ago and the susceptibility of the public to an inwardly oriented – often misanthropic – spiritualism and a privatistic withdrawal from public life into mystical or quasi-mystical belief systems.

It is precisely these belief systems that this book seeks to examine and sharply criticize. I am acutely aware that many apparently similar books have already appeared, deriding the innovative ideas generated by the radical 1960s and calling for a conservative cultural retrenchment to traditional family values, religious beliefs, conventional virtues, and right-wing political ideologies. We have more books these days on 'virtues' – cultural and social – than we know what to do with. As a lifelong social radical, I have no intention of adding to the regressive litany of woes presumably caused by radical lifestyles and values, or calling for the revival of established traditions, many of them repellent. In the 'cultural wars' that American conservatives have proclaimed in recent years, I stand basically with their opponents: women seeking full equality in a largely patricentric society; the underprivileged and victims of racial discrimination; environmentalists who are seeking to rescue our life-sustaining planet from corporate depredation; and the diminishing number of radical people who are seeking to create a rational society.

It is largely because of my commitment to these people and causes, in fact, that I have written this book. I am deeply disturbed by the conservative literature that invokes a 'traditional', usually hierarchical, hidebound past. But paradoxical as it may seem, I am also deeply disturbed by its pseudo-radical complement: the so-called 'new paradigm' or generically 'New Age' literature that 'disenchants' us with our humanity, indeed, that summons us to regard ourselves as an ugly, destructive excrescence of natural evolution – whether as a species, a gender, an ethnic group, or a nationality.

Like its conservative and traditionalist counterpart, the New Age mentality that demonizes human beings in whole or in part is not necessarily unified or coherent. Unlike many conservative traditionalists, New Age mystics celebrate the contradictions of their 'paradigm', its languid intellectual irresponsibility, and its seeming pluralism. More than one proponent of the view that humanity is a delinquent species in an otherwise amiable biosphere or 'circle of beings', as the Reverend Thomas Berry puts it, will sharply disclaim my characterization of their views.

Yet one does not have to look too far beneath the surface to find a common underlying theme that unites the highly particularistic, theistic, biocentric, postmodernist, misanthropic, and generically mystical literature. What I believe brings them together – and many of them express their views in the same journals and anthologies – is a common depreca-tion of the remarkable features that make our species unique in the bio-sphere. Whether explicitly or implicitly, they deride humanity's ability for innovation, its technological prowess, its potentiality for progress, and, above all, its capacity for rationality. I have thus found it appropriate to call this ensemble of deprecatory attitudes *antihumanism*.

Antihumanism – in sharp contrast to the humanistic ideologies advanced by rationalism, various socialisms, and some forms of liberalism – is a world view that places little or no emphasis on social concerns. The message it offers is primarily one of spiritual hygiene, personal with-drawal, and a general disdain for humanistic attributes such as reason and innovation in impacting upon the natural and social worlds. It offers no serious challenge to modern secular power. Rather, it tilts, when it does not tumble headlong, toward self-oriented nostrums – and disturbingly regressive ones at that. Antihumanists commonly extol an intuitionism supported by the mythopoeic mentality of the distant, preliterate past of our species. In varying degrees, they demean civilization, progress, and science, denying either their reality or their value as goals worthy of respect.

Above all, antihumanists deprecate or deny humanity's most distinc-tive hallmark – reason, and its extraordinary powers to grasp, intervene into, and play a guiding role in altering social and natural reality. Many antihumanists harbor a static mindset, partly the result of their reverence for a mythologized 'Nature' – sometimes seen as a realm of cyclical 'eter-nal recurrences' – in which they strive to passively *dwell* rather than actively *live* as innovative beings; and partly, too, the result of their entombment in a pantheistic 'cosmic womb', a 'night in which all cows are black' (to use a favorite aphorism of Hegel's), imbued with an out-look that dilutes active selfhood and social involvement. So wide-ranging and multifarious, in fact, are the antirational moods in contemporary Western culture that they often defy clear characterization apart from their shared antipathy for reason and the mostly intuitive nostrums with which they propose to replace it.

In exploring these moods, the reader will often be obliged to deal with criss-crossing ideas that are poorly formulated or directly expressed. Indeed, some antihumanists do not hesitate to invoke science, a *bête noire* to the more naive antihumanists, in support of their views. Nor will the reader encounter many spokespeople who synthesize coherence in their antihumanism. Elusiveness, prettified as pluralism and diversity, has become a well-cultivated art in the world we shall be entering.

Invoking the simplest rational canons of logical discourse is fruitless in a realm that regards reason *as such* as a form of tyranny or 'logocentricity'.

Not infrequently, antihumanist moods are viscerally predisposed not toward discovering truth but toward gaining ritualistic and non-rational 'insights'. Apart from the extravagant use of words like *oneness, interconnectedness, cosmic,* and *ecological,* the antihumanist vocabulary is almost willfully vague. Quite often, in a dazzling display of eclectic pluralism – a euphemism for contradiction – almost anything goes, without any regard for consistency or clarity.

I find it particularly ironic that at a time when so many of these antihumanistic books and articles exalt the need to 're-enchant Nature', the 'Planet', indeed the entire 'Cosmos', the most pronounced effect they have had is to 'disenchant' humanity itself: specifically, its unique potentiality for rationality.

Which raises a central concern of this book: the assault antihumanism has mounted against the rational faculties that make us human. For it is not specific traits of individual human beings that antihumanists attack but the general and unique attributes that *define* human beings as a species. In the end, it is our claim to be able to reason and to rationally intervene in the world around us that is under siege. The special features that make us remarkable products of natural evolution are in one way or another viewed with acute suspicion or forcefully maligned.

To unravel the ensemble of convoluted, contradictory notions that can be characterized as antihumanist, with their tangled roots in a highly intuitive psychology, is the task of this book. Each form of antihumanism, be it cultural primitivism, mystical ecologism, or a variety of postmodernism, must be examined on its own terms. Suffice it to say here that far too many antihumanists see the malaise that afflicts modern society as rooted not in irrationality, be it in the spiritual or material sphere of life, but in precisely the opposite: in rationality and a humanistic 'anthropocentrism'. Beyond this basic premise, antihumanism strays in every conceivable direction such that it defies clear categorization and logical coherence. Normally this *modus operandi* would be regarded as an intellectual failing, but antihumanism cherishes it as evidence of flexibility.

One word in particular needs explication if this book is to be properly understood. Inasmuch as I argue for a secular and naturalistic view of the world, I feel obliged to justify my use of the word 're-enchanting' in the title of this book. This word, after all, suggests a mystical bewitchment consistent with views held by many antihumanists, not humanists. My reasons for employing the word are simple: I am using it partly as a spoof, and partly as a metaphorical expression of my respect for what the human species could be and what it could achieve if it applied its intellectual faculties to the creation of a rational society.

I do not mean 'rational' here in a purified, abstract, merely philosophical sense, but rather in the sense of a lived rationality that, at its best, fosters cooperation, empathy, a sense of responsibility for the biosphere, and new ideas of community and consociation. A society guided by this existential form of reason must replace the present predatory society that I am convinced threatens the survival of human and most non-human life. It is this socially critical vision that I hope to commend to the reader, a vision I have held in more than six decades of struggle against oppression, domination, hierarchy, class rule, and the debasement of life to a mere resource for personal enrichment and greed.

For this book advocates no compromise with the *status quo* and the mentality it fosters. I am as much opposed to a humanism structured around self-aggrandizement and plunder as I am to an antihumanism structured around humanity's self-effacement in a mystical all-embracing 'cosmos'.[1] While human beings differ fundamentally from other life-forms in their ability to bring meaning and reason to the world, *precisely* because of these remarkable abilities they are ethically obliged to develop a firm sense of responsibility to non-human beings and the planet as a whole.

Indeed, this book advances a view that is based on neither a Pollyanna *philanthropos* nor a repellent *misanthropos,* but on a transcendence of both of these one-sided views. There is, I submit, an outlook that goes beyond the dichotomy of an angelic and demonic humanity to a sublation that gives due emphasis to humanity's affinities with non-human life on the one hand and to the satisfaction of its own special requirements on the other.

The current literature all too often offers readers either one extreme or another – either the biocentric or the anthropocentric – rather than a wide spectrum of views that allows for a sense of social and ecological responsibility. It is the one-sided, mutually exclusive dogmas exemplified by these two 'centricities' that I emphatically wish to transcend. Tragically, more and more people today agree with one or the other of the extreme, nonsensical notions: that human beings are inherently deleterious to almost everything around them, *or* that everything around us was 'created' exclusively for human use. I would hope that these pages provide a better map to negotiate the conflicting centricities in the modern cultural landscape.

More specifically, the void created by these extremes must be filled by a *new humanism* based on an 'ethics of complementarity', as I called it in my 1982 book *The Ecology of Freedom.*[2] There are many reasons for frustration and anger about the human condition, but there are none, I submit, for demeaning humanity, let alone for viewing its unique rational abilities as demonic. Indeed, there are good reasons to cherish our species for the splendors it has achieved, often against incredible odds, and that it certainly *can* achieve if reason in all its fullness can be brought into the world – most particularly, into the management of social and ecological affairs.

February 1995

Notes

1 Whatever its chronology, the use of 'humanism' to mean a crude anthropocentric and technocratic use of the planet in strictly human interests (often socially unspecified) has its contemporary origins in Martin Heidegger's *Brief uber den Humanismus* (Letter on Humanism), written in 1947, which gained favor among the postwar French *philosophes* of the existentialist and later postmodernist vintage.

Heidegger's very flawed and sinister *Brief* is a masterpiece of misinterpretation and irresponsible reasoning. The humanist–antihumanist dichotomy has its historical roots primarily in the postwar cynicism and nihilism of the 1950s and 1960s.

2 Murray Bookchin, *The Ecology of Freedom* (Palo Alto, CA: Cheshire Books, 1982; republished, with new introduction, by Montreal: Black Rose Books, 1991).

CHAPTER 1

Becoming human

Until recently, the belief that the human species is qualitatively different from non-human life-forms has been one of the most abiding notions of nearly all sophisticated civilizations.

The nature of this difference, to be sure, was defined in a great variety of ways. Human beings generally assigned to themselves the possession of souls, moral sensibilities, immense technical powers, and remarkable mental faculties. These traits were often melded into various combinations and ascribed to some social strata by others to distinguish various strata from one another and from the proverbial beasts in the field. Even tribal peoples, who professed to see similarities between themselves and the animals around them, indirectly gave a commanding identity to their own kind by attributing human speech, motives, and interests to animals in the anthropomorphized universe of their mythology.

Western civilization in particular singled out reason as the faculty that, more than any other, gave humanity a unique status among all other forms of life. The West saw reason as the generative source not only of logic, discourse, and reflection but also of moral awareness and empathy. The ancient Greeks gave to thought an eminence so great that it acquired almost heroic proportions, both in the classical era of Athenian philosophy and as a major legacy in the ages that followed. Socrates, designated by the Delphic oracle as the 'wisest man in Greece', became the prototypical symbol of human genius, and Western civilization saw the jurors who sent him to his death for his intellectual independence as the collective embodiment of intolerance and ignorance, men who defiled the noblest traditions of Hellenic civilization.

Even theology, Eastern as well as Western, despite its emphasis on the validity of faith over reason, commonly used reason to justify faith to its followers. Augustine's *The City of God,* Christianity's ideological bridge from the ancient to the medieval world, remains to this day a closely reasoned masterpiece of dialectic, its authority partly supplanted centuries later by the scrupulously analytical *Summa Theologica* of Thomas Aquinas.

The notion that the Middle Ages was entirely an age of faith that elbowed reason and philosophy to the sidelines of culture is a myth, invented chiefly by later rationalists to free themselves from clerical authority. The biblical crossroads between man and the gods intersects precisely at the point where Adam eats of the tree of moral knowledge, to be expelled with Eve into 'the east of Eden' by an anxious Yahweh who warns his fellow deities (or angels) that man 'has become like one of Us' – in fact, that he will become a deity – if he eats from the tree of life and becomes immortal (Genesis 4:22–24).

By the eighteenth century, reason had not only been elevated to the status of a defining human trait; it was seen as the arbiter *par excellence* for critically evaluating human social progress and moral development. Indeed, by virtue of its speculative capacities, reason had the all-important power to critically search *beyond* the past and present, to transcend the given state of affairs, and to stake out the contours of a progressive future literally defined as a rational society. Turgot, Diderot, and Holbach, among the great Enlighteners of the eighteenth century, conjoined reason with freedom in an intellectual partnership that prepared the ideological climate for the French Revolution and the emergence of modern socialism. Reason would illuminate the path to liberty, they believed, by destroying the fetters of superstition and domination. Diderot, for his part, gave to reason a suppleness and a nuanced sensibility equaled only by the greatest dialogues of Plato. A generation after Diderot, Hegel equipped reason with a system of logic that emphasized the creative dynamics of development over the arid statics of formal Aristotelian analytics.

The Enlightenment, as the rational and humanistic movement in eighteenth-century Western Europe came to be called, was appropriately named for its all-embracing rationalism. To the thinkers of the time, the world *itself* was inherently rational. Newton had shown that its physical aspects were marked by order and intelligibility; Montesquieu broadened this outlook to society and its history; Voltaire challenged the authenticity of supernatural agents; and German idealists from Kant to Hegel incarnated man from an Edenic malefactor into a creative subject who had the power to know himself and his own destiny. This sweeping vision of 'man the knower', as *Homo sapiens* (a name that dates from 1802), helped to reinforce the emerging natural sciences in their struggle against theological restrictions, fostered a belief in social progress, and nourished the technological innovations of the Industrial Revolution, whose limits, if it had any, have since bounded beyond the reach of prediction.

Classical humanism, as the humanism of the Renaissance was called, was born in the fifteenth century. Embodied in men like Erasmus and

Leonardo da Vinci, it tried to orient European sensibilities toward the intellectual achievements of the ancient world, particularly Greek culture, and its naturalistic aesthetics, in sharp opposition to the dogmatism and artistic rigidities of medievalism. But its outlook was basically retrospective. By contrast, Enlightenment humanism was born in the intellectual and scientific ferment of the eighteenth century. It was oriented not toward a pagan past but toward a rational future. It was to be embodied not only in the Encyclopedists but in the theorists of various nineteenth-century socialisms, with their shared principles of futurity and hope.

By the middle of the nineteenth century, both forms of humanism – the Renaissance and the Enlightenment – melded into what I shall call an 'enlightened humanism' that united Renaissance aestheticism with Enlightenment rationalism, an outlook that pervaded the thinking of most socialists. The formidable prestige of enlightened humanism remained triumphant for a century, despite the assaults that were directed against it by mystics, romantics, and nationalists, all of whose ideas converged in the proto-fascistic *völkisch* movement of the *fin de siècle*. In the postwar era it is due in no small part to Martin Heidegger's anti-Enlightenment and anti-rational tract, 'A Letter on Humanism' (1947), that the word 'humanism' has acquired its present-day pejorative meaning as an amoral, narrowly anthropocentric and ugly technocratic outlook.

My expanded interpretation of humanism is not free of paradoxes – indeed, of paradoxes within paradoxes. Rousseau, to cite a striking example, who was no less a rationalist than the mathematician D'Alembert, nonetheless placed an emphasis on *sensibilité* so maudlin that he may be broadly called the 'father' of much of the anti-rationalistic romanticism of the nineteenth century. Voltaire was no less a progressivist than Turgot, yet the pessimism of his novella *Candide* fed into the misanthropic attitudes of later generations. Adam Smith, still another case, absorbed the altruistic moral philosophies of Shaftesbury and Hutchinson as a young man, yet he became the voice of 'enlightened self-interest' and the amoralism of the emerging industrial bourgeoisie. All of these paradoxes came to a head in the French Revolution, whose universalistic declarations heralded the unity and fraternity of humanity, only to plummet into a strident nationalism and Napoleonic imperialism.

Within these major paradoxes lurked seemingly minor ones that emerged full-blown in the nineteenth and twentieth centuries: technological advances were rational, yet they brought terrible misery to the working classes of the Industrial Revolution. The national rights of peoples were regarded as rational, yet asserting them brought a host of parochial cultural and ethnic hatreds. The growth of cities, commerce, manufacturing, and self-interest was rational, yet they despoiled the land, wrought havoc on the natural landscape, and destroyed the very aboriginal cultures that the enlighteners in their own writings had celebrated for their 'natural virtues'.

Even as these paradoxes increased in number and intensity, fostering a sentimental and moral counterweight to the overriding ideal of value-free scientific objectivity, the arguments between the rational enlightened humanists and their anti-rational romantic critics (who may be loosely called the antihumanists of their day) were eminently ideological in the strictest meaning of the word. Ideas were pitted against ideas, however passionate the poetry of the romantics and cold the prose of the rationalists. Even as reason was denounced by romantics as 'meddlesome' or hypostatized by rationalists as 'sovereign', it was in fact reason that informed both parties to the debate. Apart from sheer rhetoric, few were prepared to challenge the validity of rationality on its own terms or to deny its powers of clarification and conviction.

In fact, the paradoxical fact that rationality was an approach shared by enlightened rationalists and romantic anti-rationalists alike became all the more marked in the late nineteenth century.[1] Both fervently parochial racists like the Comte de Gobineau and universalistic social visionaries like Karl Marx cast their views in scientific or at least rational terms, as did heated romantic nationalists like Garibaldi and sober revolutionary internationalists like Eugène Varlin. The great Western tradition of reason, indeed, of an expansive humanism that included the natural sciences, not only served as the arbiter of truth but constituted the formative core of human self-definition. Enlightened humanism retained its influence even when it was under assault by its opponents. For upon whatever grounds anti-rationalists and rationalists differed in specifics, they usually shared an implicit common concern for humanity.

In any case, the influence which the romantic anti-rationalists exercised was largely confined to an intellectual and aesthetic elite. On society as a whole, it had a very limited influence. Conventional nationalism and religion had a much stronger impact on the social attitudes and emotions of nineteenth- and early-twentieth-century Europeans, albeit generally as viscerally existential phenomena with no discursive appeal to 'man the knower'. Creditably, the most significant and intellectually demanding popular movement of the nineteenth and early twentieth centuries was formed around ideas attributed to Karl Marx, which appealed not only to the proletariat's material interests but, with varying degrees of success, to its mind and its presumed internationalism. Apart from the intellectuals who debated, often in aesthetic realms, the virtues and failings of reason, the heritage of enlightened humanism acquired a mass outreach in Marxian socialism and, to a considerable degree, in classical anarchism.

The ideological situation we face, today, is significantly different. The current crop of antihumanists are coarser, intellectually shoddier, and, alas, far more influential than the romantic anti-Enlightenment writers and poets of a century ago.

Worse, contemporary antihumanism tends to be more blurred than its predecessor in its approach to the grave concerns that face humanity and those that lie on the social horizon. If most of our ills – ecological as well as social – arise from increasingly dangerous dislocations in the existing society, the problem of how we deal with each other and with the powerful technological means that society has at its disposal for reshaping the planet is a matter of paramount importance. To slight these eminently social problems, to play down the importance of reason in resolving them, indeed, to ignore the need to achieve what socialism in all its forms called a *rational* society, is in my view suicidal. Owing to the immensity of our social and ecological problems, the turn to an irrational antihumanism serves to paralyze our capacity to act with purpose and sanity.

Indeed, at a time when the world seems to be descending into cultural and ecological chaos, to deprecate the very means for creating a rational society – notably, an enlightened humanism – should be cause for great alarm. This is especially so when antihumanism is on the point of becoming the conventional wisdom of our time. It surfaces today in ordinary table conversation as a chic state of mind from the households of American suburbia to the regal domiciles of England. Not much of this 'conversation', to use the language of postmodernism, is entirely intelligible; nor is it notable for its consistency. It is rare these days to come upon any single work that is reasonably coherent and free of juvenile exhortations and unthinking waywardness, or that tries to follow out with relative completeness the logic of its premises.

In this ideological quagmire, several antihumanist works can be singled out that typify those which fill libraries and bookstores today. Perhaps the most characteristic work that lends itself to coherent analysis – which is not to say that it is free of contradictions – is David Ehrenfeld's *The Arrogance of Humanism*.[2] Written by an academic at Rutgers University who holds numerous degrees in history and science, Ehrenfeld's book is possessed of a literacy and pithiness that are unusual in current antihumanistic literature, much of which is drenched in New Age metaphors and heady exhortations. 'When one chooses a guiding philosophy of life', Ehrenfeld sternly warns his readers, 'and the modern world has chosen humanism – one becomes responsible for *all* the consequences that flow from that choice'.[3] This demand that we follow the logic of a choice to its end is entirely laudable.

What, then, *is* the humanism of which Ehrenfeld is so suspicious? His definition is unerring in its certitude and disturbing in its implications. Humanism, we are told, is

> *a supreme faith in human reason – its ability to confront and solve the many problems that humans face, its ability to rearrange both the world of Nature and the affairs of men and women so that human life will prosper. Accordingly, as humanism is committed to an unquestioning faith in the power of reason, so it rejects other assertions of power, including the power of God, the power of supernatural forces, and even the undirected power of Nature in league with blind chance.*

In the humanist outlook, notes Ehrenfeld reprovingly, neither the 'power of God' nor the 'power of supernatural forces' exist, while the 'undirected power of Nature' can 'with effort be mastered. Because human intelligence is the key to human success, the main tasks of humanists is to assert its power and to protect its prerogatives'.[4]

Ehrenfeld's definition of humanism may be less than satisfactory, particularly when he casts adherence to humanism in theistic terms, like 'supreme faith' and 'unquestioning faith'. But inverting Ehrenfeld's definition of humanism supplies us with a pithy definition of *anti*humanism: notably, a faith in the powers of God, of supernatural forces, and of 'Nature'. Precisely what these cryptic powers and their sources *are* remains disturbingly unclear. Even more disturbing are the archaisms contained in both these definitions. Ehrenfeld seems to believe in the very powers of God and powers of the supernatural that it took enlightened minds centuries, if not millennia, to exorcise, together with necromancy, superstition, and religious fanaticism, a struggle literally waged in the torture chambers of the Church and State.

By no means is Ehrenfeld alone in criticizing enlightened humanism for its 'degoddedness' or *Entgöttering* in viewing reality. We also have it from E. F. Schumacher in his *Guide for the Perplexed* that

> *faith in modern man's omnipotence is wearing thin. Even if all the 'new' problems were solved by technological fixes, the state of futility, disorder, and corruption would remain. ... More and more people are beginning to realize that 'the modern experiment' has failed. ... Man closed the gates of Heaven against himself and tried, with immense energy and*

> *ingenuity, to confine himself to the Earth. He is now discovering that the Earth is but a transitory state, so that a refusal to reach for Heaven means an involuntary descent into Hell.*[5]

Clearly, 'faith in modern man's omnipotence' is a pejorative interpretation of the humanistic commitment to rationality. Perhaps even more explicitly than Ehrenfeld, Schumacher, the guru of 'small is beautiful' (the title of his most influential book), tilts toward the transcendental, if not the ecclesiastical. Still other antihumanist authors, such as William Irwin Thompson, Thomas Berry, and Matthew Fox, would likely have few disagreements with Ehrenfeld's and Schumacher's antihumanism.

These seemingly reflective judgments by presumably sophisticated antihumanists are often the stuff from which the crassest of vulgarities are written for consumption by the New Agers of California and, in recent years, nearly all other points of the compass. Neither Stonehenge nor the romantic cliffs of the Rhine can be excluded as a center for those 'Higher Levels', as Schumacher calls them, 'that alone can maintain [man's] humanity'.[6] Cruder forms of this extremely loose verbiage can be found snugly ensconced not only in esoteric periodicals that proclaim 'Nature' as 'the gates of Heaven' but in the Anglo-American mass media.

Consider the characteristic opening of a recent cover article in *Time*, the American mass-circulation weekly. 'How Man Began', professing to tell its readers about 'sensational' developments in human evolutionary anthropology, declares: 'No single, essential difference separates human beings from other animals – but that hasn't stopped the phrasemakers from trying to find one'.[7] Whereupon the article proceeds, presumably under a tyranny of archaeological facts, to tell us, quite inadvertently, that the differences between humans and other animals are not only essential but really quite staggering. Filtered down to ever lower layers of literacy, the article's sensationalistic opening – the facts notwithstanding – produces a vision of the human condition that is ultimately opaque, mysterious, and necromantic to millions of ordinary readers.

In contrast to nineteenth-century debates between romantic antihumanists and the enlightened humanists, rationality rarely, if ever, enters into current antihumanist affirmations. Statements that are not simply declarative are filled with theistic metaphors that seem bent on making the skeptical reader feel like a heretic who violates God-given (or Goddess-given) injunctions. Intonations replace insights, dull repetitious mantras replace the evocative poetic recitations of the old-time romantics, and reason gives way not only to intuition but to vague allusions to cryptic 'powers' that allow for no explication, much less analysis.

No less irritating is the fact that this stuff not only blurs the boundaries between the human and non-human; it obliterates the very identity of human beings in the great drama of biological evolution and their self-consciousness in the equally important drama of social evolution. Whatever the 'gates of Heaven' may be, we have no way of knowing where they are located, still less how to open them. The spiritual geography of these freely drawn and inspirationally guided maps, so currently popular in Anglo-American bookshops, constitute a cartography guided by the viscera rather than by the brain, and by visions that are more hallucinogenic than insightful. Antihumanism provides no compass for *this* world, yet it has no other world to offer, short of an imaginative one that differs in considerable detail with each guru, periodical, or book consulted.

In the light of the public confusion about the human condition, particularly with respect to humanity's identity, it behooves us to ask ourselves *who* we really are as a species and *what* would constitute a society that fulfills our potentiality as rational and creative agents in the world. Let me stress the word *potentiality*, a word I use to emphasize what we *could* be if we brought reason into our affairs rather than what we *are* today in a mad and meaningless world.

Our being as a species is closely related to our being as social creatures. To discuss them requires asking what constitutes our place in what is broadly called 'Nature' and what constitutes a rational society. Certainly, if we stumble blindly into the future with no sense of the characteristics that make us uniquely human, antihumanists would have a prima facie case for designating people a 'cancer' in natural evolution, with little promise of doing more than destroying the biosphere and most of themselves.

In trying to define our humanity as organic beings, we will not get very far unless we define words that are usually used very loosely in reference to our status in the biosphere. I refer especially to the word *Nature*, one of those very complex words that is used glibly and whose meaning becomes more elusive the more we examine it.

No one doubts that 'Nature' is, minimally, a wilderness area that one can see from a mountain top, a scenic view of valleys, fields, forests, and streams, indeed, of all that lies so magnificently and invitingly within our purview. Nature, to many people, is simply a vista free of human beings and hence 'authentically' natural. Such vistas adorn picture postcards, particularly in the Far West of the USA, and the canvases of 'nature painters'.

On the surface, this definition is partly true – and also partly false. That Nature is a vista bereft of human presence is a convention deeply ingrained in the modern mind, especially in North America, where

Nature and *wilderness* are widely regarded as synonymous. More important, the notion that Nature has eternal attributes as wilderness is so commonplace that it has become a frozen image in innumerable artistic, literary, and documentary works and a staple in a pseudo-philosophical New Age literature that extols the need to 'dwell in' and 'abide with' an unchanging, eternal 'balance of Nature'.

Yet this frozen image of Nature is extremely deceptive. The *fixity* of a breathtaking vista simply does not exist. Nature is not only dynamic at every moment of the day but, above all, is highly developmental. Plants and animals are generally not only active in maintaining themselves but are interactive in creating new eco-communities.[8] Life-forms are continually being born, maturing, and dying, entering into elaborate food webs or networks that make possible the vistas we admire.

Most important for the purposes of our discussion, what we call Nature is continually *evolving:* plants and animals vary within the same species and mutate into new life-forms. They are continually transforming themselves, at times so gradually that their evolution is completely unnoticeable; at still other times with great rapidity, in what some biologists call 'punctuated equilibria'.

What makes our notion of Nature as a mere vista particularly misleading is that it ignores *humanity's* place in the natural world. That is to say, it obscures the fact that human beings are not aliens in a dichotomy of Man pitted against Nature. Rather, human beings are a result of the long evolutionary history of the natural world.

In fact, they are a very special result of that history. They are possessed of abilities no other life-form has equaled in kind. Indeed, if Nature is a cumulative evolutionary process – in the case of organic evolution, from the earliest prokaryotic cells through eukaryotic cells and their elaboration into the aquatic, terrestrial, reptilian, mammalian, and primate groups – the word Nature becomes more than a metaphor for mere 'Being', an abstract existence.

The challenge of thinking about Nature as a cumulative evolution arises from the duality of the evolutionary process itself. On the one hand, human beings have qualities that can be found in nascent form in other animals as a result of their shared evolution. But by virtue of a twist in the evolutionary process, they have also developed well beyond their animal ancestors. They have created a new realm of evolution based on their extraordinary intelligence, anatomical flexibility, unprecedented communicative abilities, distinctly mutable and highly malleable institutions (that we can properly call society), and extraordinary capacity for innovation.

I cannot emphasize the institutional, mutable, malleable, and innovative nature of society too strongly. Society, properly speaking, is a strictly human phenomenon, one that stands in significant contrast to the genetically imprinted collectivities of so-called 'social insects' and the relatively loose, developmentally static animal aggregations of herds, troops, and similar groups. Although such animal aggregations change in population numbers and are found in a wide range of different species, animal communities undergo very little variation; nor do they possess an institutional framework formed by conscious design. Human beings, by contrast, form bands, tribes, tribal federations, monarchies, democracies, and republics, among others, each of which has richly articulated structures, intersubjective relationships, and cultures, and which can be changed by popular action, *coups*, and upheavals of one kind or another.

The majority of animals, moreover, merely dwell in their environment. If they alter that environment, they do so primarily inadvertently, merely by their presence in it, or by nascent choices from among naturally available possibilities. With a few and very limited exceptions, they do not consciously remake the conditions they find but rather try to live within them. By sharp contrast, human beings consciously act upon their environment, and with new material techniques, they intentionally try to shape it to meet their own needs. Put simply: animals generally *adapt*, while human beings generally *innovate*. This distinction is a difference not merely in degree but in kind.

Even so, our unique human capacities do not constitute a complete breach with the natural world – even as we innovate, we simultaneously incorporate our animal heritage into our lives. Indeed, one of the great problems in social development is our animalistic inertia – our conservatism – in retaining obsolete social traditions that act as a brake on much-needed social changes and innovations. Although as human beings we are vertebrates, mammals, primates, and retain certain instincts and vaguely understood impulses that are rooted in our inescapable animality, we are also capable of transcending our adaptive animal attributes and in the process becoming less animalistic than our remote hominid forebears.

If we are to advance beyond metaphorical concepts of Nature and see the organic world *as an evolutionary process,* we have to view Nature in a less simplistic and more graded way than the romantic image of a mere vista. To understand the emergence of humans and their creation of culture requires that the conventional image of Nature as the strictly organic be differentiated in such a way as to distinguish the social world from the merely biological. While acknowledging that all humans are necessarily mammals, we must also recognize that all mammals are not necessarily humans – indeed, between them is not only an evolutionary continuity but also an immense divide. Insofar as Nature includes the biological realm of animality that precedes the emergence of society, we are obliged, following the Roman orator-philosopher Cicero, to speak of biological evolution as 'first nature' and social evolution as 'second nature'. And while we wish to recognize humanity's filiations with its organic evolution or first nature, second nature evolves from and also includes first nature. By the same token, we do not dissolve the very real qualitative distinctions between human and non-human life-forms in a reductionist quagmire. First and second nature – the biological and the social – form a richly differentiated continuum in which second nature emerges from first. While each interacts with the other, second nature marks a transcendence of first nature, a sublation of an adaptive animality to an innovative humanity.

Given the distinctions as well as the continuities between first and second nature, antihumanists who view human beings merely as another animal are making fools of themselves – and have a narrowly reductionist image of the natural world as well.

If humans were merely animals that just happen to be acutely intelligent – and if intelligence were an attribute no different in kind or value from, say, the ability of birds to navigate or caribou to migrate – their strictly animalistic behavior in exercising that faculty should be cause for little concern.[9] If people are no different from other animals, why shouldn't they limitlessly populate the planet, as all animals would if they could? Rabbits, after all, might very well have overpopulated the Australian continent to the detriment of its flora and other fauna if human beings had not taken radical measures to control their reproduction rates. Or why shouldn't people devour the earth's resources, or even tear down the entire biosphere merely to gratify their immediate needs and impulses? If rationality is comparable to the navigation of birds or the migration of caribou, humans are under no obligation to behave differently from any other animal. Indeed, the fact that all non-human animal species are occupied exclusively with their own well-being and their need to reproduce should countervail the antihumanist view that ill-mannered human beings constitute an ecological cancer on the planet.

My point is that antihumanists unthinkingly *presuppose the very exceptional rational faculties human beings alone possess,* even as they denounce these faculties as the source of human 'hubris' and 'arrogance'. Indeed, even as they belittle 'faith in the power of reason and human capabilities', to cite another of Ehrenfeld's formulations,[10] they implicitly rely on reason to criticize that seemingly sinister 'faith'. That antihumanists can even communicate with other human beings on morally and religiously charged issues – that would be utterly meaningless to animals, indeed completely beyond their understanding – reveals the unstated presuppositions of their denunciations of humanism. Moreover, if they denounce reason as a 'power' supported by a misplaced 'faith', their alternative cognitive faculties – intuition? – would also require the 'power of reason' to explain why an intuitive 'faith' has any validity at all. That is to say, they must turn to reason to wriggle their way toward a belief system or any eminently *human* form of knowledge, with all its evident or concealed ways of thinking – be it a faith, belief, or insight.

Whether one chooses to anchor human knowledge in faith based on intuition or on reasoned elucidation, there is not a shred of evidence to support a belief that animals have faith in anything. Nor do we expect them to have faith, let alone act rationally, with respect to anything aside from their survival. Belief systems are beyond the competence of any known animal species apart from human beings. Ironically, we tend to judge the competence of animals in the survival game more on their 'intelligence' than on any belief systems we may impute to them – that is, on an attribute denigrated in human beings.

Finally, human beings are distinctive and different from animals because they are consciously innovative, not merely adaptive. They do not merely dwell in given habitats; they create *new* environments. Their innovativeness, like their power of reason, was not given to them by heavenly beings, mythic figures, or 'alien' visitors from another galaxy; rather, they are products in great part of biological evolution itself – of first as well as second nature.

It is to this evolutionary process – biological development and the emergence of society – to which we must turn for an understanding of what it means to be human.

Anatomically, human beings are not an abrupt branching away from a long flow of evolutionary development. Quite on the contrary, they are the outcome of trends in natural evolution that are not only explicable but are in a sense quite logical, to an extent that paleoanthropologists, even nominalistic ones, are still learning.

If biological evolution is entirely a hit-or-miss matter of chance, it is inexplicable and meaningless; unique human qualities would seem to have emerged *ab novo* with no basis in a long process of organic differentiation. If, conversely, biological evolution is predestined in unwaveringly teleological terms, so that the appearance of humanity was already inexorably prefigured from the very beginnings of life, the emergence of humanity – or any life-form – acquires a mystical dimension that presupposes the existence of the very phenomena we are attempting to explain.

Between a strictly nominalistic conception of evolution and a strictly teleological one, there is a middle and more plausible ground that is worth examining. If we think of how certain, *specific* evolutionary attributes developed, our image of their development becomes both less nominalistic and less teleological. Consider how the nervous system evolved, for example. Organisms with complex nerve networks can be traced back to the distant Devonian epoch, more than a hundred million years ago, when fishlike animals began to leave the ancient seas for terrestrial shores and the open air. These Chordata, with their spinal cords and simple brains, adapted themselves to so many different ecological niches that their ultimate occupancy of trees was quite as comprehensible as their occupancy of swamps, arid lands, caves, and the like.

In the light of the eminently attractive ecological forest niches that were open to them, the evolution of primates and their differentiation into monkeys, apes, hominoids, and hominids seems far less chancy a development than strictly empirical paleoanthropologists often lead us to suppose. Recent discoveries suggest that it was in densely forested areas – not necessarily in arid open savannahs – that bipedal primates began to evolve. Indeed, the discovery in 1994 of an ancestral fossil, *Australopithecus ramidus,* has left paleoanthropologists speculating that a bipedal link between apes and humans walked on forest floors nearly four and a half million years ago, about a million years before *Australopithecus afarensis* of 'Lucy' fame appeared, and long before savannahs emerged in areas of Ethiopia that are rich with hominid fossils today.

Is this mere accident? Possibly – in a very narrow view of natural selection. Or is it the fulfillment of a potentiality? Certainly, because such bipedal hominids *did* appear after all, they did not emerge from smoke. Their development toward bipedalism built on earlier anatomical changes that had taken place long before primates descended from tree branches to the ground. What we call 'human' patently evolved from within an immensely important tendency in biological evolution: the enormous specialization of an organ system whose development makes for greater behavioral flexibility – the *nervous* system – in contrast to highly specialized anatomic attributes such as scaled, armored hides, fanged jaws, and immense claws. Leaving aside ironclad teleology, human evolution occurred within a number of specific *tendencies* in animal development that are thoroughly consistent with Darwin's *Origin of Species,* and reveals the potentiality for *social* evolution.

Human beings are primates, a group of animals with highly flexible physical attributes. The primate body has free forearms that allow it to adapt easily to a great variety of environmental conditions. It has stereoscopic vision, which makes it possible to judge distances ranging from the most minute to the far horizon. Primates can see colors, a capability not given to mammals generally, remarkably enhancing primates' knowledge of the similarities and differences between the things that make up its environment.

Human hands, distinctly primate in origin, are puny by comparison with a lion's claws, and human arms are weak by comparison with a bear's forelegs. The relatively hairless human skin is more vulnerable than the hides of most mammals to changes in weather, insect bites, thorns, and abrasions. These anatomical failings would have made humanity's survival impossible without a brain that was ultimately capable of generalizing and memorizing to an unprecedented extent. These brains, which evolved together with a vocal apparatus, bipedalism that freed the arms for a greater variety of tasks, stereoscopic and color vision, and highly manipulative fingers, conferred on human beings an unprecedented capacity not only to survive but to radically refashion the natural environment to suit their needs.

Not all of these attributes emerged at once. Indeed, it would render biological evolution miraculous to maintain that they emerged simultaneously in a single creature. Contrary to the conventional wisdom of only half a century ago, which regarded brain development the earliest step toward human development, evidence today shows that bipedalism preceded humanity's advance beyond the mental equipment of a modern chimpanzee.

Whether bipedalism conferred rudimentary social advantages upon the earliest hominids by freeing the arms to carry food back to a family unit or a group, or to fashion simple implements, or both, is a question we may never be able to answer definitively. Greater brain power came later, as the evidence suggests, as did elaborate tool-making. Each may have had social consequences: bipedalism leading to closer association; free arms to a growing sense of responsibility to one's kin group rather than to a single or several offspring; tool-making enhancing mental astuteness.

The emergence of humanity was part of a strong overall biological trend, spanning hundreds of millions of years, that gave rise within first nature itself to a species that transcended its mere animality and produced a second, distinctively social nature, just as the development of the inorganic world had previously given rise to the organic. Having developed *within* first nature and as part of its very evolution as an animal, humanity evolved further to produce a second or social nature.

No 'faith in a higher authority', be it the 'power of God' or the 'power of the supernatural' (Ehrenfeld) or any power to 'open the gates of Heaven' (Schumacher), need be invoked to explain how – or why –

human beings, over the course of their evolution, achieved their eminently *natural* capacity to consciously alter their environment and make them more amenable to human well-being.

Nor did any of this ability evolve because primates, hominids, and humans perversely 'willed' it into existence. Throughout, natural selection shaped the human ancestral line, no less than it was shaping the ancestral lines of contemporary wolves, bears, whales, tigers, and all the furry little creatures we find so endearing and of which we feel so protective.

Natural selection worked on features that already existed, 'selecting' certain possibilities or potentialities that arose from previously advantageous developments, be they simple nerve ganglia that *could* become brains, legs that *could* become arms, a rudimentary upraised stature that *could* become fully bipedal, bones that *could* become fingers, and so forth – ranging across the anatomical and organ systems of the earlier, more generalized mammals.

Thus humanity is not some sort of freak in organic evolution. In fact, increasing subjectivity, intelligence, and physical flexibility would confer enormous advantages on *any* animal species. Early human beings initially did no more than what any versatile animal would do: they used their remarkable and developing brains to meet their own needs. If their highly generalized anatomy required still more brain power to compensate for their very limited muscle power, they fortunately continued to evolve more brain power.

The *natural* component of becoming human, then, consists in the fact that biological evolution enhanced rationality – the very ability that so many antihumanists regard as one of humanity's troubling attributes. To be a human animal, in effect, is to be a reasoning animal that can consciously act upon its environment, alter it, and advance beyond the passive realm of unthinking adaptation into the active realm of conscious innovation. A mystical faith in the 'supernatural', 'God', and 'the gates of heaven', as an alternative to reason, not only catapults humanity out of natural evolution; it creates out of pure smoke a mythic transcendental realm that severs the ties of our species to the natural world. Not only do antihumanists denigrate the naturally endowed power of human beings to reason; they open a vast chasm between the human and their revered Nature that no wispy metaphors, alluring rituals, lofty pretensions of naturalness, or mystical rubbish can fill. However much they may claim to deny that they see any opposition between human beings and the natural world, they are implicitly among its principal ideological architects today.

Finally, the supernatural, God, and the gates of heaven are crassly anthropomorphic illusions, like Disney cartoons that present talking bears, soulful deer, commanding lions, malicious wolves, and gloved mice, recreating the animal world in the most pedestrian human forms. In movies, talking lions are imparted with missions acceptable to a highly moronized public, then sent forth to carry the burdens of lionhood onto the African savannahs. Conversely, in real life, full-grown men and women try to establish an identity with wolves by childishly howling around campfires – which would probably panic any nearby wolf and cause it to rush back to its lair. Others speak as the 'representatives' of stones, rivers, and – with excessive hubris – of entire mountain ranges in a juvenile 'Council of All Beings', as though the animal world – prey and predator alike – ever created so natural an institution as parliamentary government.

Naive as these antics may seem, their impact on the human condition can easily become sinister when they are used to create atavistic movements, socially reactionary impulses, and dangerous fantasies that obstruct attempts to change an irrational society into a rational one. Such movements bear disturbing parallels to earlier movements that offered biologistic explanations for the world's troubles – movements that melded a romantic ecologism with nationalism and racialism, to make the twentieth century one of the bloodiest in history.

Having defined Nature as a cumulative evolutionary *process* and suggested humanity's place in it, we are in a better position to deal with human beings as social creatures.

Our highly complex brains, our capacity to make tools and to vocalize syllabically, our dexterous fingers, bipedal gait, and stereoscopic vision, all taken together would not provide us with startling advantages over instinctively programmed, heavily muscled, roaring, and swift beasts of prey if each of us lived isolated in forests and on savannahs. Indeed, many human attributes – such as our relatively feeble muscles and slow gait – would be outright liabilities, especially if our highly imaginative minds panicked us with fantastic as well as real fears. The distant Pleistocene world of our ancestors was anything but safe, carefree, and liberating. It does not take an abundance of knowledge to recognize how appallingly dangerous an African night is to any creature, even to animals that live in herds.

By bringing a camera with infrared lights onto the African savannah, Donald Johanson and others have dramatically shown that all hell breaks loose when the sun goes down: Hyenas attack lone lions, while lion prides attack elephant calves and even pull down a burly, formidable buffalo of enormous strength and bulk.[11]

Humans are immensely vulnerable animals – more vulnerable than arboreal primates – and our ancestors, such as Lucy, in the remote Plio-Pleistocene, were even more vulnerable than we, who at least have nearly three times the brain size for our weight than she. Our rich cultural heritage enhances our versatility in the most challenging and unfamiliar conditions. It is doubtful that lone, bipedal hominids could have survived the furious predation that normally occurs in African forests and savannahs at night without some system of common defense. And it was in Africa, in a wilder and more dangerous world than the cold northlands, that our ancestors originated.

Significantly, hominids honed to a fine degree precisely those traits that made for effective cooperation. Their traits for expression, communication, guardianship, care, and cooperation seem to have increased rather than diminished. They increasingly developed skills that depended upon cooperative activity rather than individual physical strength. If bipedalism had any value to our ancestors, it was to carry food and young juveniles – to acquire food for a group of some sort, not merely to feed oneself. Like many paleoanthropologists, I wish to emphasize that an integral part of our first nature – our biological evolution – is our ability to function cooperatively with others of our own kind. The extent to which we can call this ability social is difficult to say. It is striking that the physically strongest of the early hominids, *Australopithecus robustus*, with its massive jaws and frame, was extinct by the early Pleistocene, while the more gracile *Australopithecus afarensis*, which may have been ancestral to all *Australopithecines*, gave rise to the early *Homo* genus from which we are all directly descended. Nor was Lucy, some three and a half million years ago, any less an object of prey than baboons, chimpanzees, and other primates. What is remarkable is that the diminutive hominids of the late Pliocene and early Pleistocene were not extinguished like so many other species in those remote periods, and it is this fact that requires explaining, not simply their anatomical and cranial evolution.

By no means, in fact, did social life or second nature suddenly emerge in our species from first nature and abruptly 'disconnect' us from the natural world. Inscribed on our physical anatomy are the incipient elements of social life that make it possible for us to be sharing, cooperative, and family-oriented animals. Human first nature is shaped not only by anatomical developments that make for greater intelligence in getting food and outwitting predators – developments we might expect to find in all animals; it is also shaped, especially in early hominids, by developments that yield complex forms of consociation and interaction. For an immensely long span of time, rudimentary forms of consociation provided an advantage to one hominid line over another that was selective socially as well as naturally, much as mutual aid provided a marked advantage to one animal species over another.

To speak exclusively of natural selection without reference to the advantages conferred on hominids by social selection, then, would be simplistic. To the extent that early hominids formed social groupings without complex institutions, the two were tied together very closely. Thus traits favoring cooperation, intercourse, group protection, and scavenging-foraging (our ancestors were more likely scavengers than hunters) were 'selected' for the same survival reasons that fangs and claws were 'selected' for lions.

The earliest institutions that distinguish a society from a herd were probably structured around eminently biological facts, such as extended infantile dependence, age difference, gender distinctions, and blood ties.

The newborn human child is a strikingly unfinished and vulnerable creature. Unlike many newborn ungulates, which can rise to four legs within a matter of hours and run with the herd in a day or two, it is totally helpless at birth. It takes years for a human infant to gain the competence to care for itself. Depending upon individual differences, some thirteen years may pass before a child is sufficiently developed to function as a responsible person. During this protracted period of dependence, children retain a mental plasticity that makes it possible for them to learn a great deal of knowledge, much of which they will need to survive under very rudimentary material conditions of life.

By contrast, a newborn chimpanzee completes its infancy in half the time of a newborn baby, and it ends its juvenile phase in half the time required by a human child. Five years or so after a chimpanzee is born, it can fend for itself within its habitat more effectively than can any human child of the same age, even in simple band or tribal communities. Once it has reached maturity, however, a chimpanzee's learning capacity is very limited; a human being, on the other hand, can absorb knowledge throughout much of its life.

The protracted dependence of the human child leads to bonds of life-long commitment, even as the mother becomes occupied with the care of new and younger siblings. Sharing food, collective caretaking for the young, an abiding sense of responsibility to the infirm and to the family group as a whole – all yield a clearly discernible human family structure, to an extent that is largely unknown in chimpanzees, our closest primate relatives, among whom even the sharing of food is idiosyncratic at best (apart from the mother-offspring relationship), and the sick are actually shunned.

Given the human child's ever-increasing mental faculties, its wide-ranging emotional repertoire, and its growing sense of self-awareness, it becomes the cement, as it were, of a distinct institution, the family, together with its mother and others by whom it may be raised. The biological imperatives of childrearing for a long period of time constitute the point of departure for building an institutionalized *society*, rather than a loosely bound community.

The next major biological fact that seems to have played a constitutive role in forming early society is old age. In the demanding world of prehistory, the physical vulnerability of aging adults would tend to foster a commonality of interests among them that led to a simple, mild stratification in which they were mutually protective against neglect or abandonment by the community. In cultures that lacked writing, elders were the all important repositories of community knowledge, the heirs of the group's wisdom, which would give them an enhanced position in band and tribal communities. It was they who taught the young the arts of survival and who brought their experience to the service of the community – and made themselves indispensable as teachers. Respect for elders, often in powerful gerontocracies, is almost universal among the remaining preliterate peoples, and it is not difficult to believe that they were highly respected in early organized societies and were ultimately given privileged positions.

Of immense importance as well were the institutionalized differences in gender that emerged in early social development. Certainly, the sexes took on different material tasks. Women were responsible for child-bearing, food-gathering, and food preparation, while men engaged in scavenging, tool-making, hunting in varying degrees, and protecting the group from marauding men of other communities. Although both sexes did many things in common, the more the human tool-kit expanded and new ways of securing a livelihood emerged, the more likely it was for work to be divided functionally along gender lines so that a true division of labor occurred in most cases, even leading to a cultural division along sexual lines, in which females formed their own sororal groups and males their own fraternal groups.

Finally, the most obvious institutional forms of affinity were organized around kinship, the most universal form of relationships in contemporary preliterate communities. Just as childrearing, age differences, and gender groupings are based on biological facts, so too are relationships structured around blood ties (whether real or fictitious). Within a recognizable circle of blood brothers, sisters, parents, and other relatives, strong obligations existed that formed the sinews of social ties. One's basic allegiances were owed first to one's immediate kin, the members of one's family. These were slowly extended outward to include allegiances to cousins and to offshoots of one's group, clan, and tribe, until kinship ties became so remote that in their most extended forms, they implied no obligations at all.

We can only guess when clearly definable institutions like the family appeared in human evolution. One of the earliest hominid ancestors, *Australopithecus afarensis,* about four feet tall but clearly bipedal, appeared on the semiforested African savannahs some four million years ago.[12] It had a brain that was no larger than that of a chimpanzee. Far from resembling the 'killer ape', as Australopithecines were called years ago, the predators of other animals, *afarensis* was more likely the fairly docile, omnivorous prey of leopards and hyenas. The fact that it was undoubtedly bipedal, which qualifies it as a direct ancestor of modern human beings, provides reason to suspect that mother–child relationships in these hominids were more structured than those of chimpanzees, among whom maternal bonds to the young are relatively loose and easily separated after a couple of years. In 1976 in Tanzania, the distinguished paleoanthropologist Mary Leakey found free-striding, distinctly bipedal footprints of what appears to have been two *afarensis* adults and a child, preserved by overlays of volcanic ash. Very much like our own, they suggest close bonding among our early ancestors – possibly even a permanent family unit that walked upon ashy soil some three and a half million years ago.

The first hominid to earn the generic name of *Homo,* specifically *Homo habilis* (that is, 'handy man') appeared about two million years ago, leaving not only distinctly humanlike fossil remains but recognizable stone tools. Little more than a half-million years later, its descendant, *Homo erectus,* emerged, and with its appearance we can speak plausibly of some kind of lasting institutionalized form of social organization. *Homo erectus* clearly crafted tools and learned to use fire. Indeed, until this indisputably human species appeared, our ancestors were confined geographically to the African continent.

Erectus was not only technically versatile but, given its capacity to use fire, may have been a hunter, setting grasslands afire to trap and harvest animals, possibly stampeding herds over cliffs, and effectively defending itself against predators with torches. This constellation of developments – particularly the 'taming' of fire – must have been a turning point in human evolution. Probably, *erectus*'s main source of animal proteins and fats came from scavenging, especially using stone hammers to break open the long bones of prey animals that even hyenas, with their powerful jaws, could not crack, and consuming the rich marrow that was left behind after the animal's flesh was consumed. It is also possible that *erectus* did some hunting and fishing, built shelters, and lived an organized group existence. Finally, *erectus* was the first hominid to leave the African cradle of human evolution, migrating as far east as Java, which suggests that these humans may have known how to clothe themselves against inclement weather.

Erectus had a brain that was about two-thirds the size of its modern descendants. Within a span of about a million years, humans like *Homo sapiens neanderthalensis* (now classified as a form of *Homo sapiens*) appeared with brain sizes comparable to our own. They probably carried spears, hunted collectively, engaged in seemingly ceremonial burials, and lived in small organized communities. In the absence of any art-like remains, it is hard to say with assurance that they held complex religious beliefs; nor is it clear that they could articulate words and sentences with any proficiency. But their burial sites suggest that they may have had some kind of belief system and form of family organization.

The physical features that distinguish authentic humans from their Neanderthal cousins is more marked than the more genteel current literature on Neanderthals would have us believe. Contrary to what some paleoanthropologists have contended, it is very unlikely that Neanderthals would be indistinguishable from modern men and women if they were dressed in modern clothing. Not only were they unable to use articulated language but they would be noticeably different in their very rounded facial profiles. We have no reason to believe that they had the artistic sense that modern humans possess, or the power to generalize in such a way that their cultures resembled even the mythopoeic cultures of present-day aboriginal peoples. They were sluggishly adaptive rather than excitingly innovative, and more passive in response to the world around them than experimental and innovative. Indeed, although they were the most important human types for nearly a hundred thousand years, they left no significant evidence of artistic or ongoing technological development. Ironically, Neanderthals may well qualify as the prototypical 'primitives' revered by primitivists and ecomystics today, that lived in 'harmony' with 'Nature' – but if they did, it was in a harmony that they did not know existed, produced by their inability to change the environment in which they lived, not by any sensibility that could be called ecological.

Not until some ninety thousand years ago did our own species, *Homo sapiens sapiens,* become a clearly visible presence in the evolutionary process, essentially crossing the line between its animal ancestry and its human future. The famous Magdalenian peoples of southern France and northern Spain, who left behind the remarkable cave paintings and sculptures of some 15,000–20,000 years ago, as well as related groups in central Europe and Asia, created a definitely human-conditioned *environ-*

ment, one that they had significantly altered to meet their survival and mental needs. Theirs was no passive culture, despite obeisances made to it by modern primitivists extolling stone age ecological communities. Far from merely dwelling in a habitat, they innovated technologies unknown to any previous human community: bows and arrows, sophisticated spears and spear-throwers, weaving, elaborate decorative clothing, amulets, extraordinary depictions of themselves (males and females), and complex shelters, on the tundras of Eurasia.

As their burial sites indicate, they probably had increasingly elaborate status groups structured around elders, shamans, and outstanding hunters, and they were likely to have developed complex systems of sympathetic magic. Over time they seem to have developed rationalized techniques for making things to supply not only themselves but the growing trade networks of which they were part – even an 'assembly-line' system in one case, in which each participant made a portion of an implement that was ultimately exchanged in finished form across the European continent.

From the mammoth hunters of the Eurasian tundra to the Magdalenian foragers of southern and central Europe, *Homo sapiens* collectively produced a virtual explosion of creativity in technology and art, aggressively intervening in the surrounding world. Stone Age Man, as we like to conceive 'him', is less likely to have been a somnambulant worshiper of Nature than a wandering, curious, and immensely inventive being who hunted with vigor and tried in every way to improve his everyday lot, even to the point of exterminating existing species to meet his needs (including the need for goods to trade), then migrating into areas that contained more plentiful sources of food and other resources. The theory should not be excluded that these migrations required them to displace other hunters – that is to say, through warfare.

Clearly, no mystical reverence for Nature that gives rise to an ecological sensibility inheres in human beings like a gene in a double helix. Only an *ethical* intention to behave with a sensitive concern for other life-forms and their needs – a uniquely *human* trait – could yield an ecological sensibility that goes beyond the gratification of material needs. Such an ecological sensibility is the result not of a 'Pleistocene consciousness', to use the jargon of modern day primitivists, but of a rich civilization, of the nuanced sophistication of the human mind, and of sensitive advances in humanistic values.

An institutionalized community, composed of structured family groups, constitutes the initial biological basis of second nature. Added to this minimal society, so to speak, are institutions formed around age groups that conferred authority on the old as the repositories of wisdom, around kinship ties as the sinews of social obligation, and around an emerging division of labor based on gender differences.

These institutional bases for social life were initially grounded in biological facts: childrearing, age, blood kinship, and sexual traits. Thus it is fair to say that second nature 'eased' in a graded way out of first nature. The separation between first and second nature may have been very gradual; in fact, the quasi-biological institutions that mediated this separation – family, kinship, age, and gender – are still a major presence in modern social life, however much their institutional forms have changed over time. For all the difficulties that besiege it, the family is still regarded as the cellular tissue of society, age is still viewed as a source of wisdom, and 'blood' (often in the form of raging ethnic solidarity and nationalism) is still 'thicker than water'.

Even as these biological facts were increasingly acculturated, transporting humanity from first into second nature, their impact was as confining as it was liberating. Social structures based on blood ties, such as bands and tribes, could be very parochial. Generally they tended to deny to outsiders or strangers the customary protective rights that all the kindred members of their groups enjoyed. An outsider or stranger who visited a group or lived in its midst could be treated quite arbitrarily and might easily be killed because of a whim or a minor quarrel.

Gender differences, which probably took the form of a complementary relationship between the sexes in early human communities, ultimately led to the domination of women by men. Indeed, in almost every ancient civilization, the truly patriarchal family, in which the *eldest* male exercised life-and-death powers over *all* members of a familial or clan group, placed domestic life under an absolute tyranny. Nor did the male's authority, whether as father or husband, disappear until fairly recently, however much it was attenuated over the passage of time.

By the late Paleolithic, when *Homo sapiens sapiens* clearly replaced the Neanderthals, animistic and probably quasi-religious belief systems had become an integral part of hunting-gathering or foraging societies. Whatever meanings can be imputed to the paintings and sculptures in European caves, there is every reason to believe that they were partly if not entirely magical. By 18,000 years ago, as the last glacial period drew to an end, people were painting figures that are remarkably redolent of Siberian and American Indian shamans. Burial arrangements suggest a belief in an afterlife, and statuettes are intended to have unknown but apparently potent magical or quasi-religious powers.

To the extent that modern aboriginal cultures are a creditable guide to the past, we may speculate that *Homo sapiens sapiens* was ideologically suffused by a belief in the portentous functions of dreams, the presence of ancestral ghosts, the power of magic to assure success in hunting, and the ubiquity of demons that caused illness and death.

But if our hunter–gatherer ancestors lived in a world so 'enchanted', it was built overwhelmingly on illusions, as I cannot stress too strongly – given the specious primitivism and mysticism so much in vogue among today's bored middle classes. Needless to say, people in Paleolithic cultures experienced tangible dangers, too, from marauding groups, warfare, and the sacrifice and torture of captives – and from very real material uncertainty, dangerous predators, and early death. Indeed, judging from their remains, few if any Pleistocene peoples survived beyond the age of fifty, and only half reached twenty. There should be no illusions that Nature closed around this human world any less harshly than it did around the animal world.

Moreover, the limits imposed by first nature or the 'natural life' were not only physical but mental. Lacking syllabic writing, our early ancestors had no means of clearly recording their thoughts and experiences. Pictographs may provide a concrete story to those who inscribe and read them, but only modern syllabic writing provides the means for sophisticated generalizations that can be elaborated from one to another. Hence much that preliterate human beings knew, aside from what they acquired from experience, was handed down by word of mouth – a technique for conveying knowledge that is patently limited.

Important as spoken language is – indeed, it is one of the most important distinctions between human and non-human beings – the fund of knowledge it can provide, even in the most practical matters, is markedly limited. A preliterate community's history and experiences can reach back no further in time than to what is retained in the memory of an individual narrator. However keen the narrator's memory may be, it is immensely limited by comparison with the knowledge contained in the books of even a modest library. Moreover, the very *idea* of a history has little meaning in a preliterate society. There, events of the past take on a fabulous form that slowly drops a veil between past experience and reality, or else their memory simply fades away as one generation replaces another.

Is the prevalence of reason the sole criterion for defining our humanity? Should an ethics of complementarity, rectifying the unavoidable inequalities that exist between individuals within a community – even within the same individual at different times in the life-cycle – be ignored in the light of cold reason? Do aesthetic sensibilities, intuitions, spiritual insights, and personal uniqueness have a place in a rational society? My response would be that reason and imagination, thought and passion, have be to combined.

In sum: to become human is to become rational and imaginative, thoughtful and visionary, in rectifying the ills of the present society. By extension, our capacity for compassion *obliges* us to intervene in the evolutionary process of first and second nature and to render them a rational and ethical development. To become human, in effect, is to become Nature-rendered self-conscious, to *knowingly* and *feelingly* participate as active agents in the natural and social worlds. As the potentially conscious products of first and second nature, we are the lone agent who can meld them in a higher transcendence I have called 'free nature' that eliminates needless pain, destruction, catastrophes, and regressions.

This free nature would be a 'thinking nature', a fulfillment of the evolutionary process in the natural world that tends toward ever-greater subjectivity and flexibility in dealing with environmental challenges. Social life, far from being divided from or placed in opposition to the natural world, would then be rationally integrated with first nature as a self-conscious dimension of a new, creative, richly differentiated, and meaningful whole. These goals, rooted in the still-unfinished Enlightenment, constitute a unified vision and passion that takes full note of humanity's singularity and potential ability to ultimately create ecosocial institutions – institutions that will bring human beings into harmony with one another and humanity into harmony with the natural world.

Enlightened humanism is the hopeful message that society can be rendered not only rational but wise and not only ethical but passionately visionary. If this message remains no more than a hope today – and no movement for a rational and ecological society is possible unless it is permeated by *hope* – it would nonetheless validate my claim that humanity is the most 'enchanted' species on this planet. For only human beings can hope rather than merely exist, foresee rather than merely remember, live as active agents rather than merely dwell as passive beings, change the world for the better rather than merely accept it, innovate rather than merely adapt.

But humanity today lives in the tension between the utterly irrational society that has brought us two monstrous World Wars, the unforgivable horrors exemplified by Hitler's extermination camps and Stalin's gulags, seething nationalisms, and ethnic hatred on the one hand – *and* generous ideals of freedom, cooperation, sharing, empathy and an ecological sensibility on the other. However important sentiment, intuition, feeling, and spirituality are as part of our being, reason must always stand like a sentinel, a continual challenge and corrective, lest our animality conspire with our intelligence or cunning to yield unforeseeable terrors and unexpected horrors in our still-unfinished development as human beings.

Unfortunately, removing these tensions and failings in such a way that humanity can undertake its movement toward a rational society is more problematic today than it has ever been in the past. The very means that exist to achieve a rational society – technological proficiency, wide-ranging instruments of communication, enormous knowledge of the natural world, and great intellectual powers – can be dangerously deployed by the present irrational society against the attainment of a better world. Today, simplistic appeals to our 'intuitions' and 'spirituality', to the 'power of the supernatural', to our 'inner child', and to the 'wisdom' of various gurus are leading not only to futile introspection and an irresponsible narcissism but to social inaction.

Attaining the realm of freedom requires replacing the demonic powers that keep us in various degrees of servility – be it to the dominant political and economic powers or psychic charlatans – and presupposes the existence of freely acting rational as well as imaginative human agents. It is precisely this much-needed consciousness that is under formidable assault from the antihumanistic ambience of our time. Seldom have we been invited so insistently to regress to modes of 'Being', to use Heideggerian language, that emphasize our animality. Whether this animality takes the form of our genetic makeup, our undifferentiated 'Oneness' with an indefinable Nature, our intuitions, or our ancestral primitivity, it involves a loss of our rationality, human distinctiveness, capacity for innovation, and active agency in changing the world for the better.

These antihumanistic trends, in their intangible but all-encompassing ambience, have gained an influence that obstructs our fulfillment as a meaningful result of natural and social evolution. Until the current antihumanistic tendencies are subjected to serious criticism, we cannot even begin to address the more tangible problems of our time that antihumanism obscures and distorts. It is to this critical task that we must turn if there is to be even the remotest prospect of achieving the social fulfillment and ecological responsibilities that implicitly constitute our humanity.

Notes

1 The accusations within the antihumanist camp that their own members are enveloped in the very rationalism they denounce persists to this very day, as witness Heidegger's criticism of Nietzsche as a captive of rationalism and humanism and charges by certain postmodernists, in turn, that Heidegger was no less a product of the rationalists and humanists whom he for a time denounced. See my discussion of Jacques Derrida in Chapter 7.

2 David Ehrenfeld, *The Arrogance of Humanism* (New York: Oxford University Press, 1981).

3 *Ibid.*, p. viii.

4 *Ibid*, pp. 5–6.

5 E. F. Schumacher, *A Guide for the Perplexed* (New York and London: Harper and Row, 1977), pp. 138–9.

6 *Ibid.*, p. 139.

7 Michael D. Lemonick, 'How Man Began', *Time*, 14 March 1994.

8 The word *eco-communities* is used quite deliberately. I have deep reservations about the word *ecosystem*, except when a systems analysis of the energy flow between plants and animals is involved. Systems theory has little if any applicability to qualitative as distinguished from quantitative discussions of ecological issues. However popular it may be in mechanistic views of the natural world, systems theory cannot exhaust our knowledge of plant-animal and human interactions.

9 An argument equating the 'navigational skills' of birds with the intelligence of human beings has actually been advanced by a deep ecologist in a serious academic journal. See Robyn Eckersley, 'Divining evolution: The ecological ethics of Murray Bookchin', *Environmental Ethics*, vol. 11 (Summer 1989), p. 115.

10 Ehrenfeld, *Arrogance*, p. viii.

11 In a 1994 documentary series, *Ancestors: In Search of Human Origins*, on NOVA. The book accompanying the documentary is Donald Johanson, Lenora Johanson, and Blake Edgar, *Ancestors: In Search of Human Origins* (New York: Villard Books, 1994).

12 *Australopithecus ramidus*, discovered in north-central Ethiopia by Gen Suwa, is believed to be some 4.5 million years old. According to Suwa in the October 1994 issue of *Nature*, this hominid was bipedal and lived in a forested area; if this is true, it raises problems for theories of bipedalism as an adaptation to savannah lifeways. Some experts have reportedly declared that the fossil remains are the 'missing link' between apes and hominids. More data must be made available before the role of *ramidus* in human evolution becomes clear.

See also Derek Joubert and Beverley Joubert, 'Lions of Darkness', *National Geographic*, August 1994, pp. 35ff.

CHAPTER 2

From 'selfish genes' to Mother 'Gaia'

Among the most insidious challenges to human uniqueness today are two self-proclaimed sciences, both of which first appeared in the mid-1970s. One, sociobiology, is a form of biological reductionism that tends to ascribe human agency to our genetic makeup; the other is the planetary Gaia Hypothesis, according to which human beings are 'intelligent fleas' that feed on the pristine body of 'Mother Earth'.

That both these challenges wear the mantle of science makes them particularly insidious. Theoretically, the scientific mantle should place them at odds with the expressly anti-rational and antiscientific bias held by most antihumanists, yet they are not. The reader who finds this state of affairs inconsistent is quite justified.

But intellectual consistency has never been a hallmark of antihuman-ism, still less of mysticism, necromancy, and various forms of deep ecol-ogy. In fact, by no means are ostensibly scientific antihumanists very far apart from their anti-rational counterparts. Even legitimately scientific disciplines allow for wild extrapolations into the mystical, as witness the growing number of physicists who have recently written books profess-ing to prove mathematically the existence of a deity, a heaven, and immortality. Science and pseudo-science alike blithely drift hand-in-hand into a shared mythopoeic antihumanism. While sociobiology essentially reduces human intellectuality to a mere by-product of 'selfish genes', the sweeping planetary vision of the Gaia Hypothesis trivializes human beings as mere parasites on the Earth.

The word *sociobiology* seems to have been invented by E. O. Wilson, a professor of science at Harvard University and curator in entomology at the University's Museum of Comparative Zoology. An engaging writer with a solid reputation for research on 'social insects', Wilson's magnum opus, *Sociobiology: A New Synthesis,* was originally published in 1975.[1]

That was a strategic year in the evolution of the American environmental movement. The waning New Left in the early 1970s was still sufficiently influential to exercise a radical influence on environmentally concerned young people by focusing their attention on the social causes of ecological dislocations. To any thoughtful young environmentalist at the time, it seemed patently clear that a profit-oriented and competitive market society was plundering the planet with the serious consequences of widespread pollution and ecological dislocation.

Precisely as the New Left began to wane, a countervailing view appeared. A harshly Malthusian approach toward environmental problems emerged, principally advanced by Paul Ehrlich in 1969 in his very widely read *The Population Bomb*.[2] Ehrlich stridently linked the causes of the environmental crisis to population growth, particularly in the so-called Third World. An entomologist-cum-ecologist, like Wilson, Ehrlich significantly helped to sidetrack environmental concern away from serious social criticism and toward essentially biological issues, dealing with population growth as though people were asocial beings who mindlessly proliferated like fruit flies. Indeed, far from challenging the existing social order, Ehrlich and his increasingly numerous admirers called upon American governmental authorities to establish a bureau of population control – all the more scandalous because the demand for such a patently invasive bureau was made of the Nixon administration.

In this growing conflict between the socially critical tendency in the environmental movement and the crudely biologistic orientation, Wilson's *Sociobiology* played a major role in tilting environmentalists toward the asocial and politically inert attitudes fostered by Ehrlich. Wilson's work, to be sure, did not focus on population issues, but he clearly enhanced a narrowly biologistic approach toward environmental problems by reducing human behavior to the restrictive operations of genetic selection and emphasizing their role in shaping the human condition. Since 1975 his views have increasingly sedimented themselves into the minds of many literate people, particularly scientists, and they are becoming the received wisdom in a wide diversity of fields, from anthropology to social theory.

Sociobiology is basically the theory that animal behavior – and for the purposes of our discussion, human behavior – is overwhelmingly determined by the species' genetic makeup. This theory is not particularly new: ever since genetics became recognized as a scientific discipline, some geneticists have always ardently privileged the role of genes in determining human social and mental traits.

But in the 'nature versus nurture' debate over the respective roles of inherited as against socially conditioned traits, contemporary sociobiologists have added several new twists. E. O. Wilson and Richard Dawkins, an Oxford University ethologist, have imparted a veritably metaphysical quality to 'the gene', endowing it with extraordinary autonomy, often at the expense of the organisms it presumably 'controls'.

For Wilson as for Dawkins – whose popular work, *The Selfish Gene,* also appeared in 1975,[3] genes are ends in themselves more than means that contribute to the functioning of a given species. Species seem to exist mainly to perpetuate genes, to foster their well-being and development. Species, in effect, are primarily the media for genetic evolution – a crudely reductionist view that has far-reaching implications for biology and ethics.

Consider, for example, Wilson's observation on the opening page of *Sociobiology* that an 'organism does not live for itself', nor is its 'primary function ... to reproduce other organisms; it reproduces genes, and it serves as their temporary carrier'.[4] Whether knowingly or not, Wilson essentially reduces human beings, with all their personality traits, willfulness, passions, and intellectuality, to molecular units with an intentionality of their own. His sweeping contentions advance a narrowly biochemical and genetic teleology that places fully developed and complex organisms at the service of self-perpetuating and developing DNA molecules. Indeed, in one of Wilson's pithier statements, an 'organism is *only* DNA's *way* of making more DNA'.[5]

Nor did Wilson modify this simplistic view of organisms three years later in his Pulitzer prize-winning *On Human Nature,*[6] despite stormy debates about the soundness and reactionary implications of his 'synthesis.' In *On Human Nature* we learn that '*no species, ours included,* possesses a *purpose* beyond the imperatives created by its genetic history. Species may have vast potential for material and mental progress but they lack any immanent purpose or guidance from agents *beyond their immediate environment or even an evolutionary goal* toward which their molecular architecture automatically steers them.'[7]

What is clearly disturbing about these passages is that Wilson's teleological bias is simply causality reduced to the narrow molecular level. He exhibits little appreciation of any evolutionary tendency that imparts value to subjectivity, intelligence, creativity, and ethics, apart from the service they perform to the well-being of genes. Indeed, where cultural and subjective attributes exist, they are mainly the work of genes, which are 'intent', as it were, on perpetuating their own kind through behavioral traits favorable to themselves. Entire levels of organic development are dissolved into DNA, much as a reductionist in physics might dissolve all phenomena into atomic or subatomic particles.

With the tunnel vision characteristic of so many sociobiologists, Robert Wright, in *The Moral Animal: The New Science of Evolutionary Psychology* (1994),[8] suggests that compassion, love, parenting, and the like have genetic sources, so that ethical behavior merely serves a genetic self-interest that cannot be grounded in humanistic principles and sentiments. Using this kind of reasoning, one may claim that there are genes for capitalism, socialism, conservatism, liberalism, racism, sexism, and fascism.

And if one is a sociobiologist, why not ascribe social forms to humanity's genetic makeup? Societies and movements that have used sociobiologistic ascriptions in their ideology have indeed existed. But by what magic wand do sociobiologists decide that some societies and ideas are genetically determined while others are not? How to determine the extent to which a society or idea is biologically offensive? Is it based merely on the personal inclinations of the sociobiologist? For many sociobiologists, in fact, the mere existence of various social phenomena like capitalistic egoism and socialistic altruism seems to suffice as proof that our genes are responsible for them. Indeed, in Wilson's view,

> the human mind is constructed in a way that locks it inside this fundamental [genetic] constraint and forces it to make choices with a purely biological instrument. If the brain evolved by natural selection, even the capacities to select particular esthetic judgments and religious beliefs must have arisen by the same mechanistic process. ... The essence of the argument, then, is that the brain exists because it promotes the survival and multiplication of the genes that direct its assembly. The human mind is a device for survival and reproduction, and reason is just one of its various techniques.[9]

Self-evidently, Wilson is placing the cart before the horse – the autonomy of the gene before the seemingly heteronomous organism it steers so automatically. Radically inverting Wilson's formulation, we can far more plausibly claim that genes which abet the increasing sophistication of brain power and the mind tend to *free* a species, like humanity, from iron genetic constraints such as sociobiology would impose upon it. Given sufficient rationality in human beings, we can more plausibly claim that they have evolved a degree of free will, intentionality, speculative insight, and ethical standards so that their behavioral traits are effectively removed from their dependence on the 'molecular architecture' that is supposed to 'automatically steer' them.

This view, so easily justified by humanity's ideals, aspirations, and social development, helps us to recognize the fact that we have developed as a species into a realm of second nature – a moral, intellectual and social realm that sociobiology crudely reduces to molecules arranged in a double helix. That sociobiologists are obliged to offer obeisances to non-genetic factors in accounting for human behavior is due less to the flexibility of their views than to the untenability of their simplistic biologistic premises. For if their premises were consistently carried to their logical conclusion, highly advanced mammals and human beings would indeed be reduced to mere vehicles for DNA with a metaphysical autonomy of its own.

Wilson's mechanism and reductionism are often as crude as Descartes's machine-like view of the body, however liberally he sprinkles his pages with caveats, personal opinions, and asides designed to soften the genetic tunnel vision of his argument. His *chef d'oeuvre*, *Sociobiology*, is riddled with behavioral constraints that rest on genetic predeterminations, indeed with anthropomorphic metaphors that seem to impart to genes an intellectuality and intentionality that properly belong in the realm of culture and to complex forms of social life.

The first chapter of *Sociobiology*, for example, is entitled 'The Morality of the Gene', a phrasing that beguiles the reader to suppose that genes are not only sovereign in determining the behavior of all life forms but, given the sizable number of amoral people in the world, possess a self-awareness beyond that of the very animals they presumably 'construct'. This grossly unwarranted phrasemaking, I would hold, is more misleading than clarifying.

It is highly unlikely that human beings could transcend their 'molecular structure' if, as Wilson explains in *On Human Nature*, 'the [human] intellect was not constructed to understand atoms or even to understand itself but to promote the survival of human genes'[10] In fact, the human intellect was 'constructed' not only 'to understand itself' but to understand the world and even the cosmos upon which it reflects – indeed to create art, music, literature, and philosophy, which in no way serve to perpetuate the existence of its 'molecular structure'.

The title of Richard Dawkins' book, *The Selfish Gene*, speaks for itself. To most literate people, selfishness is a distinctly psychological orientation, not simply a metaphor for biological self-maintenance and self-preservation. Nor is there any reason to believe that Dawkins is using the term as a metaphor. The opening pages of the book disabuse us of the suspicion that Dawkins regards genes as anything but crass egotists. 'The argument of this book is that *we*, and all other animals, are *machines* created by our genes,' writes Dawkins; '. . . I shall argue that a predominant quality to be expected of a successful gene is *ruthless* selfishness.' Moreover: '[t]his gene selfishness will usually give rise to selfishness in *individual* behaviour.'[11] Thus morality has a simplistic one-to-one relationship with genic morality, rooted in molecular 'selfishness' that allows for no independence on the part of living beings.

Lest this dazzling concept be left to stand on its own precarious ground, Dawkins quickly modifies it. 'However, as we shall see,' he adds, 'there are special circumstances in which a gene can achieve its own selfish goals best by fostering a limited form of altruism at the level of individual animals. "Special" and "limited" are important words in the last sentence. Much as we might wish to believe otherwise, universal love and the welfare of the species as a whole are concepts which simply do not make evolutionary sense.'[12]

This is an extraordinary passage – partly because of the unstated conditions it presupposes, and partly, too, because it seems to worsen rather than mitigate the Dawkins claim that genic selfishness usually gives rise to human selfishness. In Dawkins' world, genes are not only selfish but manipulative to boot. They have subtle ways – these devilishly clever DNA molecules! – of getting *us* to behave in seemingly altruistic ways, on behalf of their own egotistical ends. If this conclusion seems like a distortion of Dawkins' views, the reader who consults Dawkins' book is regaled with chapter titles like 'The gene machine', 'Genemanship', and, of course, the 'Immortal coils' of DNA.

I will not try to second-guess Dawkins, Wilson, or for that matter any sociobiologists on whether they impute any real morality, emotional state, or intentionality to genes apart from their specific biochemical functions. If the selfishness of a gene is causally related to human selfishness, and a gene can exhibit the guile to use individual altruism to serve its own egotistical ends, I fail to see what doubts remain about the autonomy sociobiologists impute to human genic equipment.

Yet in the closing pages of a book structured almost consistently around a genocentric interpretation of animal behavior, Dawkins suddenly reverses his entire thrust. Making no discernible argument so far as I can see to support his case, he singles out humans to advance the claim that culture can indeed supplant the authority of genetics over a wide range of behavior. After some two hundred pages of support for the sovereignty of selfish genes, the reader suddenly learns that almost all of Dawkins' contentions can be annulled by the human species. 'Are there any reasons for supposing our own species to be unique?' he asks. To which he responds with a proud 'yes.'[13]

What, it may be asked, gives us this privilege? 'We have the power to defy the selfish genes of our birth,' Dawkins responds,

> *and, if necessary, the selfish memes [units of cultural transmission] of our indoctrination. We can even discuss ways of cultivating and nurturing*

pure, disinterested altruism — something that has no place in nature, something that has never existed before in the whole history of the world. We are built as gene machines and cultured as meme machines, but we have the power to turn against our creators. We, alone on earth, can rebel against the tyranny of the selfish replicators.[14]

Dawkins' 'memes', in fact, are the cultural analogues of genes, transferred from the biological to the social by means of the same naive atomism that characterizes Wilson's 'molecular machinery'. Like genes, memes are mimetic replicators; they duplicate cultural traits by means of imitation, just as genes duplicate biological traits by means of sexual reproduction. Accordingly: '[j]ust as genes propagate themselves in the gene pool by leaping from body to body via sperms or eggs, so memes propagate themselves in the meme pool by leaping from brain to brain via a process which, in a broad sense, can be called imitation.'[15]

Not surprisingly, given sociobiology's highly deterministic way of thinking, they too have a life of their own.

When you plant a fertile meme in my mind you literally *parasitize my brain, turning it into a vehicle for the meme's propagation in just the way that a virus may parasitize the genetic mechanism of a host cell. ... Imitation, in the broad sense, is how memes can replicate.*[16]

But what of their 'copying-fidelity'? After all, a song, which Dawkins regards as a meme, is altered ever so slightly each time it is sung until, perhaps, it no longer sounds like its original. Here, Dawkins acknowledges 'I am on shaky ground'.[17] Indeed, taking Dawkins' forceful comparisons of selfish genes and selfish people too seriously causes the ground beneath us to shake. Before long we are confused over what is metaphor and what is not in this thoroughly curious argument. In a grand finale, Dawkins tells us that 'we must not think of genes as conscious, purposeful agents. Blind natural selection, however, makes [!] them behave rather *as if they were purposeful,* and it has been *convenient,* as a shorthand, to refer to genes in the language of purpose. ... [But] the idea of purpose is *only* a metaphor, but we have already seen what a *fruitful* metaphor it is.'[18] The same, I suppose, could be said for memes, which, like genes that struggle with rivals, compete with each other in the 'computers' that are 'human brains.'[19]

The Selfish Gene, which opens with an association between genetic selfishness and human selfishness, closes by producing a certain vertigo — it may be a geno-mimetic reaction — caused by Dawkins' failure to explain where his metaphor ends and his reality begins. 'Genes have no foresight,' he warns us. 'They do not plan ahead. Genes just *are,* some

genes more so than others, and that is all there is to it.'[20] Genes and
memes float in the air with the same stability of a kite in a hurricane.
Such stirring acknowledgments of humanity's uniqueness are rare.

What we certainly learn, even with Dawkins' memes, is that culture is
reducible to biosocial atoms – cultural particles, so to speak – that are no
less reductionist than genes. This close analogy between culture, indeed
of society in its broadest sense, and genes is as stifling as a genetic interpretation of human behavior.

That *The Selfish Gene* plays into the antihumanist leveling of human
beings to all biota, despite Dawkins' protestations of human uniqueness,
is suggested by Robert L. Trivers' foreword to the book. Trivers, who
seems to enjoy Dawkins' highest esteem, is at pains to inform us:

> *There exists no objective basis on which to elevate one species above
> another. Chimp and human, lizard and fungus, we have all evolved over
> some three billion years by a process known as natural selection. Within
> each species some individuals leave more surviving offspring than others, so
> that the inheritable traits (genes) of the reproductively successful become
> more numerous in the next generation. This is natural selection: the non-
> random differential reproduction of genes. Natural selection has built us,
> and it is natural selection we must understand if we are to comprehend our
> own identities.[21]*

So much for human uniqueness – and memes. Antihumanists nevertheless belie their very act of leveling human beings to the simplest organisms by burdening our species with the extraordinarily unique
responsibility of, as Trivers put it, 'understanding' sweeping biological
facts 'if we are to comprehend our own identities'. Although humans are
'objectively' interchangeable with chimps, in Trivers' view, only *our*
species, it would seem, is competent to understand that all-encompassing
reality or comprehend its own identity. Chimps may lack even a knowledge of death, as recent evidence has shown, let alone a comprehension
of natural selection. But antihumanist protocol insists that there is no
objective basis for elevating humanity over the most elevated of apes in
the primate world.

Wilson seems far less equivocal than Dawkins about humanity's inability
to transcend its genetic ensemble through culture, even through morality. He asks:

> *Can the cultural evolution of higher ethical values gain a direction and
> momentum of its own and completely replace genetic evolution? I think*

not. The genes hold culture on a leash. The leash is very long, but inevitably values will be constrained in accordance with their effects on the human gene pool. The brain is a product of evolution. Human behavior – like the deepest capacities for emotional response which drive and guide it – is the circuitous technique by which human genetic material has been and will be kept intact. Morality has no other demonstrable ultimate function.[22]

If Wilson's views are ultimately unequivocal, he nonetheless peppers the most dogmatic passages in his book with highly equivocal sentences. To the question of whether '*higher* ethical values' – not mere customs, opinions, or moral injunctions – can transcend the grip of genocentricity, Wilson responds with an opinion, then proceeds to graduate his opinion into a fact by asserting that 'genes hold culture on a leash'. It may be a 'long leash', to be sure, but even 'higher ethical values' (which Wilson has mutated into mere 'values') are 'inevitably' constrained by 'the human gene pool'. Conclusion? 'Morality has no other demonstrable ultimate function' than to keep 'human genetic *material*' intact.[23] These careless remarks, taken from his strategic chapter, 'Altruism', in *On Human Nature*, reveal how Wilson advances a mere opinion to support his genocentric approach – then changes the subject.

In the debates that followed the publication of *Sociobiology,* Wilson's capacity to mingle dogmatic statements with equivocal adjectives and subclauses, often shifting the scope of his arguments and backtracking to less committed positions, made it virtually impossible to subject his views to critical interpretation. Amidst a flurry of claims that his critics 'misinterpreted', 'maligned', or 'misstated' his ideas, Wilson managed to wear so many different ideological hats that it was often impossible to determine the head they covered. We shall see that this game of musical chairs is played out repeatedly in sociobiology and even more outrageously in other antihumanist works.

The subject of altruism vexes sociobiologists for obvious reasons: its existence militates against the image of selfish genes (a term Wilson also uses as well as Dawkins) that ostensibly produce selfish individuals. In that case, *why* do human beings ever behave altruistically at all? *How* can selfish genes explain the common fact that people exhibit concern for others, indeed for individuals whom they do not know as well as their immediate circle of friends?

In no small part, the answer to these questions depends upon how we define altruism. *Webster's Third International Dictionary* calls it 'uncalculated consideration of, regard for, or devotion to others' interests, sometimes in accordance with an ethical principle.' This reasonably balanced definition patently applies to the majority of altruistic acts, from personal charity to a commitment to social ideals, whose memes are perhaps too intertwined with genes and other memes to be extricable.

By contrast, sociobiology's definition of altruism is far removed from the balanced and commonplace. Wilson's *On Human Nature* defines altruism as '*self-destructive* behavior performed for the benefit of others. Altruism may be entirely rational, or automatic and unconscious, or conscious but guided by *innate* emotional responses.'[24] His elucidation of altruism is one of the most genocentrically convoluted arguments I have encountered in the antihumanistic literature.

Thus the chapter titled 'Altruism' opens with an allusion to the ambiguities of religious martyrdom and its high estate in Christian precept. It seems the Church found it difficult to reconcile an elite of martyrs with its belief in the deity's egalitarian view of humanity as a whole. Wilson thereupon obliges us to 'drop to all fours', as Voltaire once caustically remarked that the 'noble savage' in Rousseau's writings inclined him to do, by showing that altruism usually becomes selfishness. 'We sanctify *true altruism* in order to reward it', he observes, 'and thus to make it less than true, and by that means to promote its recurrence in others. Human altruism, in short, is riddled to its foundations with the *expected mammalian ambivalence*'[25] – a sufficiently ambiguous expression if there ever was one!

Whether rewarding true altruism makes it less than true I cannot say. What does Wilson regard as true altruism? The really authentic stuff, I take it, is 'self-destructive behavior performed for the benefit of others',[26] as his glossary claims, as exemplified by Christian martyrs. Thus, true altruism is depicted as a form of grisly self-sacrifice – as, for example, saints boiled in oil by pagan barbarians or thrown to lions.

But is this really true altruism? Martyrs to Christianity or, for that matter, Islam and other crusading religions, were probably less concerned with 'the benefit of others' than they were with their personal salvation and the rewards (in the case of Islam, very material ones) of a future life.

Lest we are too puzzled by the phrase 'expected mammalian ambivalence', Wilson quickly plunges into portrayals of the most *supreme* kinds of true altruism: soldiers who bodily throw themselves upon live enemy hand grenades to shield their comrades, who rescue others from battle sites 'at the cost of certain death to themselves', and other such fatal decisions.[27] Very few such cases are illustrative of 'expected mammalian ambivalence', least of all in attempts to 'rescue others' in battle situations with the certainty of being killed.

But let us agree that passion, a pure impulse whether of anger or affection, can inspire true altruism, as can a genuine, sober concern for the well-being of other human beings. In fact, the most *sustained* examples of altruism occur in daily social life. Altruism is also found in people who engage in struggles for freedom, be they the volunteers who join armies to oppose tyranny and social privilege at grave risk to their lives, or the revolutionary *dinamateros* in the Spanish Civil War of 1936–39 who exploded Francoist tanks with dynamite strapped to their own waists. We need not turn to warfare to find extraordinary examples of altruism – take for example the civil rights workers who drove into the American South in racially mixed buses and faced armed white mobs, vicious police, and police dogs in civil rights marches.

Wilson takes no note of such commonplace examples of everyday altruism. Indeed, a reflective and abiding concern for social justice and freedom is perhaps a *truer* expression of sustained altruistic behavior than are impulsive actions, heroic as they may be, which are likely to be driven by the passions of the moment. Is it possible that such everyday and abiding behavior reveals 'a transcendental quality that distinguishes human beings from animals', to use Wilson's words? Perhaps it does, 'to put the best possible construction on the matter,' Wilson generously advises us, but he then warns that 'scientists are not accustomed to declaring any phenomenon off limits'[28] – a gratuitous remark, I may add, since few responsible people would want scientists, like Wilson himself, to take recourse to the transcendental as they perform their work.

Whereupon Wilson proceeds to survey presumably altruistic forms of animal behavior ('minor' altruism, to be sure) in robins, thrushes, and tit-mice, who alert one another that a hawk is approaching, by changes in posture (crouching) or acoustical signals (whistling). Is this *altruism*, or is it self-protection? Or fear? Alas, we lack the ability to penetrate into the minds of robins, thrushes, and titmice, but Wilson somehow seems to know that instead of issuing a warning to alert other birds, 'the caller would be wiser not to betray its presence but rather remain silent.'[29]

Allow me to suggest that attributing altruism to birds is too anthropo-morphic to allow for credulity. It is no less anthropomorphic for Wilson to tell us that in three recorded cases at the Gombe Stream National Park in Tanzania, chimpanzees have taken over the care of the orphaned infants of their deceased siblings. Is this altruism, or is it a sibling recogni-tion that might be expected in an ape that has been called man's closest cousin?

Far more striking, in fact, is what our 'closest cousins' do *not* do that human beings do with extraordinary frequency. They never share food, except for meat after a kill, which is idiosyncratic at best: it normally requires a great deal of 'begging' and cajoling on the part of the hunter's companion to gain the meat. Equally important, chimpanzees normally distance themselves from an ill or injured member of their group and leave them to survive their infirmities on their own. They exhibit no knowledge of death: when they capture prey, such as a pig or an infant baboon, chimpanzees have been known to literally eat it alive, despite the victim's struggles and cries before a vital organ of its body is chewed away.

I am not trying to characterize chimpanzees as 'cruel', a value-laden term that has no meaning in the non-human world. Chimpanzees are busy being chimpanzees. I am, however, criticizing anthropomorphic primatologists for overemphasizing the extent to which chimpanzees are like people, searching out qualities in them that render them affines of humans, and attributing to them moral responsibilities and cognitive abilities that they probably do not possess. A very considerable amount of material has been published about chimpanzee 'wars' and 'sacrifices' that reads far too much human behavior into a species that is removed from humans by more than five million years of evolutionary development.[30]

Wilson's authority on the mindless world of genetically programmed bugs is unquestionable, although his beguiling stories about 'kamikaze attacks' by bees on intruders and African termite 'soldiers' whose 'caste' members 'are quite literally walking bombs' seem too metaphorical.[31] Even Wilson, I should note, does not accept an equivalence between the behavior of insects and that of human beings; indeed, he prudently warns that 'sharing the capacity for *extreme sacrifice* does not mean that the human mind and the "mind" of an insect (if such exists) work alike.'[32]

But Wilson's point is that inasmuch as kamikaze bees and soldier termites, like all creatures capable of making the 'extreme sacrifice' for the common good, systematically self-destruct and hence do not pass on their own genes to others, these 'self-sacrificing' or 'altruistic' bugs make it possible for their 'more fertile brothers and sisters to flourish'. In fact, there are *two* kinds of genes among the many that control insect behavior: 'selfish genes' *and* 'altruistic genes'.[33] And if we are to accept the title of Christopher Will's recent book on genetics, there are 'wise genes' as well.[34]

But how can self-destructive altruistic genes ever survive the harsh imperatives of natural selection when they exist in 'competition' with the self-perpetuating selfish genes? Wilson invokes 'kin selection' to meet this challenge: that is, genetically governed behavior by which individuals sacrifice themselves to enhance the survival of their kin, who possess altruistic as well as selfish genes. And with kin selection at hand, Wilson now feels that it is 'natural, then, to ask whether through kin selection the capacity for altruism has also evolved in human beings'.[35]

Wilson's response, of course, is an unqualified yes. Among humans, he allows, 'the form and intensity of altruistic acts are to a large extent culturally determined'. Actually, they would seem to be 'culturally determined' to an *immense* extent, or as Wilson puts it: 'Human social evolution is *obviously* more cultural than genetic.' To one who has read so far in *On Human Nature*, culture's power over genetic imperatives would not at all be 'obvious', and, in fact, lest we take Wilson's fleeting emphasis on culture too seriously, we learn that 'the underlying *emotion,* powerfully manifested in virtually *all* human societies, is what is considered to evolve through genes'.[36]

What is vexing about this passage, all its backtracking aside, is that human altruism, conceived as a concern for other people and the human condition generally, is by no means reducible to the underlying emotions that are considered to evolve through genes. Indeed, innumerable thinkers and many revolutionary social movements in the past were guided not by kin selection but by great ideals, be they 'Life, Liberty, and the Pursuit of Happiness' or 'Liberty, Equality, and Fraternity'. For profoundly cultural reasons they evoked strong passions in many idealists and produced passionate social upheavals, guided by great ideas that had no evident association with genes or memes. Yes – human genetic equipment was involved in the *emergence* of passions, as were hormones like epinephrine. But the evolution of these passions, their sophistication, and the extent to which they powered ideas rooted in intellection were too evidently cultural to reduce to genetic influences.

What is fundamentally wrong with Wilson's genocentry is that concepts such as 'selfishness' and 'altruism' presuppose the existence of a culture that gives them *meaning* and a morality that explains why primordial 'underlying emotions' can be active in *social* causes. If one reduces society from a human phenomenon to mere aggregations of living things – not only *organisms* but genes and memes – culture is inconceivable. We would have a collection of living beings, but not a *society* organized into mutable institutions.

Sociobiology, with its atomized genes and memes, patently deals with collections, aggregations, and heaps of organisms rather than with authentic societies characterized by a radically different level of association and organization of superficially discrete beings – specifically, *human* beings. Human beings exist in relationships with each other that are not defined by genes alone, if at all. In this respect, sociobiology is not *social* at all. It deals with biology, specifically with genetics, and gives them a social patina, generally by using anthropomorphic metaphors. It describes genes not only as 'selfish' but as 'altruistic' and even as 'wise'. Given this luxurious moral life of genes, it seems impossible that we are more than mere 'genetic machines', and yet we plainly are, just as we are not simply atoms, electrons, or protons.

Inasmuch as genes determine human development, aggression, sexual behavior, altruism, and religion, to cite the principal concerns of *On Human Nature,* how are modern humans to cope with a genetic ensemble that evolved when human beings, according to Wilson, were 'Ice-Age hunter–gatherers'? How can we readjust our glacial genes to deal with the era of the information superhighway? The answer, Wilson tells us, is 'an exercise of will'.[37] Where will this 'will' come from? Perhaps it will come from a gene that makes for obduracy, intentionality, purpose, and who knows what other willful character traits that lurk in the human genome, not to speak of one that will evolve. If evolutionary genetics places a high premium on adaptation, as do all theories of natural selection on which Wilson relies, the genetic sources of will may be uncertain indeed.

But by what right can Wilson claim that the human genetic ensemble was shaped by Ice-Age hunter–gatherers when a substantial proportion of *Homo sapiens sapiens* never left the warm climate of Africa in which they evolved? Indeed, they may never have encountered the glaciation that covered much of the northern hemisphere through the Pleistocene. Amusingly, Wilson's theory might be mistakenly seen as a risible converse of that of Professor Leonard Jeffries of the City College of New York, the chairman of the school's African-American studies program, who has gained considerable notoriety for emphasizing that blacks, evolving in sunny climates, have 'shiny genes' by comparison with the 'dull genes' of white 'ice people', apparently rendering Africans innately superior to Europeans.

Such genetic ping-pong would be silly were it not redolent of reactionary ideologies that are less sophisticated than modern sociobiology. Needless to say, an animal's genetic make-up plays a major role in guiding its behavior. The simpler the life-form, the more thoroughly genes determine its actions and the more limited is its genetic repertoire.

Sociobiologists are at their worst when they try to deal with social phenomena. In Wilson's glossary, the definitions – and their implications – of words like *society, hierarchy, dominance, aggregation, band, caste, communal,* and *competition*, reveal his orientation toward social structures and ethical phenomena. Where these concepts have clearly social premises, Wilson tends to restrict them to narrow biological definitions, in a reduction of social phenomena to genetics that obscures the discontinuities as well as the continuities between biology and society.

Consider, for example, Wilson's definition of *society,* which he describes as 'a group of individuals belonging to the same species and organized in a cooperative manner.'[38] Only a devout acolyte would fail to require Wilson to explain what he means by *organized* and *cooperative,* two culturally, philosophically, and ethically laden words that have far-reaching implications in social theory. Different societies have been *organized* and *cooperative* in very different ways – as despotisms, democracies, republics, monarchies, patriarchies, and the like. Nowhere does Wilson tell us what kind of cooperation and organization he means. What would seem to count, in his definition, is whether a society's form of cooperation and organization make it genetically fit to survive the challenges of natural selection.

All of Wilson's effusions about his liberal beliefs to the contrary, sociobiological thinking is crude. Yet given the increasing fascination of scholars and the public with genetics these days, sociobiology is making its way into many social disciplines that were once distinguished for a relative degree of sobriety. To cite only one of many examples: a recent issue of *Current Anthropology,* a highly reputable scholarly quarterly, contains a discussion article entitled 'On Human Egalitarianism', in which the authors, puzzled by the virtual ubiquity of egalitarian values and institutions among hunter–gatherers, assume that the 'ancestors of *H. sapiens*' were innately 'hierarchically oriented', and that 'cultural elaborations of food sharing, pair bonding, and egalitarianism [are grounded] in inherited tendencies', in natural selection rather than consciousness.[39] So widespread is sociobiology today that we are now told that apparently there are genes for hierarchy and domination on the one hand and genes for egalitarianism and food sharing on the other. Perhaps one set of genes is dominant and the other is recessive, or perhaps dominance depends upon the adaptive advantages the genes confer in natural selection. Whether consciously or not, the proponents of such sociobiological interpretations – and they are growing steadily in number – diminish the role of ethics and social relations in determining human behavior and social development.

Hierarchy is in fact a social term – hierarchies are found nowhere in first nature. A hierarchy is based on domination by institutionalized strata, such as gerontocracies, patriarchies, warrior sodalities, shamanistic guilds, priestly corporations, and the like over subjugated strata who are visibly underprivileged on an ongoing basis. To dissolve hierarchies into the person of an alpha chimpanzee, gorilla, or baboon, as so many primatologists do, is to make a mockery of a term which has its origins in pyramidal ecclesiastical structures. A hierarch goes with an institution such as a monarchy, bureaucracy, or even a stable patriarchal family – relationships that are not institutionalized in the animal world.

Protests by sociobiologists to the contrary notwithstanding, they eventually do reduce human beings to 'gene machines', and by extrapolation, they deal with society, mind, and great social ideals from a preponderantly genocentric viewpoint. We do not have to turn to Max Weber to lament the 'disenchantment of the world'; it is very much under way because of the genetic noose sociobiology is tightening over humanity and its greatest endeavors.

Before leaving the realm of the genetic, let us examine the so-called 'microcosmos' itself, as seen through the eyes of two antihumanists who dismiss human beings and their achievements as mere by-products of bacteria and cells.

This thesis has been strongly promoted by Lynn Margulis, professor of biology at Boston University, who, in a book entitled *Microcosmos: Four Billion Years of Microbial Evolution* written in collaboration with Dorion Sagan, really puts humanity in its trivial place.[40] Indeed, the real wonders of biotic evolution, Margulis and Sagan argue, are the microorganisms that have been on the earth for five-sixths of organic evolution, in contrast to humans, who have been around for only one thirtieth of 1 per cent of that time. Bacteria hold first place in the drama of life – whereas we humans are 'a sort of mammalian weed, with all our accomplishments and personality we are still the result of aeons of microbial evolution'[41] – which presumably puts us in our place.

Precisely why Margulis and Sagan selected microbes over the more basic and older chemicals that make up life is puzzling. Carbon, so indispensable to the formation, sustenance, and evolution of organic things has been in the universe for many billions of years, much closer to twelve billion than to a measly four or five. Certainly hydrogen, no less important than carbon, has been around even longer. Amino acids have been around for so long that a figure as small as four billion hardly does justice to their longevity. Are they less important to life than microbes are to recently arrived humans?

This numbers game rests on the omnipresent fallacy of mistaking a necessary condition for advanced life-forms for their sufficient condition. There is nothing stunningly new in the fact that cells of one kind or another are needed to produce multicellular life-forms. Nor is there anything stunningly new in the fact that microbes of a vast variety and in staggering numbers are necessary to render complex multicellular life-forms functional. Yes, the earth would be covered with nothing but

FROM 'SELFISH GENES' TO MOTHER 'GAIA'

debris if wastes were not broken down, recreated, and reworked by microbes, just as it would be very messy indeed without trillions of ants to reprocess detritus into forms usable to ants and other life-forms.

One may reasonably wonder, to be sure, how much of a mess would exist in the first place if complex animals were not present to produce it. Even more troubling, why would microbes be of any interest at all if they did not produce, facilitate, and help – as well as injure through disease – complex life-forms that engage in a good deal more than the biochemical and reproductive activity of microbes – such as *thinking,* for example? or exhibiting acute *self-consciousness*? or *knowing* the world, or *exploring* it, or exercising *will*?

When microbes can do these exceptional things, they may indeed be considered the marvels of life. Yet Margulis and Sagan seem to give primacy to microbes largely because they are indispensable to the development and existence of such biota as mammals, primates, and of course, human beings. Indeed, as one chapter of their book breathlessly follows another, describing how during dramatic environmental changes organic molecules combine to produce cell membranes, DNA, RNA, anaerobic cells, and aerobic ones, we are always reminded that human beings are dependent upon microcosms and their ability to survive human depredations.

Thus we are told with much aplomb that 'the visible world is a late-arriving, overgrown portion of the microcosm, and it functions only because of its well-developed connection with the microcosm's activities. ... Grasping as best we can the formidable powers of the biosphere in which we live out our lives, it is difficult to retain the delusion that without our help nature is helpless. ... We may pollute the air and waters for our grandchildren and hasten our own demise, but this will exert no effect on the continuation of the microcosm' which, in fact, 'is still evolving around us and within us. You could even say ... that the microcosm is evolving *as* us.'[42]

It is a novelty to learn that many people these days harbor the 'delusion that without our help nature is helpless'. Margulis and Sagan engage in the usual overstatement of humanistic views all the more easily to demolish them. It is no less a novelty to learn we, like all multicellular life-forms from jellyfish to wolves, are simply an 'overgrown portion of the microcosm'. That we cannot function without microcosms is a trite biological fact; their activities in maintaining the earth, the biosphere, and even our digestion of food are well-known facts of paramount importance. But why not include all the chemical elements that make up our genes and protoplasm?

Margulis and Sagan seem to confuse 'information' with wisdom, intelligence, and innovation. We are told:

> For sheer scope, human information systems have only just begun to approach the ancient bacterial systems which have been trading bits of information like a computer network with a memory accumulated over billions of years of continuous operation. As we move from a purely medical view of microbes to an understanding of them as our ancestors, as planetary elders [!], our emotions also change, from fear and loathing to respect and awe. Bacteria invented [!] fermentation, the wheel in the form of the proton rotary motor, sulfur breathing, photosynthesis, and nitrogen fixation, long before our evolution. They are not only highly social beings, but behave as a sort of worldwide decentralized democracy. Cells basically remain separate, but can connect and trade genes with organisms of even exceedingly different backgrounds. Realizing that human individuals also remain basically separate but can connect and trade knowledge with very different others may be taking a step toward the ancient wisdom [!] of the microcosm.' [43]

This passage, to speak frankly, is entirely anthropomorphic. We have no reason to believe that the parallels that Margulis and Sagan draw between microcosmic attributes and human behavior have anything in common, that microbes exhibit any ability that compares with the foresight that went into invention of the wheel, institutionalized social relations, 'a worldwide decentralized democracy', reflective 'wisdom', and self-conscious individuality.

Having indulged in this paean to microbial inventiveness, wisdom, and democracy, Margulis and Sagan invite us to regard 'man' as 'the consummate egotist'.

> Human beings are not particularly special, apart, or alone. ... It may be a blow to our collective ego, but we are not masters of life perched on the final rung of an evolutionary ladder. ... Objective scholars, if they were whales or dolphins, would place humans, chimpanzees, and orangutans in the same taxonomic group. There is no physiological basis for the classification of human beings into their own family (Hominidae – the manapes or apemen), apart from that of the great apes (Pongidae – the gibbons, siamangs, gorillas, chimps, and orangutans). Indeed, an extraterrestrial anatomist would not hesitate to put us together with the apes in the same subfamily or even genus. [44]

To argue down this taxonomic rhetoric demeaning the human species as a mere primate would be an insult to the reader's intelligence. Neither whales nor dolphins can ever be objective scholars for a multitude of anatomical, environmental, and even mental reasons that actually explain why human beings *are indeed unique* and why apes must be placed in a separate taxonomic family. Indeed, evolutionary biologists can easily make fools of themselves when they use microbiology, anatomy, and taxonomy to subvert the uniqueness of human beings, whose biological evolution has opened up cultural development.

Still, Margulis and Sagan do not deny us the benefit of a few homilies. We should be consoled to know that if human beings became extinct, if even all primates disappeared, 'the microcosm would still abound in those assets (e.g. nervous systems, manipulative appendages) that were leveraged into intelligence and technology in the first place.'[45] These 'assets' would not be nervous systems or 'appendages', however, since Margulis and Sagan seem to regard any microbial trait, such as flagella, as means of communication comparable to a nervous system and a means of locomotion comparable to bipedal walking. Alas, flagella do not constitute arms or legs; they are simply whiplike appendages that give greater motility to microbes and cells. One might, with equal superficiality, regard the wind as a means of communication for the earth and waves as seaside vocalizations.

So abundant are 'human' characteristics among microbes that should it come to pass that humanity is destroyed by a nuclear bomb and its radioactive fallout, Margulis and Sagan console us with their 'doubt that the overall health and underlying stability of the microcosm would be affected. ... Nor would the destruction of the ozone layer, permitting entry of torrents of ultraviolet radiation, ruin the microbial underlayer. Indeed, it would probably augment it, since radiation stimulates the bacterial transfer of genes.'[46]

I will not dwell on the various scenarios Margulis and Sagan offer for a 'future supercosm' in which, among other possibilities, technology gains such autonomy that it masters humans rather than the reverse and carries 'the wet, warm environment of the pre-Phanerozoic [or Present Era] microcosm into a future as fascinatingly nonhuman as the past.'[47] Exactly what will constitute 'fascination' or who will be 'fascinated' when human beings are not around remains something of a puzzle – unless computers are given the emotional as well as the mental equipment to replicate these distinctly human attributes.

If sociobiology has effectively reduced human beings to 'gene machines' and microcosmology seems to reduce them to bacteria, the Gaia Hypothesis reduces them to 'intelligent fleas that infest' Mother Earth or, more theistically, 'Gaia'. The image of humanity as fleas appears in James Lovelock's stridently antihumanistic 1988 book, *The Ages of Gaia: A Biography of Our Living Planet.*[48]

Much of the science Lovelock brings to the Gaia Hypothesis (as he called it on the inspired suggestion of a novelist friend, William Golding) seems to be basically sound. Dating from the 1970s, it advances the hypothesis that life over the course of organic evolution has interacted very creatively with its inorganic or abiotic environment. The earth as we know it today and as it has been for many millions of years was not in any sense 'given' to human beings; life-forms played a decisive role in creating it. Thus 'the atmosphere, the oceans, the climate, and the crust of the Earth are regulated at a state comfortable for life because of the behavior of living organisms'. Specifically, a homeostatic mechanism of feedback loops between the earth's biota and its abiotic environment keeps the acidity, temperature, oxidation state, and 'certain aspects of rocks and waters' constant at any given time. This close coupling of biota and its environments suggests that the planet's biosphere and its abiotic realm actually *constitute* a distinct system, 'Gaia'.[49]

This thesis is plausible and inviting. But like a number of earlier Gaians, Lovelock, in my view, is a reductionist – albeit on a more cosmic scale than sociobiologists and microcosmologists. And he is a misan-thrope. 'There is no clear distinction *anywhere* on the Earth's surface between living and nonliving matter,' he tells us. 'There is merely a hier-archy of *intensity* going from the "material" environment of the rocks and the atmosphere to the living cells'.[50] Bypassing the graded but highly qualitative differences between non-living and living 'matter' for a sim-plistic 'hierarchy' of energy levels, Lovelock's notion of Gaia exhibits no real concern for or interest in specific life-forms. Given the confusion that permeates New Age thinking, the fact that the Gaia Hypothesis is even more simplistic than Descartes' view of life has not deterred its acolytes, including Lynn Margulis, from hailing it as a new view of reality.

Admittedly, the biosphere is indispensable to the existence of Gaia, but Gaia nonetheless 'is not a synonym for the biosphere. ... Still less is Gaia the same as the biota, which is simply the *collection* of all individual living organisms.' Calling biota a *collection* is indicative of a quantitative antihu-manist orientation that sees 'heaps' and 'aggregates' rather than self-transformative organisms that defy the narrow physicalist mentality of positivistic scientists. Yet for Lovelock Gaia emerged with life in its earliest forms 'and extends into the future *as long as life persists'*.[51]

Lovelock's *The Ages of Gaia* contains an interesting account of the Earth's evolution, from its Archeon to its Middle and Modern age, in which we finally arrive at 'man' and 'his' doings. The fact that, for Lovelock, specific life forms are merely the fleeting cells of a superorgan-ismic body permits his antihumanism to run riot. 'Our humanistic concerns about the poor of the inner cities or the Third World,' he declares, 'and our near-obscene obsession with death, suffering, and pain as if these were evil in themselves – these thoughts divert the mind from our gross and excessive domination of the natural world.' With the social insight of a Margulian microcosmologist, Lovelock declares: 'Poverty and suffering are not sent; they are the consequences of what *we* do.'[52]

The identity of Lovelock's ubiquitous *we* here is surprisingly cryptic. Perhaps it includes the disempowered masses of the 'inner cities or the Third World', who 'grossly and excessively dominate the natural world' as much as Lovelock appears to give a damn for humanity. Or perhaps it includes the competitive and immensely empowered bankers, industrialists, stockbrokers in all their sinister mutations, political mafias, and similarly privileged strata who have brought societies around the world to virtual ruin.

Amid his dismissal of the distractions created by social issues, Lovelock the biologist rather contemptuously tells us: 'Pain and death are normal and natural; we could not long survive without them.'[53] What Gaia doth deliver, this we must suffer in the name of a biologism that overrides social abuses, perhaps even social horrors.

Lovelock's Gaia Hypothesis might pass for mere amoralism, which would be troubling enough in the age of Auschwitz, were it were not so banal. 'When we drive our cars and listen to the radio bringing news of acid rain,' Lovelock advises, 'we need to remind ourselves that we, *personally*, are the polluters. ... We are therefore accountable, *personally*, for the destruction of the trees by photochemical smog and acid rain. We are responsible for the silent spring that Rachel Carson predicted.'[54] Indeed, 'we' are absorbed in a 'city life [that] reinforces and strengthens the heresy of humanism, that narcissistic devotion to human interests alone'.[55] Not only is humanism a heresy, but cities – that is, the one *universalizing* medium by which humanity began to overcome its barbarous parochialism and ethnic hatreds – are a blight.

Not surprisingly, Lovelock exhibits little concern for such humanistic problems as pollution, nuclear power plants, and other environmental dislocations, his pious references to Rachel Carson's warning of a 'silent spring' without birds notwithstanding. 'Gaia, as I see her, is no doting mother tolerant of misdemeanors, nor is she some fragile and delicate damsel in danger from brutal mankind,' we are firmly advised. 'She is stern and tough, always keeping the world warm and comfortable for those who obey the rules, but ruthless in her destruction of those who transgress. Her unconscious goal is a planet fit for life. If humans stand in the way of this, we shall be eliminated with as little pity as would be shown by the micro-brain of an intercontinental ballistic nuclear missile in full flight to its target.'[56]

These strident remarks are meant to defend the author from the charge that he is a 'champion [of] complacence' who claims that 'feedback will always protect the environment from any serious harm that humans might do'.[57] One could, in fact, make a very persuasive case that pollution is a form of natural selection, in which 'Gaia,' 'ruthless in her destruction of those who transgress' her 'rules' or 'unconscious goal' is merely another natural phenomenon among the many that have doomed countless species to extinction. Yet Lovelock's cosmic antihumanism takes on strong theistic features, however much he bases his hypothesis on science. In his 'testament built around the idea of Gaia,' confesses Lovelock, 'I have tried to show that God and Gaia, theology and science, even physics and biology are not separate but a single way of thought.'[58] Having obscured the boundary between science and religion rather definitively, Lovelock wanders through citations from Jacques Monod (a stern materialist and determinist), and Erich Jantsch and Ilya Prigogine (advocates of system self-development), concluding that 'for the present, my belief in God rests at the stage of a positive agnosticism',[59] after which he drifts into quasi-philosophical fantasies of an island five hundred million years from now, in which bionic 'philosophers' and speechless vegetative males have neither the means nor the need to argue about the origins of life to understand the evolution of Gaia.

Lovelock's personal predilections and aspirations aside, what is surprising is that his works on Gaia have been earnestly embraced by a huge number of New Age 'spiritualists', whose understanding of his views leaves much to be desired. Once it leaves the plausible domain of earth science, *The Ages of Gaia* is so much at war with itself, so contradictory, and so anthropomorphic, that anyone looking at it from the standpoint of consistency and coherence may well be astonished that so many Gaians populate the privileged middle-class world of the late twentieth century.

Between the selfish gene, the sovereign microcosmos, and Gaia, there appears to be little room for human uniqueness as a product of evolution, no belief in the potential nobility of the human spirit, indeed, no authentically *naturalistic* grounding for great social ideals and ecological insights. Reason barely factors in Wilson's and Lovelock's elucidations of sociobiology and Gaia, respectively, only biochemistry and a vaguely conceived 'science' that becomes a euphemism for mind. Nearly all the works on sociobiology, microcosmology, and Gaia that essay the Olympian project of 're-enchanting' the world depict humanity variously as gene machines, an assemblage of microbes, or intelligent fleas. If this is not an edifying characterization of the human species, as bad an image or worse emerges from other parts of the contemporary repertoire of antihumanism.

Notes

1 E. O. Wilson, *Sociobiology: A New Synthesis* (Cambridge: Harvard University Press, 1975).

2 Paul Ehrlich, *The Population Bomb* (New York: Ballantine Books, 1968).

3 Richard Dawkins, *The Selfish Gene* (New York: Oxford University Press, 1976).

4 Wilson, *Sociobiology*, p. 3. How 'new' this 'synthesis' is can be argued at considerable length. Many of Wilson's notions were previously advanced by the quasi-romantic biologistic movements of central Europe during the 1920s, movements that took an exceptionally reactionary form between 1914 and 1945 and that fed directly into National Socialist ideology.

5 *Ibid.*, p. 3, emphases added.

6 E. O. Wilson, *On Human Nature* (Cambridge: Harvard University Press, 1978).

7 *Ibid.*, p. 2, emphases added.

8 Robert Wright, *The Moral Animal: The New Science of Evolutionary Psychology* (New York: Pantheon Books, 1994).

9 Wilson, *On Human Nature*, p. 2, emphases added.

10 *Ibid.*, pp. 2–3.

11 Dawkins, *Selfish Gene*, p. 2, emphasis added.

12 *Ibid.*, pp. 2–3.

13 *Ibid.*, p. 203.

14 *Ibid.*, p. 215.

15 *Ibid.*, p. 206. Here Dawkins explains the origin of the word *meme* as follows: 'We need a name for the new replicator, a noun which conveys the idea of a unit of cultural transmission, or a unit of *imitation*. "Mimeme" comes from a suitable Greek root, but I want a monosyllable that sounds a bit like "gene". I hope my classicist friends will forgive me if I abbreviate mimeme to *meme*.'

16 *Ibid.*, pp. 207–8.

17 *Ibid.*, p.209.

18 *Ibid.*, pp. 210–11, emphasis added.

19 *Ibid.*, p. 211, emphasis added

20 *Ibid.*, p. 25. We are also warned by Dawkins on page 95 that he is exercising 'license' in 'talking about genes as if they had conscious aims' and in an earlier passage on page 59 he tells us that 'they do not think at all'. But much of Dawkins' account is couched in words like *selfishness, loyalties, aims,* and *goals,* so that a few disclaiming sentences here and there barely serve to support his contention that he has not attributed unwarranted intentionality to his 'immortal coils'.

21 Robert L. Trivers, 'Foreword', in *Ibid.*, p. v.

22 Wilson, *On Human Nature,* p. 167, emphasis added.

23 *Ibid.*, p. 167, emphasis added.

24 *Ibid.*, p. 213, emphasis added.

25 *Ibid.*, p. 149, emphasis added.

26 *Ibid.*, p. 213.

27 *Ibid.*, p. 149.

28 *Ibid.*, p. 150.

29 *Ibid.*, p. 151.

30 For an eminently readable critical review of the primatological material that is being inflicted on the public by

researchers like Goodall, the reader would do well to consult Lord Zuckerman's caustic 'Apes R Not Us', in *The New York Review of Books* (30 May 1991), pp. 43–9.

31 Wilson, *On Human Nature,* pp. 152–3.

32 *Ibid.*, p. 152, emphasis added.

33 *Ibid.*, p. 153.

34 See Christopher Wills, *The Wisdom of Genes: New Pathways in Evolution* (New York: Basic Books, 1989).

35 Wilson, *On Human Nature,* p. 153.

36 *Ibid.*, p. 153, emphasis added.

37 *Ibid.*, p. 196.

38 Wilson, *On Human Nature,* p. 221.

39 David Erdal *et al.*, 'On Human Egalitarianism: An Evolutionary Product of Machiavellian Status Escalation', *Current Anthropology,* vol. 35, no. 2 (April 1994), pp. 169–70. In a laudatory account of Wilson's achievements in the *Boston Globe Magazine,* Scott Allen aptly describes sociobiology today as 'a fast-growing field of science'. Today, indeed! In the 1970s, when progressive social sensibilities still had a voice in the United States, Wilson was justly criticized by a wide spectrum of scientists and political activists for speculating that 'even with identical education and equal access to all professions, men are likely to play a disproportionate role in political life, business, and science', as Wilson said in *The New York Times* in 1975.

40 Lynn Margulis and Dorion Sagan, *Microcosmos: Four Billion Years of Microbial Evolution* (New York: Simon & Schuster, 1986).

41 *Ibid.*, p. 228.

42 *Ibid.*, pp. 66–7.

43 *Ibid.*, pp. 95–6.

44 *Ibid.*, pp. 193, 195, 214.

45 *Ibid.*, p. 236.

46 *Ibid.*, pp. 238–9.

47 *Ibid.*, p. 262.

48 James Lovelock, *The Ages of Gaia: A Biography of Our Living Planet* (New York: Bantam Books, 1988). On human beings as 'intelligent fleas', see p. 155.

49 *Ibid.*, p. 19.

50 *Ibid.*, p. 40, emphasis added.

51 *Ibid.*, p. 19, emphasis added.

52 *Ibid.*, p. 211, emphasis added.

53 *Ibid.*, p. 211.

54 *Ibid.*, p. 211, emphasis added.

55 *Ibid.*, p. 210.

56 *Ibid.*, p. 212.

57 *Ibid.*, p. 212.

58 *Ibid.*, p. 212.

59 *Ibid.*, p. 217.

CHAPTER 3

The new Malthusians

A narrow biologistic mindset that has reduced human beings to gene machines, microbes, and intelligent fleas need make little further effort to view people as the biotic equals of fruit flies, whose high reproductive rates are often adduced by popular writers on demography to warn of the dangers of unlimited human population growth.

A population of fruit flies, however, is very easy to decrease or elimi- nate. We can swat them, starve them, or diminish their numbers with pesticides. Such ways of dealing with population problems, as they are called, can give rise to a rather unsavory cast of mind. Viewing human beings as merely another animal species – such as fruit flies – creates an ideal setting for thinking about how their numbers can be reduced by foul means as well as fair.

One does not have to be a sociobiologist, microcosmologist, or a Gaian to think this way – although it does help. The idea of coercively diminishing human numbers has a long pedigree in the history of reac- tionary ideologies. Antihumanistic demographics begin to seem plausible once we begin to diminish humanity's uniqueness and evolutionary stature by viewing people merely as animal organisms which can be delivered over to their destiny – the harsh laws of natural selection. We can then claim that the social factors that lead to hunger, famine, and disease are actually biological, in the name of, say, ecological imperatives.

The most impressive success story in fostering this way of thinking over the past two generations has been a small book, *The Population Bomb,* written by a then-relatively obscure Californian entomologist, Paul Ehrlich, and first published in May 1968.[1] The year of its publica- tion was a climactic one in the history of the New Left. Following the uprising of French students in the famous May–June events of that year and the general strike that swept France, the New Left was beginning to abandon its earlier 1960s populist doctrine of 'participatory democracy' by the autumn of 1968 and was veering sharply toward a doctrinaire, largely authoritarian Marxist–Maoist orientation that completely marginalized it on its own campus spawning grounds. Gradually a reaction against radicalism – and ultimately against humanism – sets in, making biologistic interpretations of social problems a fairly common viewpoint.

These sectarian maladies notwithstanding, radical sentiments remained fairly strong in the 1970s. Indeed, the possibility of combining the lingering libertarian features of the early New Left with an emerging environmental public consciousness opened the realistic possibility of developing a *social* ecology movement: one that clearly singled out the profit-oriented, competitive market system as the principal source of environmental degradation and that raised the need for a radical restructuring of society along free and ecologically oriented lines.

Based on my own experience as a very active participant in this momentous period, I can say that if there was any single work that aborted a confluence of radical ideas with public environmental concerns, it was Paul Ehrlich's *Population Bomb*. By the early 1970s, Ehrlich's tract had significantly sidetracked the emerging environmental movement from social critique to a very crude, often odious biologism the impact of which remains with us today.

The shift that Ehrlich's book produced was eminently suited to the Cold War ideology and suffocating reactionism of the Nixon administration. Whatever Ehrlich personally thought he was doing, the crudity of the book's message, indeed its ugly misanthropy and antihumanism, provided an ideological prop for highly regressive political views. For years thereafter, the book served as something of a reactionary manifesto for narrowly biologistic interpretations of demographic and ecological issues.

The one-paragraph-long opening of *The Population Bomb,* entitled 'The Problem', remains, in my view, an offensive set of observations such as is rarely encountered in the unsavory demographic literature of recent times.[2]

Ehrlich describes a taxi trip he, his wife, and daughter made through a New Delhi slum, where, to his shock 'one stinking night', his cab's passage was impeded by throngs of people. 'People eating, people washing, people sleeping', Ehrlich exclaims with revulsion. 'People visiting, arguing, and screaming. People thrusting their hands through the taxi window, begging. People defecating and urinating. People clinging to buses. People herding animals. People, people, people, people.'

People living in New Delhi's slums have been known to do many other things, such as carve beautiful artifacts, make love, practice humane religious beliefs, play, dance, sing, laugh, and socialize with each other with great warmth. Despite the desperate conditions of the India's poor, an earthy cultural vitality persists among them. Certainly Ehrlich saw what *he* seems to have wanted to see – people begging, defecating, urinating in the streets of a terribly impoverished area of the city that is notoriously lacking in shelter and means of transportation, and that still suffers from disparities of wealth and status deeply rooted in an ugly history of European colonialism.

Our worthy entomologist from the academic groves of California then goes on to declare: 'As we moved slowly through the mob, hand horn squawking, the dust, noise, heat, and cooking fires gave the scene a hellish aspect. Would we ever get to our hotel? All three of us were, frankly, frightened.' Having negotiated their way through the inferno, this middle-class Californian family found itself in the comforts of a fairly modern hotel, after which Ehrlich opined that 'since that night I've known the *feel* of overpopulation.'[3]

This depiction of extreme poverty is so offensive, so elitist, and so arrogant that any humane reader of the book might well regard it as a moral nightmare. Regrettably, most readers seemingly did not. Although Ehrlich later did suffer reproaches from a small number of critics, their numbers were relatively few, and his book became immensely popular, as its long publishing history indicates. Indeed, Ehrlich still figures as an eminent figure in the ecology movement today, and in recent years he has gained favor among the same liberals and radicals whom one would expect to have found his *Population Bomb* completely repugnant, even as he has lauded reactionaries such as Garrett Hardin.

The remaining pages of *The Population Bomb* offer us little respite from the antihumanism and arrogance of its opening chapter. 'Too many cars,' we learn, 'too many factories, too much detergent, too much pesticide, multiplying contrails, inadequate sewage treatment plants, too little water, too much carbon dioxide – all can be traced easily to *too many people*.'[4] The emphasis is Ehrlich's – and one feels obliged to ask, *all*? In view of the relatively small number of cars and factories in late 1960s India, is Ehrlich possibly thinking of California, where cars, factories, and excessive pollution were major problems for decades before his epiphany in New Delhi?

Leaving aside some of Ehrlich's science fiction scenarios, we are told that family planning will not suffice to reduce population numbers. It is not enough to offer couples the 'means' to control the birth of children, since they may, after all, 'plan' to have too many. Stronger measures are required. 'Everywhere' in the Third World, 'people *want* large families. They *want* families of a size that will keep the population growing – whereupon Ehrlich regales the reader with statistics that show that Third World women who seek guidance in family planning are mainly those who have already had several children. But then, Ehrlich brightly cautions, 'remember that planned, well-spaced children will starve, or vaporize in a thermonuclear war, or die of plague just as well as unplanned children.'[5] This statement was egregiously false – family planning has done a great deal to reduce rates of population growth. For all the noxious methods that Indira Gandhi's government used to force sterilization on India's poor and despite China's scandalously restrictive measures, in many places women embrace technologies to limit the number of their offspring and recover their humanity as someone who is more than a reproductive factory.

How are Americans to overcome their propensity for large families, in Ehrlich's view? Aside from bringing their own population numbers and growth-rates down, 'we are ... going to have to adopt some *very tough* foreign policy positions relatively to population control, and we must do it from a psychologically strong position.' Thus: '[m]any of my colleagues feel that some sort of *compulsory* birth regulation would be necessary to achieve such control. One plan often mentioned involves the addition of temporary sterilants to water supplies or staple food. Doses of the antidote would be carefully rationed by the government to produce the desired population size.' 'Rest easy,' Ehrlich assures the shocked reader; the scientific means for instituting this salutary solution are not 'even open to us, thanks to the *criminal* inadequacy of biomedical research in this area.'[6]

Still, 'it might be possible to develop such population control tools, although the task would not be simple.'[7] If there is a will, there is a way. But then, Americans would not stand for it. In a breathtaking shift in perspective, we pass from authoritarian solutions (for the Third World?) to financial solutions (for the First World). The US tax structure could be changed to reward citizens for not having children and to punish those who do, Ehrlich proposes. Additionally, we might also consider higher taxes on such perilously dangerous items as 'layettes, cribs, diapers, diaper services, and expensive toys', with due allowance that 'the essentials be available without penalty to the poor (just as free food now is).'[8]

Ultimately, however, we must face up to the fact that these and other such measures 'would need coordination by a *powerful* governmental agency. A federal Department of Population and Environment (DPE) should be set up with the power to take *whatever steps are necessary* to establish a reasonable population size in the United States and put an end to the steady deterioration of our environment.' This agency 'would promote intensive investigation of new techniques of birth control, *possibly leading to the development of mass sterilization agents.*' Indeed, the DPE 'would encourage more research on human sex determination, for if a simple method could be found to guarantee that first-born children were males, then population control problems in many areas would be somewhat eased' – since cultural biases usually favor having sons instead of daughters – especially 'where couples with only female children "keep trying" in hope of a son.'[9] Readers in the 1990s who care to commend Ehrlich for foreseeing current sex-selective technologies are welcome to do so, but the logic of this practice is self-evident, as is revealed by recent sex-ratio figures in China that abnormally favor the birth of male over female babies. I may add that the extent to which outright female infanticide has increased in China as well as gender-detection techniques, has disconcerted some of the most resolute of Western 'population bombers'.

As for American foreign policy cast in the form of 'population control', Ehrlich urges his readers to accept 'the concept of "triage" borrowed from military medicine. The idea is briefly this: When casualties crowd a dressing station to the point where all cannot be cared for by the limited medical staff, some decisions must be made on who will be treated.' Accordingly, 'all incoming casualties are placed in one of three classes': those who are mortally wounded and should be left to die; those who can survive irrespective of how quickly treatment is given; and those for whom immediate treatment may be a matter of life or death.[10]

Even though we are far from any immediate demographic apocalypse, American aid to famine-stricken or destitute countries, Ehrlich suggests, should be guided by the principle of triage. Indeed, what seems to determine whether a country should be denied food and medicine is its fertility rate. Following William and Paul Paddock, two cold warriors whose 1967 book *Famine – 1975!* never lived up to its predictive title, Ehrlich perhaps unwittingly casts population control policies along the Cold War alignments of the day. We might give food aid to Pakistan, he suggests, under 'the tough-minded leadership of President Ayub Khan', who, Ehrlich neglects to tell us, was the notoriously authoritarian *General* Muhammed Ayub Khan, who came to power in a military *coup* against a constitutional government and ruled by decree, despite the facade of democratic 'elections'.[11] Pakistan, not coincidentally, was on the American side of the Cold War – in contrast to non-aligned India, which Ehrlich suggests (in agreement with the Paddocks) should be denied American food under the triage system.

In Ehrlich's dazzling view of social and political reality, 'there is no rational choice *except* to adopt some form of the Paddocks' strategy as far as food distribution is concerned. ... The Paddocks deserve immense credit for their courage and foresight in publishing *Famine – 1975!*, which may be remembered as one of the most important books of our age' – nothing less![12] Doubtless such architects of the Cold War as John Foster Dulles and Allen Dulles would have heartily agreed, albeit for reasons that have nothing to do with demographic considerations.

More or less anticipating the authoritarian measures of Indira Gandhi in India and the Communist totalitarians in China, Ehrlich reproves the American government for opposing the suggestion of an Indian official, Dr S. Chandrasekar, that all Indian males who fathered three or more children should face compulsory sterilization. Verily, he declares: 'we should have applied pressure on the Indian government to go ahead with the plan. We should have volunteered logistic support in the form of helicopters, vehicles, and surgical instruments. We should have sent doctors to aid the program by setting up centers for training para-medical personnel to do vasectomies. Coercion? Perhaps, *but* coercion in a good cause' – at which point Ehrlich expresses astonishment at 'the attitudes of Americans who are horrified at the prospect of our government insisting on population control as the price of food aid.'[13]

Forced sterilization in the name of a good cause may look uncomfortably like authoritarian measures taken by some of the more reactionary regimes in recent history. If his good cause entails the forcible sterilization of a Third World people – or any people, for that matter, who happen not to accept the demographic apocalypse that explodes on the pages of *The Population Bomb* – such authoritarian measures would produce immeasurably worse problems in the social and political spheres than the ones they were intended to solve. Coercive measures here or harsh demographic policies there do not usually come in bits and pieces, like candy bars from a slot machine. They are adopted in a general authoritarian context whose logic leads to more encompassing social controls in ever more spheres of life, with a growing state apparatus to enforce them.

As it turned out, Ehrlich's predictive abilities were imprecise at best. Extrapolating from a number of his premises and forebodings some twenty-five years ago, we should now be wracked worldwide by famines, shortages of raw materials, and rising prices. The planet's basic resources should be largely depleted, and demographically induced starvation should be haunting wealthy and poor regions alike. During my lecture tours in the late 1960s, members of Zero Population Growth (ZPG) would raise dire warnings that the immediate future was terribly portentous.'Not only would there be famines, civil wars induced by hunger, and intolerable congestion, but fortunate would be the Americans who found some living space on man-made islands in the world's oceans.

Actually, between 1950 and 1990, worldwide grain production nearly tripled, increasing from 631 million tons to 1,780 million tons, at an average rate of some 29 million tons annually. Beef and mutton production rose 2.6 times, from 24 million tons to 62 million. The supply of fish rose nearly five times, from 22 million to 100 million tons. Nearly all the major mineral resources rose at comparable or higher rates. All of these increases by far outstripped population growth and – potentially, in a more rational society – might have amply met the needs of the world population. The famines that swept over areas of Africa were induced more by political conflicts and World Bank policies than by desertification and lack of land. Today, as new agricultural and industrial technologies emerge, it would be naive to make the inflexible predictions that many Malthusians have advanced over the past twenty-five years, just as it would be naive for so-called 'Cornucopians', who see population growth as a desideratum – to claim that the larger the number of the people on the planet, the better.[14]

Ehrlich's assertion in *The Population Bomb* that 'population is far outstripping food production' proved, in fact, to be grossly erroneous.[15] Nor was the harshness of his recipes for India matched in the advice he offered his American readers. 'There are some very distinguished economists who do not feel that our capitalist system must be fueled by an ever-growing population or ever-continuing depletion of resources (both of which are impossible anyway),' he prudently noted. 'There, in fact, seems to be no reason why the GNP [gross national product] cannot be kept growing for a very long time *without population growth*' – which indeed would be entirely possible if the business community could induce consumers to buy several motor vehicles, television sets, computers, and so on, per family.[16] Which would, of course, raise serious problems about the waste of resources, despite the multitude of recycling centers that have sprung up in recent years. In short, the GNP could grow and grow – but what, alas, would be the fate of the planet as industry turns soil into sand, oceans into sewers, forests into timber, and devastates the planet in the process? The social myopia that marks *The Population Bomb* is nothing less than appalling: a rising GNP is yearned for, amid panic that population growth will deplete planetary resources!

The book found readers across political, social and cultural lines with the carelessness of an infant scrawling on a blank page. It educated people to regard the causes of hunger as resource depletion rather than exploitation, civil war, political instability, and economic greed; imminent resource depletion, in turn, was grossly exaggerated and projected into the near future. Where Ehrlich could even remotely or indirectly 'biologize' a social cause that was producing a deterioration in the human condition, he seemed to do so with gusto, as have his admirers among the quasi-mystical tendencies in the environmental movement. Ehrlich has since retreated from the crassly coercive positions he advanced in *The Population Bomb* (and *How to Be a Survivor*, written more than a decade later), yet biological reductionism still pervades his writings. The social conditions that make for population growth and stabilization generally take a back seat to a zoological outlook that nuzzles closely to some extremely unsavory political views.

Not only did *The Population Bomb* sell some two million copies in numerous reprintings, but Ehrlich personally became a *cause célèbre*, appearing on television shows, at widely heralded conferences, and on the lecture circuit. He addressed thousands of adoring listeners and either directly or indirectly aided in the formation of a particularly rancorous organization, Zero Population Growth (ZPG), of which he became chairman. In sidetracking public discussion of the social sources of environmental deterioration – notably, global corporate capitalism, with its plundering of forests, natural resources, and, significantly, the labor force of underprivileged countries – it set the narrowly biological agenda that increasingly marked the environmental movement in the 1970s and 1980s. ZPG zealots and neo-Malthusians dismissed criticism of the social and economic irrationalities of the decade as 'leftist dogma' or 'radical sectarianism'.

The slogan that came to forefront of the 1970s – one that by no means has faded – was '*People* are Pollution', a theme that pervaded an appreciable part of the educational curriculum in American elementary and high schools. Two sixth-graders in Kensington, Maryland, for example, composed a poem that drew approval from the growing 'population bombers' and budding misanthropes of the time:

> If we didn't have people
> We wouldn't have pollution,
> Get rid of people
> That's the only solution.

Meanwhile the New York Museum of Natural History organized an 'environmental exhibition' in which schoolchildren were trotted past one case after another that showed wanton environmental damage. The last exhibit (if memory serves) was headed: 'The Most Dangerous Animal of All'. It consisted of a full-length mirror, in which visitors could see themselves in the full splendor of their terrifyingly human attributes. When I lingered near this distasteful exhibit, nothing impressed me more than the sight of a middle-class white teacher explaining to a black child the 'meaning' of the mirror and the title that surmounted it. Ehrlich, alas, had done his work only too well.

By no means was Ehrlich alone in his views in 1968; nor has he been the most chilling and coercive of the 'population bombers' in the checkered history of demography. The antihumanistic message of *The Population Bomb* dates back most notably to the publication of Thomas Malthus's *An Essay on the Principle of Population* in 1798, known more briefly today as *On Population*.[17]

The influence of Malthus's work lasted much longer than its author's own life, as he died in 1834. Indeed, it gave rise to a militant credo, Malthusianism, that enjoys a vigorous existence even in the closing decade of the twentieth century. To ignore the influence of *On Population* would be to ignore its socially malignant ramifications, which have nourished some of the most reactionary ideologies of the nineteenth and twentieth centuries.

On Population remains an unsavory, class-oriented, and often cynical tract, despite some mitigating observations Malthus made over the course of seven revisions. Although its admirers often see it exclusively as a work on population, it is actually an ideological diatribe against the humanistic tradition of the Enlightenment. Aimed against such distinguished Enlightenment theorists as the English anarchist William Godwin and the French progressivist Marquis de Condorcet (Thomas Paine's *Age of Reason* is a minor target), Malthus's tract is not only an expression of concern over population growth; it is a pessimistic attack upon the egalitarian ideals of his two principal targets and their belief in humanity's capacity to significantly improve itself. Like the theories of many sociobiologists today, Malthus's views subvert the belief that human beings are anything more than simple brutes. Not only must their numbers be kept under control by fair means or foul; people must be kept severely in tow psychologically by their well-to-do betters and by the harsh constraints of natural law.

Malthus's attack on William Godwin's 'system of equality' – and on Godwin's belief that the 'amelioration of society to be produced merely by reason and conviction – drips with sarcasm. 'In short,' Malthus declaims after a tongue-in-cheek devotional to Godwin's humane and rational society, 'it is impossible to contemplate the whole of this fair structure, without emotions of delight and admiration, accompanied with ardent longing for the period of its accomplishment.'[18]

Having delivered his breast of 'delight and admiration' for Godwin's vision, Malthus quickly turns to a misanthropic evocation that subjects such reasoned and humane utopianism to withering scorn. 'Man cannot live in the midst of plenty,' we are told *ex cathedra*. 'All cannot share alike in the bounties of nature. Were there no established administration of property [i.e. the state], every man would be obliged to guard with force his little store. Selfishness would be triumphant. The subjects of contention would be perpetual. Every individual mind would be under constant anxiety about corporal support, and not a single intellect would be free to expiate in the field of thought.'[19] These are the standard arguments that have been used from Aristotle to Hobbes to justify ruling classes and, in Hobbes's case, the state.

Condorcet's belief in 'the indefinite perfectibility of man' is treated in much the same way as Godwin's belief in an egalitarian society based on reason: it is rejected largely on grounds of natural law and its immutability. 'The constancy of the laws of nature and of effects and causes is the foundation of all human knowledge,' Malthus writes, 'though far be it from me to say that the same power [i.e. the deity] which framed and executes the laws of nature, may not change them all "in a moment, in the twinkling of an eye."' Following this nod to the deity, Malthus advises his reader:

> All that I mean to say is that it is impossible to infer [such a change] from reasoning. If without any previous observable symptoms or indications of a change, we can infer that a change will take place, we may as well make any assertion whatever and think it as unreasonable to be contradicted in affirming that the moon will come in contact with the earth tomorrow, as in saying that the sun will rise at its usual time.'[20]

Accordingly: 'population, when unchecked, increases in a geometrical ratio. Subsistence increases only in an arithmetical ratio. ... By that law of our nature which makes food necessary to the life of man, the effects of these two unequal powers *must* be kept equal.'[21] Malthus's conclusion is not only descriptive, based on assumptions or 'postulata', as he puts it; it is also prescriptive, a guide to human action.

Although in later editions of his essay Malthus imparted some value to the efficacy of 'moral restraint' by individuals in controlling their own reproductive behavior, he never retracted the conclusions that logically followed from his earlier steps. Thus, history presumably demonstrates that 'the superior power of population cannot be checked without producing misery or vice'. Indeed, charitable behavior by the rich 'contribute[s] frequently to prolong a season of distress among the poor, yet no possible form of society could prevent the almost constant action of misery upon a great part of mankind, if in a state of inequality [as existed in Malthus's time], and upon all, if all were equal' – as in Godwin's egalitarian social vision.[22]

Thus: '[t]o prevent the recurrence of misery, is, alas! beyond the power of man', and all parish poor laws meant to alleviate this inexorable destiny of the poor serve only to deceive them.[23] Indeed, we are told with pious concern, 'Famine seems to be the last, the most dreadful resource of nature. The power of population is so superior to the power in the earth to produce subsistence for man, that premature death must in some shape or other visit the human race. The vices of mankind are active and able ministers of depopulation. They are the precursors in the great army of destruction; and often finish the dreadful work themselves.'[24] Between original sin ('the virus of mankind') and the workings of the mundane world (the limited 'bounties of nature'), Malthus manages to leave us no alternative: neither heaven nor earth can come to our aid.

If the 'preventive checks' that thinking people deploy cannot inhibit the production of large families, diminish vice, and make for a better life, Malthus holds, then inexorable 'positive checks' on population growth come into play. These positive checks

> *are extremely various, and include every cause, whether arising from vice or misery, which in any degree contributes to shorten the natural duration of human life. Under this head, therefore, may be enumerated all the unwholesome occupations, severe labour and exposure to the seasons, extreme poverty, bad nursing of children, great towns, excesses of all kinds, the whole train of common diseases and epidemics, wars, plague, and famine.*[25]

The poor generally come in for a drubbing at Malthus's hands:

> *A man who is born into a world already possessed, if he cannot get subsistence from his parents on whom he has a just demand, and if the society do not want his labour, has no claim of right to the smallest portion of food, and, in fact, has not business to be where he is. At nature's mighty feast there is no vacant cover for him. She tells him to be gone [from his place at her table] and will quickly execute her own orders, if he do not work on the compassion of some of her guests.*[26]

This is a compassion that Malthus, often tongue-in-cheek, derides. Indeed:

> *Hard as it may appear in individual instances, dependent poverty ought to be held disgraceful. Such a [moral] stimulus seems to be absolutely necessary to promote the happiness of the great mass of mankind; and every general attempt to weaken this stimulus, however benevolent its intention, will always defeat its own purpose. If men be induced to marry from the mere prospect of parish provision, they are not only unjustly tempted to*

> *bring unhappiness and dependence upon themselves and children, but they are tempted, without knowing it, to injure all in the same class with themselves.*[27]

Malthus's later disquisitions on humanity's moral sense and its capacity to voluntarily control population growth and invent technologies that could increase food production are more than overshadowed by his heartless, class-oriented hunger politics. From the first edition of the essay to the seventh, Malthus mercilessly accepts the 'positive checks' that reduce population.

Indeed, in the second edition of *On Population,* Malthus proposes horrendous 'positive checks' that stigmatize his ideas as utterly unfeeling. Nonetheless they had a considerable influence on the antihumanistic demographic and sociobiological literature that has appeared more recently. 'In all old states,' Malthus tells us, 'the marriages and births depend principally upon the deaths, and … there is no encouragement to early unions so powerful as a great mortality.'[28]

To insure that the poor do not reproduce, Malthus proposes quite concretely that far from

> *recommending cleanliness to the poor, we should encourage contrary habits. In our towns we should make the streets narrower, crowd more people into the houses, and court the return of plague. In the country, we should build our villages near stagnant pools, and particularly encourage settlements in all marshy and unwholesome conditions. But above all, we should reprobate specific remedies for ravaging diseases; and those benevolent, but much mistaken men, who have thought they were doing a service to mankind by projecting schemes for the total extirpation of particular disorders.*[29]

These prescriptions were written, let me note, by a Christian parson who gained considerable honor not only in his day but also in our own.

Like a growing rhizome with innumerable offshoots, Malthusianism brought forth demographically based and racist social theories that have beleaguered humanity ever since. The ideology, even as Malthus formulated it in 1798, already nourished the mean-spirited egotism, 'free enterprise', and a vicious exploitation of the poor that found such vivid expression in the socially critical novels of Dickens and Eliot. England soon became not only the industrial center of the world but its human charnel house, where the bones of grossly exploited men, women, and children were to be deposited in vast numbers to the ever greater glory of profit. Robert Owen, a truly benevolent manufacturer of the period (whom Malthus criticized) showed at his factory in New Lanark that relatively decent working conditions did not conflict with the making of substantial profits. Visitors from different parts of England and abroad readily celebrated this enlightened industrialist for his human and economic successes – only to return home and visit a veritable hell upon their own working class with little regard for Owen's practices.

Such Victorian hypocrisies were not the product of Malthus's demographic views, but the *Essay on Population* provided an ideological patina for the notorious brutality of English orphanages and poorhouses, and the execution of poor people for what we today would regard as relatively minor offenses. Above all, it justified the ruthless exploitation of the industrial working class in the decades that followed. Malthusian ideology was employed very effectively to buttress the mean-spiritedness of the time and support the crass exploitation of factory and farm labor, often with a zealotry that was devoid of feeling for human welfare and the simplest of moral decencies.

Charles Darwin's use of Malthus's theory of population in *The Origin of Species* was added an even more chilling tenet to what could, by then, be called *social* Darwinism. By no means was Darwin responsible for the ideological transformation that his theory of natural selection underwent. But with acolytes like Herbert Spencer *et al.*, natural selection became a ruling-class social ideology of enormous influence. Dissolute scions of British noble houses, predatory bankers and industrialists, even small proprietors and manufacturers with 'expectations', and various strata of the labor aristocracy could now conceive of themselves as 'nature's elect', the product of natural selection and the 'survival of the fittest' transposed to the social realm.

Accordingly, the 'failures' in the competitive game of British capitalism – notably the working classes and the poor – were seen disdainfully as the inevitable victims of evolution's onward march toward selecting more 'fit' individuals. Natural law itself dictated their exploitation for the glory of enterprise and profit – or their disposal on the scrap heap of humanity once they could no longer fulfill their responsibility to the naturally endowed elite, selected for survival and success.

Moreover, social Darwinism was transposed from the domain of domestic affairs to world affairs, providing the rationale *par excellence* for imperialism – the 'improvement' of the dark races of the world who lived in demonic 'barbarism'. There seems to be an infinite capacity, deeply rooted in tribal dependencies and a darkly primitivist sense of parochialism, to regard outsiders or strangers as non-human and thus as potential enemies. Starting as early as the fifteenth century, Europeans and later Americans had engaged in a genocidal frenzy against native peoples on both continents of the New World and the enslavement of African tribal people. Now, in the eighteenth and nineteenth centuries, armies marched forth from Europe to 'tame' the 'uncivilized' continents of the planet, presumably a 'noble' calling for which the conqueror, colonizer, and missionary deserved a 'just reward'. The barbarities that Britain, France, Belgium, Portugal, and Germany inflicted on the territories they claimed and conquered in Africa and Asia read like the horrors Dante described in the lower depths of hell. Even after the slave trade was abolished, imperialist practices were greatly reinforced by social Darwinist ideologies. Profoundly influenced by Malthusian doctrines, almost no restraint was placed on the cruelties that the so-called Age of Imperialism inflicted on the dark regions of the earth, as the literature and vernacular of the time called today's Third World.

The sense of imperial destiny that social Darwinism imparted served this Euro-American barbarism very effectively. The French transformed the homebred British version into a vulgarized mission to spread the Enlightenment, even the ideals of their great Revolution, to the 'less endowed' peoples of the world. The German version took on a specifically racial form, celebrating the virtues of Teutonic Man over all other ethnic groups, particularly people of color. Empire, dressed up as the 'white man's burden', became in all its various nationalistic mutations specific forms of social Darwinism, each with its barely concealed roots in Malthus's notion of 'fitness' – namely the ability of the 'able' to survive and 'feast' at the table of nature.

That the number of places at Nature's table on which to feast were limited, as Malthus had opined, inexorably raised the question of who was most fit from a *eugenical* standpoint to find a seat. It was asked which racial traits were worth fostering through breeding techniques and which were not. Flat or hooked noses were apparently not, especially if they were attached to people with the brown or black skin so common in the 'dark lands' of the world. Eugenics, whatever its scientific value, was quickly socialized into insidious racial ideologies. Concepts of 'desirable' and 'undesirable' races came so much into vogue that at the turn of the century, even a Socialist like Jack London celebrated his sturdy Anglo-Saxon lineage. Nietzsche's 'blond beast' became a metaphor for Germanic virtues that many of the Kaiser's troops carried in their minds as they marched into the trenches of the Western front in 1914.

Nearly all social Darwinist, eugenicist, and nationalistic racism, as well as myths of the 'white man's burden', are deeply rooted in Malthus's writings, reaching their apogee in the last quarter of the nineteenth century and the first half of the twentieth.

Ideologically, this medley of views provided the rationale for the terrible slaughter that occurred in Europe between 1914 and 1918, initiating what Arno J. Mayer has called the 'thirty years war' of the twentieth century – the three decades that immersed a suffering humanity in blood until 1945.[30] Prior to 1914, only one institution seemed capable of countervailing Europe's drive toward self-annihilation: the Socialist or Second International. Its anthem, 'The Internationale', called upon the working classes of the world to maintain a steadfast class solidarity in the interests of humanity as a whole. In ringing prose, Marx and Engels's *Communist Manifesto* declared that the proletariat had no country, and it closed with with the slogan: 'Workingmen of all countries, unite!'

The collapse of the Second International in August 1914, when the French and German socialist parties voted in favor of war credits for their respective countries, provided tragic evidence of the power of nationalist sentiments, even within the working class itself. A primal tribalism had reasserted itself, and for more than four years of terrible slaughter it retained a vigorous hold upon the armies of the Allies and Central Powers.

This tribalism was shaken to its foundations by the promise of a new socialist future which the Bolshevik Revolution of October 1917 seemed to initiate. In proclamation after proclamation, the new Soviet regime upheld, to its lasting credit, an unwavering internationalism in the face of Euro-American national chauvinism. The years that immediately followed the Bolshevik Revolution were heady with hopes for achieving a new worldwide solidarity between the working classes of the belligerent countries and a revolutionary restructuring of society along rational and humanistic lines.

Indeed, seldom had history been imbued by so striking a sense of universality, of the 'fraternity' heralded by the Great French Revolution in 1789, and of a cooperative dispensation of human affairs. In the span between the First and Second World Wars – one of the most decisive periods in the history of humanity – repeated social upheavals posed the crucial question of whether the Enlightenment and its humanistic ideals could be embodied in a rational society. The radical political hopes of the 1920s and 1930s reached their climax in the Spanish Civil War of 1936, the most ideologically charged class struggle of the twentieth century. This conflict, virtually ignored in history textbooks today, placed upon the agenda of the modern era all the ideals that various socialisms had spawned, from the closing years of the French Revolution up to the Second World War. The crushing of the revolution in Spain – in a struggle that lasted nearly three years – marked the end of an era of classical socialism and, above all, internationalist universalism.

The Second World War, its claim to support the 'Four Freedoms' in the Atlantic Charter of 1940 notwithstanding, was fought out along largely chauvinistic and nationalistic lines. Still, never before in history had a bloc of Allied powers – the Western democracies – confronted so radically antihumanist a foe as German National Socialism. There is no historical precedent for the systematic extermination of European Jews. I refer not only to the immense number of lives that were claimed by the Nazi camp system and the special execution squads in German-occupied Poland and Russia; the past had seen numerically comparable massacres in, say, the Mongol invasions of Eurasia. Nor was the Nazi attempt to exterminate an entire people entirely without precedent in the ancient world. But National Socialism conducted its genocidal policy against the Jews on an *industrial* basis, in which millions of people were 'processed' to their deaths through a camp system that was essentially an abattoir more ruthless and inhumane than a typical slaughter-house.

Malthusianism, eugenics, social Darwinism, and racial nationalism contributed profoundly to producing the reality of Auschwitz by creating an outlook that made it possible to regard human beings as pestiferous animals. Denied all personality, individuality, recognition, and subjectivity, European Jews in particular were beaten, shot, and gassed as though they were bothersome fruit flies or fleas. National Socialism, ideologically similar to the sociobiological images of human beings so widespread today, can be regarded as the practical culmination of Malthus's view that the poor are merely objects to be systematically starved, afflicted with disease, and driven to death wholesale.

Barely had the Second World War come to an end and its dreadful genocidal tallies had been made, when neo-Malthusianism, eugenics, and 'scientific' racism emerged with all the ferocity that had marked its existence in the decades that preceded the war.

Eugenics, whose abuse accounts for the racist American immigration laws of 1924 that privileged, supposedly 'northern' European immigrants over eastern and southern Europeans, created a new basis for the Malthusian literature of the interwar period and resurfaced in the late 1940s in the United States. Barely two years after the Second World War came to an end, Guy Irving Burch and Elmer Pendell published *Human Breeding and Survival: Population Roads to Peace and War*.[31] Even while trials for crimes against humanity – the mass murder of millions of Jews and Gypsies – were still going on, this book discoursed on 'social bases' of using sterilization to attain 'peace goals'.

Burch and Pendell repeated an old Malthusian class orientation:

> *Looking toward a possibly economic test, are persons who are on relief to*
> *be encouraged to reproduce while they are on relief, as they have been? ...*
> *Are their children more likely to be social burdens than are the children of*
> *those who are in better control of their own environment? ... Is it reason-*
> *able to ask other citizens to pay more taxes in order that relief recipients*
> *may reproduce?*[32]

The passage shares a very close linguistic kinship to the reactionary
verbiage of the right-wing groups that had gained so much prominence
during the years directly preceding the Second World War. That it has
persisted for over half a century and is gaining an extraordinary prominence in the 1980s and 1990s, not only among right-wingers but among
some liberals, is evidence of its tenacious hold on the public mind.

It is hard to regard the 'economic test' to which Burch and Pendell
allude as strictly economic. The mid-1940s were a time of sweeping
social and cultural dislocation in the United States. Millions of people
had been demobilized from the military, and many rural southern blacks
were migrating to northern cities. To prepare for the postwar era, all of
them required a host of welfare measures, from direct material assistance
to government-subsidized educational programs.

The reader of their 1947 book would be justified in feeling uneasy that
the authors quote approvingly from the writings of H. L. Mencken, who
had achieved considerable notoriety for his misanthropy, elitism, and
cynicism.

> *In basing sterilization on social criteria such as criminality, low earnings,*
> *poor health, and lack of education, H. L. Mencken has probably gone*
> *farther than anyone before him, in suggesting a large-scale use of the*
> *economic test [for the right to have children].*
>
> *In the* American Mercury *for August, 1937, he observes that in gen-*
> *eral the sterilization laws apply only to persons who are defective in some*
> *gross and melodramatic way. Said he: 'Let a resolute attack be made upon*
> *the fecundity of all the males on the lowest rungs of the social ladder, and*
> *there will be a gradual and permanent improvement.'*[33]

Whereupon the authors coolly discourse on the practicability, as advanced
by Mencken, of offering a financial reward to 'prospective steriles' that
would doubtless 'result in a stampede to the sterilizing physicians'. Owing
to their shiftlessness and infirmity, we are to suppose, the poor and unedu-
cated would be only too eager to make a hundred or even twenty-five
dollars to be sterilized (the remuneration suggested by Mencken).

Mencken had belonged to the generation of the 'roaring twenties', one of the most racist and nativist decades in the United States. The generation that fought the Second World War, it might be supposed, had outgrown the influence of the Menckens and their kind. But by the closing years of the 1940s, a public debate arose on the need to control world fertility rates by almost *any* means. Scarcely a year after the Burch and Pendell book appeared, William A. Vogt, chief of the Conservation Section of the Pan-American Union, attracted considerable public attention with his particularly acerbic Malthusian tract, *Road to Survival*,[34] a postwar precursor of Ehrlich's *Population Bomb*. This book was graced by an introduction by Bernard Baruch, whose reputation as a confrère of American presidents seemed to give the book a semi-official imprimatur.

'It is certain that, for all practical purposes,' Vogt wrote, 'large areas of the earth now occupied by backward populations will have to be written off the credit side of the ledger' – that is, left to die of starvation.[35] 'Perhaps the greatest asset' of Chile, Vogt wrote, 'is its high death rate', while 'the greatest tragedy that China could suffer, at the present time, would be a reduction in her death rate.' Since China 'quite literally cannot feed more people', Chinese 'men and women, boys and girls, must starve as tragic sacrifices on the twin altars of human reproduction and uncontrolled abuse of the land's resources.'[36] Thus, Vogt argued, it was incumbent upon the newly established United Nations not to 'ship food to keep alive ten million Indians and Chinese this year, so that fifty million may die five years hence.'[37]

As if to anticipate the pollution exhibition at the Museum of Natural History of 'The Most Dangerous Animal', Vogt directed his harshest criticisms against 'The Dangerous Doctor':

> The modern medical profession, still framing its ethics on the dubious statements of an ignorant physician [Hippocrates] who lived more than two thousand years ago – ignorant, that is, in terms of the modern world – continues to believe it has a duty to keep alive as many people as possible. In many parts of the world doctors apply their intelligence to one aspect of man's welfare – survival – and deny their moral right to apply it to the problem as a whole. Through medical care and improved sanitation they are responsible for more millions living more years in increasing misery. Their refusal to consider their responsibility in these matters does not seem to them to compromise their intellectual integrity.[38]

Vogt's attack on medical attempts to save lives is all the more callous when it is placed in the context of the Second World War period. To a world traumatized by Nazi genocide, it seemed more than ever that the value of human life had to be esteemed and honored as a moral recompense for the sixty or seventy million people whose lives had been brutally claimed by warring powers over a span of some five years. Much of Europe and Asia had been reduced to a cemetery – a devastating consequence that had to be countervailed psychologically by a new respect for human life.

What made Vogt's book particularly repellent was its revival of the antihumanistic mindset, advancing a moral cost-accounting principle in dealing with matters of life and death – a principle that was to be raised repeatedly in the postwar Malthusian literature. Survival issues, for all practical purposes, were translated into a social ledger of debits and credits, as though human beings were mere commodities whose value was to be inscribed or erased by virtue of their usefulness to American self-interest in world affairs. Starvation, famine, disease, and poverty were seen primarily in *amoral numerical* terms, with complete disregard for the uniqueness, creativity, and personality of the individual.

Yet nearly every specific prediction Vogt advanced in his book proved to be wrong. The newly established Socialist [Labour] government of Britain did not, as Vogt predicted, plunge the country into famine between 1948 and 1978. Nor did the Japanese and Germans outbreed the 'carrying capacity' of their lands and succumb to famine, as Vogt suggested. Preceding Ehrlich by some two decades, Vogt, his nose highly sensitized to various demographic odors, argued: 'Anything we do to fortify the stench – to increase the population [of Europe] – is a disservice both to Europe and ourselves.'[39]

Around the same time, Garrett Hardin of the University of California at Santa Barbara entered the demographic debate with his own eugenic recipes. In his *Biology: Its Human Implications,* published in 1949,[40] Hardin was vexed by the lack of concern over the hereditary nature of individual IQ. To allow environmental factors an influence on human intelligence, in Hardin's view, was to disallow the results of animal experimentation altogether and espouse for humans a 'doctrine of exceptionalism that is repugnant to scientists'.[41]

A strong dehumanizing thrust runs through even the seemingly neutral observations in Hardin's writings, resonating as they do with an elitist bias that is distinctly unsavory. Consider, for example, the way Hardin treats the matter of 'charity' in a later (1951) edition of *Biology:* 'When one saves a starving man, one may thereby help him to breed more children. This may be a good or a bad thing, depending upon the facts.' Precisely what the 'facts' are that distinguish 'a starving man' from one who is affluent and well-fed – his class status, social misfortunes, and lack of privilege – remains unstated.

> Some people maintain that very poor people are, on the average, less able and intelligent than the rich, and that their deficiencies are, in part, due to hereditary factors. Others maintain that pauperism [sic] is exclusively a matter of bad luck; or that paupers are better genetic material than millionaires. There is a need here for indisputable facts; but whatever the facts, aid to paupers undoubtedly has genetic consequences.[42]

Amazingly, Hardin may not know what the facts are, but he seems to know without doubt that assistance to paupers 'has genetic consequences'.

To readers in the early 1950s, a statement of this kind, however equivocal, would have left a strong impression that poverty is the result of genetic failings. As the recent publication of Charles Murray and Richard Hernnstein's *The Bell Curve* shows,[43] a genetic explanation is now settling into racially oriented studies of IQ as well as material deprivation. Given the very complex social, political, and cultural factors that interact to produce economic disparities for different sectors of a given population, any genetic relationship between poverty and wealth can be justly dismissed as specious.

As might be expected, Hardin's view of Malthus is cloyingly reverential. The parson and the professor are cheek-to-jowl on most of the basic tenets of Malthus's famous essay. Hardin's reverence for the parson is not merely declarative but poetic. Thus he declaims:

> Malthus! Thou shouldst be living in this hour:
> The world hath need for thee: getting and begetting,
> We soil fair Nature's bounty.[44]

Around the time these tender lines were penned, Malthusians, in fact, were flourishing all over the place, but the literary abandon Hardin exhibited in a collection of readings, presumably for university students, makes his tribute to Malthus unique, at the very least.

It was not until 1968, however, that Hardin's views reached a wider public with his 'The Tragedy of the Commons'.[45] Published in a distinguished scientific journal, the paper became one of the most widely reproduced works in the Malthusian environmental movement of the late 1960s and is still regarded as a classic among antihumanist spokespeople and movements in the English-speaking world. Hardin's basic contention was that 'a finite world can support only a finite population; therefore population growth must eventually equal zero.' In a common pasture that several herdsmen share, 'it is to be expected that each herdsman will try to keep as many cattle as possible on the commons'. Wars, disease, and poaching keep the number of cattle down for some time, but ultimately, 'each herdsman seeks to maximize his gain'. Although all the herdsmen doing this will lead to overgrazing and the destruction of the commons, 'each man is locked into a system that compels him to increase his herd without limit – in a world that is limited', which must lead to ruin for all, indeed to widespread pollution as well as resource exhaustion. Judging from this scenario, one would suppose that Hardin would put capitalism in the dock because of its drive for endless accumulation and expansion.

Alas, this was not the case. In Hardin's view, it is not corporate interests and the market economy that are devouring the commons; it is *people,* more precisely, 'population density', which 'overloads natural chemical and biological recycling processes'. Since 'freedom to breed will bring ruin to all', so 'the *only* way we can preserve and nurture other and more precious freedoms is by relinquishing the freedom to breed, and that very soon.'

By the summer of 1987, Hardin's genteel poetry had mutated still further into bitterly antihumanistic verbiage, comparable to that of Vogt and Ehrlich. In *The New York Times* in 1987, Hardin declaimed, 'There's nothing more dangerous than a shallow-thinking, compassionate person. God, he can cause a lot of trouble.'[46] Shallow thought and compassion, in this case, meant the desire to aid starving children in Ethiopia. 'Since Ethiopia has far too many people for its resources,' Hardin declared, 'if you give food and save lives and thus increase the number of people, you increase suffering and ultimately increase the loss of life.'

Hardin was echoing a theme from the hunger politics of Malthusianism that had been resonating for decades in antihumanism generally: a species that has exceeded the 'carrying capacity' of its ecosystem should in fact be permitted to starve – partly to 'strike a balance with Nature'; partly, too, to weed the fit from the unfit in the struggle for survival. Sometimes it was adorned with genteel qualifications, but not so with Hardin.

Finally, Hardin coined what he calls the 'lifeboat ethic'. The biosphere in Hardin's view is akin to a lifeboat of survivors from a sinking ship – perhaps one whose more privileged passengers have secure places in the lifeboat. Those who are flailing in the water must be kept out if the lifeboat is not to sink. This 'ethic' rests on undisguised self-interest. Far from constituting a description of the human condition as we know it today, it is a prescription of what the human condition *should* be, as Hardin seems to see it, in the biosphere.

I have focused on Malthus, Vogt, Ehrlich, and Hardin because of their wide influence: views akin to theirs are all too frequently found in anti-humanist literature. That their demographic predictions have been nearly consistently erroneous has not dampened the conviction of contemporary Malthusians and antihumanists that their explanations for the ills of the modern human condition are sound. Yet to allow ourselves to be guided by triage and the lifeboat ethic is to open our thinking to the potentially genocidal and immoral mentality that has made the twentieth century one of the bloodiest in human history.

What are the facts about population growth? Recent demographic data (1990–92) do not support the thesis that population growth is 'out of control', although the constant revisions in population statistics and projections make it far from clear which demographic data are credible. A widely distributed brochure prepared by Zero Population Growth in February 1993, for example, assures the reader with much bombast that the present world population of 5.5 billion will 'double in approximately 39 years', presumably to 11 billion by 2032, assuming 'the current growth rate continues'. This reckless and apocalyptic assumption tends to panic rather than to clarify.

Thereupon the brochure pits jobs against the environment and an open immigration policy against a restrictive one, with minimal evidence of *why* such an opposition is inherently necessary. Indeed, a strong argument could be made that increased population can give rise to more jobs. Still, ZPG warns ominously: 'The Population Bomb Is Still Ticking', indeed with each tick of a metronome ('at 176 ticks per minute'), 'the world's population grows by another person (i.e. *net* growth, not just births)'. Returning to the fruit fly image of demographic projections, the ZPG brochure warns that 'if current population growth rates continue, the world will become so densely populated that by the year 2537' – a truly dazzling sprint into the future – 'there will be only one square meter per person'.

We have heard similar 'projections' before – for the 1970s, 1980s, and 1990s, if not for the year 2537 (the exactitude of this date is truly marvelous!). Not only have most of them proven wrong, but the most recent data contradict ZPG's predictions. According to a report released in March 1993 by the European Population Conference in Geneva, birth rates in the most populous areas of the continent have declined so precipitously that there will be 100 million fewer Europeans by 2043 than there are today. Italy's population is expected to shrink from 54 million to 40 million; in the northern part of the peninsula, despite high marriage rates and low divorce rates, the fertility rate is already less than 1.0 per cent. (It requires 2.1 per cent simply to reproduce a given population without a decline.)

Greece's fertility rate has dropped from 2.2 per cent to 1.4 per cent – a rate that will lead to an absolute decline in the population if it continues. Such negative fertility rates are occurring in Germany, Denmark, Norway, France, Spain, and most dramatically, in many Eastern European countries, especially, Russia, where the decline is precipitous. Only in Poland, Turkey, Sweden, Iceland, and Ireland 'is the population expected to increase naturally', observes an article in *The European* of 1 April 1993, 'and even among these, there are signs of moves toward smaller families'.

What of the 'Third World' – that is, Ehrlich's UDCs, or industrially underdeveloped countries? The soaring predictions of growth advanced by antinatal demographers has not been substantiated. In Egypt, the average number of children for each woman has declined from 5.3 to 4.6 (1980–88); Morocco, from 5.8 to 4.0 (1979–92); Kenya, 8.3 to 6.5 (1977–89); Cameroon, 6.4 to 5.9 (1978–91); and Sudan, 6.0 to 4.8 (1978–89). In impoverished Bangladesh, the average number of children for each woman has dropped from 6.1 to 5.5 (1975–91); Colombia, 4.7 to 2.8 (1975–90); El Salvador, 6.3 to 4.6 (1978–88); Indonesia, 3.2 to 3.0 (1987–91); and Thailand, 4.6 to 2.3 (1975–87).[47]

Unlike Western Europe, where demographic declines are usually a product of economic and educational advances, declines in the Third World have been correlated with 'vigorous' efforts to encourage family planning and the use of contraceptive devices like condoms – precisely the measures Ehrlich deprecated as insignificant thirty years ago in *The Population Bomb*. In what Steven W. Sinding, director for population sciences at the Rockefeller Foundation, and Sheldon J. Segal, a staff member at the Population Council, call a 'contraceptive revolution', women in Third World countries 'are averaging 3.9 children ... a stunning change' from the more than six children they had a decade and more ago. 'The global population's growth rate has declined faster than many experts thought possible in the late 1960's. This decline has come mainly as a result of the voluntary use of public and private family planning services, not through coercive measures some advocates once thought necessary.'[48] Ironically, India's birth rate declined from 5.3 in 1980 to 3.9 in 1991, while Pakistan, so often favored at India's expense by the triage and 'population bombers' of the Cold War era, retains its traditionally high birth rate owing to Islamic religious scruples.

The impact that such marked declines in Third World fertility figures may have on the grim predictions of ZPG, the United Nations, and the 'population bombers' is unclear. But only a generation ago few if any neo-Malthusians seemed to think that Western Europe was capable of reaching zero or negative fertility rates. As it turns out, Europe vindicated the demographic principle that improved living standards and education *did* lead to population diminution. The demographic declines registered in the Third World have very different sources.

Certainly some Third World countries have used very ugly techniques to 'persuade' families to reduce the number of children they have. China has not been alone in imposing involuntary methods that require each couple to have only one child. The principal victims of these methods have been women, particularly in agrarian areas and among the poorest classes of society. For a while, getting Third World women – and men – to allow themselves to be sterilized was a lucrative business that provided a fairly good bonus for so-called 'agents' of family planning organizations and governmental institutions. In still other countries, such as Brazil, where the average number of children for each woman dropped from 5.75 in 1970 to 3.2 in 1990, it was desperate poverty, neglect, and often illness that led to this sharp decline. In Russia, economic destitution and disease threaten to literally depopulate entire areas of the country – this, I may add, in a land that has already suffered the terrible afflictions of Stalinist and Nazi genocide.

But there are other signs that women in the Third World are taking their reproductive destiny into their own hands, due in great part to their growing desire to carve out lives of their own rather than allow men and archaic traditions to determine their behavior and future. At least half of all Third World women in the early 1990s are using contraception, an immense increase from the one in ten who used contraception during the mid-1960s. This drop, it is generally believed, is the result not simply of improved living conditions – which are ultimately of decisive importance – but of improved education, as Kenya's dramatic efforts to improve literacy among both sexes suggest. To an extent almost unknown in sub-Saharan Africa, about half of Kenyan women and three-quarters of Kenyan men are literate. Nor is it possible to ignore the growing urbanization of the world, particularly the Third World. City dwellers in Thailand, for example, have only 1.6 children per couple, compared with 2.4 in rural areas.

I am not trying to argue that urbanization on the massive scale it is occurring today is desirable or ecologically sound. My own books on this subject have long argued that we need new types of communities – towns and cities – that are scaled to human and ecological dimensions.[49] What I am emphasizing is that many dismal population projections and images of demographic apocalypse are not only highly uncertain; they are often very flawed. They have been used to create an antihumanistic ambience among environmentally concerned people that is worse, in terms of its moral effect, than the most outlandish and direst predictions advanced by the Ehrlichs, Hardins, and ZPG acolytes.

Still another compelling issue has not been confronted in the debate around population. Given a market-oriented society that professes to identify economic expansion and profit with progress, *would an appreciable reduction of population yield a corresponding decline in production, in the waste of natural resources, or in the consumerism on which the modern economy depends?* Can we blame the ecological despoliation of North America, large parts of Europe, and particularly the former Soviet Union on population increases when, in fact, population in these areas has been relatively stable over the past few decades? Indeed, let me put the issue as bluntly as possible: If the American population were halved from what it is today, *would American corporations halve their output, their destructive ecological impacts, and their appetite for ever-larger profits?*

This question, I submit, can be answered only in a context much broader than extrapolations of the fertility rates of fruit flies and other bugs. Human beings, let me reiterate, are not simply insects, rabbits, or deer; their potentiality for conscious agency makes them unique in the biosphere. Far more relevant to models of human demography is the social milieu in which population issues arise, specifically, the compatibility between a growth-oriented market economy and a viable and sound environment.

That Ehrlich waxed over the possibility that the gross national product (GNP) could merrily continue to grow 'for a long time *without population growth*' reveals, in its own way, the social mypoia that characterizes antihumanists who are prepared to reduce population by any means with little concern about the disastrous ecological impacts of capital expansion.

'Population bombers' have addressed demographic issues in narrowly statistical terms, based on a highly simplistic, indeed static, ecological notion – the 'carrying capacity' of a region or country. This seemingly fixed capacity, so far as human beings are concerned, is actually very much a function of technological development and social relationships that, in turn, involve such searing issues as the material security, productivity, creativity, and the status of people – women no less than men – not of the crude biologism fostered by Ehrlich, Hardin, and their admirers.

Ecology would be ill-served as a cause as well as a discipline (social as well as natural) if it became a mere justification for a pseudo-naturalism that takes little or no account of human agency and the social factors that profoundly determine the environment in which we live.

Notes

1 Paul R. Ehrlich, *The Population Bomb* (New York: Ballantine Books, 1968).

2 This opening paragraph was deleted in later, revised editions of *The Population Bomb.*

3 Ehrlich, *The Population Bomb* pp. 15–16.

4 *Ibid.*, pp. 66–7.

5 *Ibid.*, p. 83.

6 *Ibid.*, pp. 135–6, emphsis added.

7 *Ibid.*, p. 136.

8 *Ibid.*, p. 139.

9 *Ibid.*, pp. 138–9, emphases added.

10 *Ibid.*, p. 159.

11 Ehrlich, *Population Bomb*, p. 160.

12 *Ibid.*, pp. 160–1. Happily, the Paddocks' book has been completely forgotten. 1975 came and went with no famine that could be attributed to population size and fertility rates.

13 Ehrlich, *Population Bomb,* p. 165–6.

14 Recent declines in the world grain harvest, which the 'population bombers' have been only too quick to celebrate as evidence of lasting food shortages, seem to be due mainly to weather conditions in the United States, which resulted in a heavy loss of corn. Per capita availability of grains have been fairly steady, generally hovering around 323 kilograms. Meat and fish output has also held steady. Aquaculture, still relatively marginal, holds enormous promise as a source of food if serious attempts were made to develop it.

15 Ehrlich, *Population Bomb,* p. 177.

16 *Ibid.*, p. 150.

17 Thomas Malthus, *An Essay on the Principle of Population*, originally published in 1798. Except where indicated, all references herein are to the original 1798 version as republished in Gertrude Himmelfarb, ed. *On Population* (New York: Modern Library, 1960).

18 *Ibid.*, p. 64.

19 *Ibid.*, p. 66.

20 *Ibid.*, pp. 59–60.

21 *Ibid.*, p. 9, emphasis added.

22 *Ibid.*, p. 17.

23 *Ibid.*, p. 38.

24 *Ibid.*, pp. 51–2.

25 *Ibid.*, p. 160.

26 T. R. Malthus, *An Essay on the Principle of Population,* 1803 edition, ed. Patricia James, vol. 2 (Cambridge: Cambridge University Press, 1989), p. 127.

27 Malthus, *Population*, p. 367.

28 *Ibid.*, p. 506.

29 *Ibid.*, pp. 506–7.

30 Arno J. Mayer, *The Persistence of the Old Regime: Europe to the Great War* (New York: Pantheon, 1981), p. 3.

31 Guy Irving Burch and Elmer Pendell, *Human Breeding and Survival: Population Roads to Peace and War* (New York: Penguin Books, 1947)

32 *Ibid.*, p. 97.

33 *Ibid.*, p. 99.

34 William F. Vogt, *The Road to Survival* (New York: William Sloane Associates, 1948).

35 *Ibid.*, p. 47.

36 *Ibid.*, pp. 186, 224–5.

37 *Ibid.*, pp. 281–2.

38 *Ibid.*, p. 48.

39 *Ibid.*, p. 211.

40 Garrett Hardin, *Biology: Its Human Implications* (1949), as cited in Allan Chase, *The Legacy of Malthus: The Social Costs of the New Scientific Racism* (1975; Urbana, Chicago, and London: University of Illinois Press, 1980).

41 *Ibid.*, p. 372.

42 *Ibid.*, p. 375.

43 Charles Murray and Richard Herrnstein, *The Bell Curve: Intelligence and Class Structure in American Life* (New York: Free Press, 1994).

44 Garrett Hardin, 'To Malthus', in Garrett Hardin, ed. *Population, Evolution, Birth Control: A Collage of Controversial Readings*, (San Francisco: W. H. Freeman & Co., 1969), p. 88.

45 Garrett Hardin, 'The Tragedy of the Commons', *Science*, vol. 162 (13 December 1968), pp. 1243–8.

46 John Noble Wilford, 'A Tough-Minded Ecologist Comes to Defense of Malthus', *The New York Times*, 30 June 1987.

47 *The New York Times*, 3 January 1994; the data are based on a report by Bryant Roby *et al.* of *American Demographics* magazine.

48 Steven W. Sinding and Sheldon J. Segal, in 'Birth-Rate News', *The New York Times*, 12 December 1991.

49 See especially my *The Limits of the City* (New York and London: Harper and Row, 1979; reprinted by Montreal: Black Rose Books, 1986); *Remaking Society: Pathways to a Green Future* (Boston: South End Press, 1990); and *From Urbanization to Cities* (formerly *Urbanization Without Cities*) (1986; London: Cassell, 1995).

CHAPTER 4

From ecomysticism to angelology

Sociobiologists, microbiologists, Malthusians, and among the Gaians James Lovelock profess to be scientists who are dealing with facts and statistical projections. As such, their ideas and conclusions are open to critical analysis, to acceptance or rejection based on scientific criteria. If their views and conjectures are found to be incorrect, they may be modified or rejected on the basis of the evidence.

Alas, such intellectual responsibility is absent from religion generally, and particularly in the burgeoning credos of ecological mysticism, or ecomysticism. To attempt to critically explore contemporary ecomysticism is to enter a hall of mirrors, wherein we encounter a host of multiple reflections, double-takes, confusing images, and false leads that are mercifully absent in sociobiology, Malthusian demography, Margulis's microcosmology, and Lovelock's Gaia Hypothesis. We may think that Wilson, Malthus, Margulis, and Lovelock are wrong in their use of data and their extrapolations, but at least their premises and conclusions can be checked.

By contrast, mysticism generally celebrates its very imperviousness to rational analysis. Explicitly *anti*-rational, it makes its strongest appeal to the authority of belief over thought. Reason, mystics usually tell us, is cold, objective, indifferent, and, according to some of its feminist critics, even masculine. Not so with mystical outlooks, we are told, which are warm, subjective, caring, and feminine. Mystics enjoin us to 'listen' to our intuitions and feelings, to live with a sense of mystery about the world and our 'interconnectedness' with the 'whole' that surrounds us.

*Eco*mystics, in particular, tend to add a quasi-ecological dimension to mysticism by imparting a preternatural dimension to the interconnected natural world. They commonly advance a spirituality that is little more than outright spiritualism, adorned with expressions like 'reverence' and 'adoration'. Dressed in ecological trappings, such spiritualism has the dubious advantage of being so 'global', even 'cosmic' in its outlook that 'nature', conceived either as a deity or as a pantheistic, all-embracing

'Oneness', vastly overshadows human beings. One may literally get lost in this ecomystical shuffle. What at first glance seems like a generous approach to the natural world sometimes conceals a highly deprecatory view toward one of natural evolution's own species, notably humanity.

Which is not to say that all ecomystics are necessarily misanthropes, unsympathetic to the human condition. In the best of cases, many of them are essentially conservationists, imbued with a sensitive regard for the well-being of animal and plant life, which they see as a continuation of their concern for social justice. Hardly anyone with a sense of responsibility to the natural world can fault them for attempting to deepen public concern for the loss of wildlife, forests, and unsettled land. This laudable impulse is eminently desirable in a time of growing ecological devastation.

But still others advance far more than a conservationist viewpoint. They propound a quasi-religious philosophy that is explicitly antihumanistic. Even as their outright spiritualistic beliefs immunize their intuitive views to rational inquiry, their explicitly anticivilizatory and antitechnological views yield a far-reaching deprecation of humanity and its interventions in a presumably pristine natural world.

This description of ecomysticism is by no means extreme or tendentious. The attributes I have touched upon appear very clearly in the body of views called 'deep ecology', as named by the Norwegian philosopher Arne Naess in a 1972 lecture.[1]

Naess's brief, often obscurely worded lecture advances seven theses that are actually more proclamatory than expository. He makes very little attempt to argue out his conclusions but instead essentially announces them under the catchy name of the 'the deep ecology movement' – in contrast to 'the shallow ecology movement', which he views with unmistakable disdain. Where the shallow ecology movement is simply occupied with a 'fight against pollution and resource depletion' and seeks to preserve 'the health and affluence of people in the developed countries', the deep ecology movement, according to Naess, sees all living things, including humans, as 'knots in the biospherical net or field of intrinsic relations'.[2] His use of the word *movement* in 1972 was at best metaphorical; there were no deep ecology and shallow ecology *movements* in the English-speaking world when the article was written. Naess's names refer to two of several environmental tendencies that were beginning to attract public attention. Indeed, deep ecology was virtually unknown until the late 1970s and early 1980s.

Nor was Naess's distinction between the anti-pollution and antiresource-depletion activities of environmentalists and something 'deeper' an original theory. A similar distinction had been made in a multitude of books and articles throughout the 1960s, not only in my own writings but in those of Barry Commoner, Leo Marx, and René Dubos. Nor was it fair on Naess's part to confuse Western economic affluence with the very reasonable concerns of 'people in developed countries' for their health.[3] By the late 1960s, a very sizable literature – and mounting evidence – had appeared in the United States and Europe on the dangers that food additives, heavy metals, pesticides, nuclear wastes, and exotic chemicals presented to public well-being.

In fact, by the early 1970s, American environmentalists (or what Naess called shallow ecologists), were very deeply concerned with the environmental impact of 'the affluent society'. They made symbolic protests like the public burial of automobiles – naive gestures, perhaps, but expressly demonstrative actions against 'consumerist' values. What they lacked was not an explicit opposition to consumerism or affluence but a clear understanding of the profound social sources of pollution and the destruction of wildlife habitats.

Nor did 1970s environmentalists have to be told about the need for biological diversity and symbiosis – themes that form one of Naess's theses in his *Inquiry* article. Such ideas had been percolating within anarchic New Left ecological tendencies since the mid-1960s, and a literature was emerging that stressed the need for diversity as a basic requirement for ecological well-being. Naess's thesis on local autonomy, decentralization, and 'soft technologies' was also old hat by 1972; I had personally advanced it in a comprehensive inventory of alternative energy sources like solar, wind, and geothermal power as early as 1962.[4]

Finally, it is worth adding that apart from his general references to decentralization, diversity, and symbiosis, little in Naess's remedies for the environmental crisis distinguished his ideas from the reformist activities of shallow ecologists. Indeed, deep ecology was quite tame in its vision of a new social dispensation. But Naess and his acolytes during the 1970s, confined to their fastnesses in the academy, were basically isolated from the new ecological trends – technological, communitarian, and political – that were emerging in the United States. Their writings reveal little lived contact with the international environmental movement that was unfolding. If deep ecology was a movement, it was overwhelmingly a cerebral one that had little interaction with groups actively trying to expand public consciousness of environmental hazards and indeed of the need to change society's way of interacting with the natural world.

From a theoretical standpoint, in what way did Naess distinguish deep ecology from shallow and other ecologies?

Naess's formulation that constituted deep ecology's most distinctive contribution to environmentalism was 'biospherical egalitarianism'. What Naess meant by this expression was 'a deep-seated respect, or even veneration, for ways and forms of life'.[5] 'To the ecological field-worker,' Naess added, '*the equal right to live and blossom* is an *intuitively* clear and obvious value axiom.'[6] In the closing sentences of his two-paragraph thesis, Naess went on to address the extent to which such respect and reverence are important for the quality of human life, indeed, 'the deep pleasure and satisfaction we receive from close partnership with other forms of life', as well as the 'alienation' we feel from each other in the absence of such a 'partnership'.

What is striking about these passages is precisely the intuitive basis on which they rest and the extent to which Naess's 'biospherical egalitarianism' – or what was later called 'biocentrism' by his acolytes – is oriented toward our own human, perhaps even anthropocentric 'pleasure and satisfaction' in living in 'close partnership with other forms of life'. In this respect, Naess's rather anthropocentric concern for human pleasure and satisfaction is exceptional among the many people he and his followers were to win over to deep ecology and their wildlife and conservationist concerns.

In time, Naess elaborated his position of 'biospherical egalitarianism' into a self-proclaimed biocentric *ethic* that professed to intuitively endow every life form with an unquestionable 'intrinsic worth' or 'intrinsic value'. In a 'biospherically egalitarian world', according to this ethic, human beings are intrinsically of no greater (or lesser) value, than *any* life-form, be it a wolf, bear, eagle, or fruit fly. Like all other animals, Naess allowed in his later writings, human beings have a 'right' to kill other life-forms to meet their 'vital needs' – which raises the very arguable question of what constitutes human vital needs. To this question Naess and his acolytes were essentially to respond by asking us to reduce our needs and 'live simply' – which again raises the question of what one means by simply. In Naess's *Inquiry* paper, all of these arguable issues were resolved with a catchy slogan: 'Live and let live' – apparently with the exception of predation to acquire food and meet other vaguely stated needs.

In fact, many deep ecology acolytes used this slogan to justify – in theory, at least – a minimalist, indeed primitivist vision of human interaction with the natural world. Which is not to say that all deep ecology theorists necessarily gave up their computers, sophisticated binoculars, and other high-tech accoutrements of the 'affluent' society in favor of a 'primitive' lifestyle. But interference with the ways of 'nature' was viewed askance. Indeed, the world view of primitive or primal peoples –

who, it was assumed, lived in a joyously simple partnership with and love for the virginal world around them – became a model for contemporary ecological visions of behavior and reality.

Naess, for his part, enjoined deep ecologists to 'fight against economic and cultural, as much as military, invasion and domination', and to oppose 'the annihilation of seals and whales as much as to that of human tribes or cultures'.[7] Such injunctions, too, were becoming the conventional wisdom of environmental groups in the 1970s throughout much of the Western world, not only in the United States but in Britain and Germany, where Naess's *Inquiry* paper was virtually unknown. Indeed, so embedded were antimilitarist and conservationist views in the conventional wisdom of environmentalists by the 1960s and 1970s that, when wedded to the New Left activism of those decades, they acquired a radical political and social form.

There is precious little in Naess's *Inquiry* paper that was not old hat at the time he wrote it. Even Naess's biocentrism, seemingly the most original feature of the paper, had become the stock in trade of conservationists influenced by the writings of John Muir and his conscious or unconscious devotees. Yet despite its brevity, Naess's paper unavoidably – and perhaps deliberately – raised but left unanswered a number of problems that still haunt the deep ecology movement to this very day.

Why did such a patently simplistic and singularly unoriginal body of views as deep ecology take root in the first place – initially in the United States and later in Europe?

To a great extent, it was the very simplicity – indeed, the simple-minded message – of Naess's ecological philosophy that made it attractive. Deep ecology makes no great intellectual demands upon its followers. Its intuitions and a priori concepts, usually presented as simple homilies and metaphors, make it accessible to anyone who vaguely 'loves nature'. More a mood than a body of ideas, deep ecology derives its message from the same intuitive materials that have long been exploited by assorted gurus, shamans, priests, fakirs, and dubious psychotherapists. Deep ecology, in effect, makes its appeal to the heart rather than to the head, and little intellectual effort is required to absorb its maudlin message of how to live the 'simple life' and behave 'ecologically'.

But what accounts for its rise to popularity, rather than the similar, equally intuitive ecological tendencies that surfaced almost simultaneously with it? One of Naess's more staid academic admirers, Warwick Fox, explains its influence as the result of a remarkably successful public relations job. As Fox observes:

the ecophilosophy community's acceptance of the shallow/deep ecology dis-
tinction is due far more to the powerful advocacy that the distinction
received from a couple of writers from 1979–80 on, rather than to any
kind of collective decision on the part of the ecophilosophy community. In
other words, as with so many ideas, the shallow/deep ecology distinction
was effectively thrust *upon its relevant intellectual community rather than*
'elected to office'.[8]

The 'couple of writers' to whom Fox alludes are two Californian academics, George Sessions and Bill Devall, who zealously promoted deep
ecology among a newly emerging environmental professoriat at academic
conferences and particularly through Sessions' newsletter *Ecophilosophy* in
the mid-1970s. In Fox's view, if a given 'typology' (Naess's, in this case)
finds 'a couple of persuasive, committed, industrious, and eloquent supporters where the other typologies did not ... you have the beginnings of
an identifiable intellectual movement/grouping/school.'[9]

Indeed, so important were Devall and Sessions to the promotion of
deep ecology that Fox, in his highly sympathetic account of the movement, observes that the two men

are generally, and rightly, acknowledged by ecophilosophers, first, as being
almost wholly responsible for having introduced Naess's distinction
[between deep and shallow ecology] to the ecophilosophical community (in
about 1979–80); second, as being very largely responsible, along with
Naess, for having influenced the ecophilosophical community in general to
the point where reference to Naess's typology became accepted as standard
within the space of a few years (by around 1983–84); and, third, as
being very largely responsible – again, along with Naess – for having
influenced a number of individual ecophilosophers to the point where these
individuals now identify themselves and/or are identified by other
ecophilosophers as deep ecologists *– or, at least, as close relatives.*[10]

In fact, Devall's and Sessions' promotion of deep ecology occurred overwhelmingly within the framework of a collegiate-professorial world during the late 1970s, in backwoods campuses like Sierra, Pitzer, and
Humboldt Colleges. Sessions' general appeal may have been more the
result of his interest in Spinoza and Whitehead than in Naess, whose
work he does not seem to have known until 1973. Naess, in turn, apparently attracted Sessions because of their shared interest in Spinoza. Devall
appears to have followed Sessions more as a wilderness conservationist
than as an ecological theorist.

In any case, in journals, bulletins, conferences, and seminars, academics
generally deal with other academics. Like any professional coterie, they

cite one another's works and form clubby enclaves, quite apart from the movements – social or environmental – that swirl around their campus world. Not surprisingly, deep ecology in the late 1970s and early 1980s was mainly a campus-oriented phenomenon. Its following seems to have been composed mainly of teachers and the students they influenced, many of them were locked into their own disciplines with only glancing contact with the actual environmental movements around them.

But of the greatest importance to deep ecology's rise – far greater than Sessions' and Devall's efforts in promoting it – was the ideological climate that followed the decline of the New Left, a climate that favored intuitive and mystical notions. These notions had already existed in the 1960s counterculture, which had mixed sporadic political activism with an abiding fascination for Asian mysticism. With the demise of the New Left, the counterculture's mysticism literally exploded in California in the 'New Age'. As the tidal wave of mysticism, with all its narcissistic by-products, rolled across the Sunbelt, it created a cultural region that can be justifiably called the Mystical Zone of the United States.

Judging from the writings of Devall and Sessions, their academic cloister did not render them immune to the mystical viruses that were exploding in the collegiate and countercultural worlds of their region. Drenched in Taoist, Buddhist, pagan, magical, and generically mystical notions, the California air has proverbially produced eclectic versions of the occult, indeed, of the cultic, to an extent that gives it few equals elsewhere in the Western world.

The New Left of the radical 1960s had more or less steadied the various spiritualisms that flourished in that culture area by freighting them with political ballast. Mere intuition alone did not suffice to fight institutionalized racism in the South or to protest the repression of free speech in northern universities, let alone to maintain a viable political organization on campus. At the national level, overheated notions of imminent social revolution created a degree of political zealotry that overshadowed the more or less zany religious cults that flourished in California's bohemias.

Once the secular constraints that the New Left imposed on California's counterculture were removed, however, the mindless spiritualism of the Mystical Zone reclaimed its traditional territory. Worse still, it rebounded militantly against the high politicization of the decade from which it had been expelled; partly as an anodyne for the anomie, the meaninglessness and deadening mediocrity that marked American life in the 1970s and 1980s; partly too as a highly profitable source of income for the gurus who supplanted New Left organizations. Ideas – and the need to think them out or seriously deal with them, which the New Left had at least professed to demand in its debates and factional conflicts – were increasingly replaced by the fantasy world that the Mystical Zone had nourished over previous generations. Vaporous 'feelings' displaced the 'mindbending' challenges of rationality, while the delights of mythopoesis and mystery displaced the cold demands of secularity and intellectual clarity.

Quite bluntly, the late 1970s were an ideal time for deep ecology to take root in California, indeed in the Mystical Zone generally. It was an ideal slogan for reprocessing, in typical Sunbelt fashion, into a *Weltanschauung* superficial enough for anyone to adopt and spiritually uplifting enough to offer a restful soporific for all troubled souls. Indeed, deep ecology was an excellent analgesic for the intellectual headaches of a culture that felt more at home with Disneyland and Hollywood than with political radicalism.

Nor was the Mystical Zone, which pioneered deep ecology, alone in seeking relief from the demanding political and intellectual tribulations of Western civilization. The antihumanism, mysticism, and misanthropy that are now sedimented into present-day culture have long roots in the social decay of our time. Deep ecology is a symptom of that decay even more than it is one of its causes.

What eventually catapulted deep ecology from the campus into the broader public realm was a conservationist direct action movement – Earth First! – that gave Naess's notion of 'biospherical egalitarianism' or 'biocentrism' headline quality.

Inspired by Edward Abbey, whose books such as *Desert Solitaire* had gained a wide audience of nature-oriented readers, a number of fairly young wilderness enthusiasts in the American southwest embarked on a direct-action 'monkeywrenching' campaign to preserve and, if possible, enlarge as much of 'primordial' America as they could. The concept of monkeywrenching came from Abbey's popular novel, *The Monkey Wrench Gang* (1975), in which a conservationist band of saboteurs wander through American deserts, demolishing billboards and earth-moving equipment, and ultimately plan an ill-starred attempt to blow up the Glen Canyon Dam.

Earth First! was ostensibly founded by five men in April 1980 – David Foreman, Mike Roselle, Howie Wolke, Bart Koehler, and Ron Kezar – of whom four came from conservationist organizations and one, Roselle, from a New Left-antiwar activist background. Judging from Foreman's *Confessions of an Eco-Warrior,* the name Earth First! was chosen to express the primacy of the planet above such 'humanistic' notions as 'People First'.[11] Foreman, at one time a Barry Goldwater admirer and political conservative, is credited with inventing its name and Roselle is credited with designing its logo – a clenched fist in a circle. If Foreman's title denoted his misanthropic attitude toward the human species, Roselle's logo reflected the influence of the leftist tradition from which he ostensibly derived some of his social views; he later broke with Foreman presumably because of his misanthropy.

Organizationally, Earth First! never became more than a very loosely formed tendency within the environmental movement. In fact, most of its activities in the United States were essentially theatrical. More rhetorical than real, with its slogans favoring 'monkeywrenching' and 'ecotage', the group made headlines because of its threats to sabotage lumbering operations. Its colorful guerrilla theater antics at lumbering sites, in which supporters dressed in animal costumes and carried large, decorative banners, were mediagenic photo-opportunities that made the front pages of newspapers.

Earth First! also became an excellent and much-needed target for industry's cries against 'environmental extremists', which tended to give a 'terrorist' patina to the entire environmental movement. In fact, the Earth First! tactics of sitting before bulldozers, occupying tree branches, and blockading small tracts of forest land were largely symbolic: the movement was generally more of a media creation than a serious challenge to polluters, lumbermen, and developers. To be sure, Earth First!, at least while Foreman led it, added a sharper edge to the demands of conventional environmental organizations and even embarrassed them, but its achievements, in fact, were modest, and after much infighting, the extent to which Earth First! can still be said to be a stable or definable movement is arguable.

In its 'heroic' days, however, Earth First! members and supporters shared certain views that were expressly antihumanistic. Although its members–supporters (the distinction is difficult to make) had diverse environmental agendas, its most articulate and best-known leaders were avowed Malthusians and even crude misanthropes. Their New Left tactics and logo notwithstanding, they advanced no serious criticism of the social *status quo*. As a number of their most articulate spokesmen were to emphasize, Earth First! regarded social issues as 'humanistic' – they concerned the much-despised human species, not the furry or feathery nonhuman ones. By the early 1980s – whatever the clenched fist logo that appeared on its periodical, *Earth First!*, may have originally meant – the periodical's editors and principal writers had adopted deep ecology as their theoretical framework, and the periodical opened its pages to deep ecology's leading proponents in the United States – Bill Devall and George Sessions.

In 1980 and 1981, in fact, it would have been hard to decide whether deep ecology was a movement or an academic ripple. Inasmuch as Naess's *Inquiry* article was unknown beyond a few campuses even in California, deep ecology's influence seemed to depend upon the number of people who read Sessions' newsletter, *Ecophilosophy,* or were privy to hearing Devall's papers at academic conferences. Oddly enough, even Naess, who did not meet Sessions until 1978, used the phrase *deep ecology* rather sparingly. It was Devall who, according to Warwick Fox, 'elaborated the basic ideas of deep ecology at greater length [than Naess] *under the name of deep ecology* and surveyed and classified much of the existing literature in terms of its points of contact with these ideas.'[12]

In a second series of newsletters, Sessions – even more than Naess – seems to have established the 'typology' that currently passes under the name of deep ecology. Despite his penchant for a Spinozistic pantheism and Asian quietism, Naess retains strong roots in his background as a logical positivist, which is to say that he often takes recourse to precise mathematical and logical definitions, so akin to the analytical formalism that constituted his earlier philosophical training. By contrast, Sessions is so patently mystical that his writings contrast markedly with those of Naess. As Fox observes:

> Under deep ecology [Sessions] classified Christian Franciscans (as opposed to Benedictine resource stewardship); the philosophy of Spinoza; the later philosophy of Martin Heidegger; the pantheistic ecophilosophy of Robinson Jeffers; Aldo Leopold's ecosystem-oriented ethics; John Rodman's ecological resistance/ecological sensibility; Eastern process philosophy (Taoism and Buddhism); Western process philosophy (Heraclitus, Whitehead, and, for Sessions, Spinoza as well); the ecological wisdom of various tribal cultures.[13]

In short, this 'typology' is an eclectic hodgepodge. Spinoza allows for no comparison with Heidegger, and that Taoism and Buddhism can be regarded as 'process philosophies' is, to put it mildly, arguable. But what most of – although by no means all! – these philosophies have in common is a strong mystical undertow more characteristic of Californian notions of 'wisdom' than Norwegian notions of analytical sobriety. Moreover, apart from Spinoza, who by no stretch of the imagination can be regarded as 'biocentric' (indeed, quite the contrary is true) and possibly one or two others, many of the proto-deep ecology thinkers Fox lists are essentially anti-rationalists.

Thus, precisely what constituted a wide-ranging or coherent theory of deep ecology was anything but clear – a problem that beleaguers it to this day. The deep ecology literature was confined for years mainly to academic papers and Sessions' newsletters. By the early 1980s, in fact, no single volume had yet appeared in English that could be called a definitive deep ecology book. To the extent that deep ecology has since become an 'established' ecophilosophy, it was primarily among some two hundred or so professors and/or their students whom Sessions and Devall could reach with their newsletter and conference papers. Despite growing support today, many academic environmentalists viewed deep ecology with considerable skepticism or rejected it outright. For the rest of the Mystical Zone, deep ecology was more of a rumor that denoted deep thinking than a movement or coherent outlook.

Not surprisingly, the phrase *deep ecology* first appeared as the title of a book which was in an anthology edited by Michael Tobias in 1984.[14] Tobias seems to have used it as a catchall phrase to denote any insight that seemed more searching than the popular environmentalist literature of the day. Not until 1985 did Devall and Sessions write and edit a collage entitled *Deep Ecology: Living As If Nature Mattered,* making a definitive statement of deep ecology available to the English-reading public.[15] The book was indeed definitive, for it reflected the eclectic typology of deep ecology that Sessions had formulated more than any book on the subject since.

By their own admission, the central theses of Devall's and Sessions' *Deep Ecology* are 'two *ultimate norms* or intuitions which are not themselves derivable from other norms or intuitions ... *self-realization* and *biocentric equality.*'[16]

Like Naess before them, Devall and Sessions use the terminology of 'intuitions', not reasoned reflection. Intuitions constitute our 'sense' or feelings about something. As a momentary personal apprehension, they are notoriously unreliable; indeed, they constitute precarious grounds upon which to base any outlook, much less the veritable *Weltanschauung* that deep ecology professes to offer. It is my intuition, for example, that Devall's and Sessions' intuitions are outrageously wrong – which says nothing whatever about the validity, soundness, or insightfulness of either my or their conflicting intuitions. Lacking divine guidance, I fail to see how this conflict can be resolved except by the intuitions of our readers.

It should come as no surprise, then, that Devall and Sessions tell us that their two ultimate norms 'cannot be validated, of course, by the methodology of modern science based on its usual [!] mechanistic assumptions and its very narrow [!] definition of data.'[17] This loaded and highly pejorative statement encloses deep ecology's 'norms' in a closet beyond the reach of critical analysis, immunizing deep ecology to the 'methodology' of science and the challenge of reasoned argument. By casting aside reason, deep ecologists may dismiss – presumably intuitively – any method or data that are critical of their views.

In the process, deep ecology appeals to an increasingly popular but erroneous image of scientific method as 'mechanistic' and confines its terrain of inquiry to a 'very narrow definition of data'. This antiscientism may go over well in the scented ashrams of the Mystical Zone, but 'the methodology of science' merely requires experiential proof that various ideas are *real,* not divinations spun out by mystical gurus with or without Ph.D.s. In other words, the methodology of science constitutes a minimal objective criterion by which we may judge ideas on the basis of *reality* and not on the basis of the self-proclaimed insights of spooks. This is no trivial problem in a world increasingly beset by supernatural, manipulative, and, dangerously authoritarian intuitions that range from experiences with angels to fascistic fears of racial 'pollution'.

Nor is the methodology of science always mechanistic. Apart from what is commonly called 'scientific method', a phrase that I believe requires restatement, the specific *techniques* associated with scientific analysis often vary from science to science. Hence deep ecology plays upon a popular prejudice that 'the methodology of science' is confined to 'a very narrow definition of data'. Cosmology today is such a sweeping, extravagantly creative, and even dialectical field of study that to call its methodology narrow is, to put it gently, evidence of gross ignorance. Its ever-changing and expanding vision of the origins, nature, and future of the universe defies some of the most imaginative plots dreamed of in science fiction.

Chemistry, in turn, with its 'dissipative structures', is the scientific discipline *par excellence* for deriving systems theories, in which some of the most mystical of the Mystical Zone's theorists dabble. Biology, for its part, abounds with a wealth of speculations and experiments that make the insights of deep ecology's founders seem singularly unimaginative. Paleoanthropology, ethology, and geology all have thrown more light on the marvels of the natural and human worlds in single papers than can be found in all the tomes on spiritualism and deep ecology in New Age bookstores.

What Devall and Sessions seem to be telling us, in effect, is that *they* have an ideology, called deep ecology, that rests on *their* intuitions, and that to challenge *them* is to be captive to the narrow and mechanistic method *they* impute to the sciences. Worse still, their intuitions cannot be judged by rational criteria, which presumably originate in a narrow and mechanistic methodology. And herein lies the rub: we cannot, by Devall's and Sessions' criteria, enter into a rational or scientific exploration of their intuitions because to do so would challenge the authority of their personal faith.

Thus, for Devall and Sessions to claim that their intuited norms are 'arrived at by the deep *questioning* process and reveal the importance of moving to the philosophical and religious level of *wisdom*' is rhetorical.[18] No 'deep *questioning* process' can rest exclusively on intuition, least of all that of Arne Naess, to which they are referring here. If Devall's and Sessions' 'deep questioning' cannot be supported by experiential reality, other than what *they* regard as valid experience, it simply cannot be challenged. One cannot attain a 'philosophical and religious wisdom' without acknowledging the *premises* of objective knowledge (which include science) and the need for logical consistency, both of which stand at odds with the privileged claims of intuition. A questioning process that is insulated from rationality and experience can hardly be said to involve very much questioning at all. Nor is one intuition true and its contrary false if both rest *merely* on a personal belief.

This is no trivial matter. It took thousands of years for humanity to begin to shake off the accumulated 'intuitions' of shamans, priests, chiefs, monarchs, warriors, patriarchs, ruling classes, dictators, and the like – all of whom claimed immense privileges for themselves and inflicted terrible horrors on their inferiors on the basis of *their* 'intuited wisdom'. Once we remove the imperatives of rational inquiry that might challenge their behavior and the scientific criteria of truth that might challenge their mystical claims to insight, social elites are free to use all their wiles to subjugate, exploit, and kill enormous numbers of people on the basis of unsupported belief systems, irrational conventions, and purely subjective views of society and the world.

A multitude of intuitions and irrational belief systems are returning to the foreground in the closing years of this century. From mystical divinations to ethnic hatreds, these belief systems have grave implications for the future of modern society and the way people view reality. That deep ecology has contributed to this regressive trend with hortatory claims that are strictly subjective, even personalistic, and often reactionary cannot be ignored – and must be seriously probed.

Of the two 'ultimate norms' Devall and Sessions intuit, the first, 'self-realization' is the more wayward.

In the counterculture of recent years, few terms have been tossed around more frequently than this eminently Western philosophical, religious, and psychological expression. If self-realization means anything, it certainly implies the *free* development of a person's distinctive and individual potentialities. This Euro-American image of selfhood and individuation has been centuries in the making. Devall and Sessions dismissively caricature it as 'the modern Western *self* which is defined as an isolated ego striving primarily for hedonistic gratification or for a narrow sense of individual salvation in this life or the next.'[19]

Western culture has nurtured a sense of individuality that is vastly *more* than isolated, hedonistic, and materially egoistic. Indeed, self-realization as a fulfillment of individual intellectual and spiritual potentialities was a major goal, if not *the* major goal, of thinkers such as Socrates, Plato, Aristotle, Aquinas, the Renaissance thinkers, Luther, the French Enlighteners, Hegel, Marx, and Freud, among many others, whose names are conspicuously absent from Devall's and Sessions' book.

The reason these names do not appear in their book is obvious. By 'self-realization', Devall and Sessions leave little doubt that they mean a certain type of *religious* notion of the self that can more properly be called *self-effacement.* We have to shed, as they put it, the 'modern Western *self*' and return to the traditional *Asian* notion of the individual, who *disappears* in a '"self-in-Self" where "Self" stands for organic wholeness'. More precisely, we have to return to a self for whom 'the phrase [sic!] "one" includes not only me, an individual human,' Devall and Sessions emphasize, 'but all humans, whales, grizzly bears, whole rain forest ecosystems, mountains and rivers, the tiniest microbes in the soil, and so on.'[20] Subsumed in the unending natural cycles of ahistorical cosmologies, this self (or more precisely, the lack thereof) is divested of control over its destiny. Historically, such a self was long subjugated to despotic monarchs and lords – all of whom have spoken in the name of a 'natural order', 'natural forces', and a divine or 'cosmic' power, ideologies that drained peasants, craftspeople, and slaves of the will to transform their destinies, not to speak of the spirit of revolt.

This self-*abnegating* notion of individuality resonates with precisely the animal deities and spirits that humanity had to eventually exorcise in order to render social life secular and divest itself of imperial rulers who claim 'naturally' endowed powers for themselves. A 'self-in-Self' that 'realizes' itself as part of an unthinking 'community' of 'whole rain forest ecosystems, mountains and rivers, the tiniest microbes in the soil, and so on' has not *merged* its identity with a larger cosmic whole; it has *lost* its identity, its distinctively *human* qualities as well as individual contours.

Moreover, imputing a notion of the self to non-human beings and even inorganic entities presupposes a very anthropomorphic treatment of these phenomena, which cannot constitute a self in any meaningful sense of the term. The 'and so on' invites us, once we have imparted selfhood to mountains and rivers, to think of the barren moon, the stars, interstellar space, and galaxies – in terms of a degree of 'self-in-Self', perhaps in 'harmony' and 'interconnected' with the entire cosmos!

This rhetorical recycling of Taoism and Buddhism, and their Western filiations, into a vulgar Californian spiritualism leads us, almost unerringly, to the other 'ultimate norm' on which deep ecology rests: 'biocentric equality'. Simply put:

> The intuition *of biocentric equality is that all things in the biosphere have an equal right to live and blossom and to reach their own individual form of unfolding and self-realization within the larger Self-realization. This basic* intuition *is that all organisms and entities in the ecosphere as parts of the interrelated whole,* are equal in intrinsic *worth*.[21]

This stunning doctrine literally defines deep ecology. 'Deep' it is in every sense – not only in the intuitions that the authors and their acolytes hold, but in the many presuppositions they make.

If the self must merge – or *dissolve,* as I claim – according to deep ecologists, into rain forests, ecosystems, mountains, rivers 'and so on', these phenomena must share in the intellectuality, imagination, foresight, communicative abilities, and empathy that human beings possess, that is, if 'biocentric equality' is to have any meaning.

On the other hand, we may decide to agree with Robyn Eckersley, a champion of biocentrism, that no such abilities are necessary, that the 'navigational skills of birds' are themselves on a par with the wide-ranging intelligence of people.

> Is there not something self-serving and arrogant in the (unverifiable) claim that first nature is striving to achieve something that has presently reached its most developed form in us – second nature? A more impartial, biocentric approach would be simply to acknowledge that our special capabilities (e.g. a highly developed consciousness, language and tool-making capability) are simply one form of excellence alongside the myriad others (e.g. the navigational skills of birds, the sonar capability and playfulness of dolphins, and the intense sociality of ants) rather than the form of excellence thrown up by evolution.[22]

Whether birds have navigation *skills* – which assumes conscious agency in negotiating their migratory flights over vast distance with clear geographical goals – or primarily tropistic reactions to changes in daylight and possibly the earth's magnetic fields of force, need not occupy us here. What counts is that Eckersley's state of mind, like that of deep ecologists generally, essentially debases the intellectual powers of people who, over previous centuries, consciously mapped the globe, gave it mathematical coordinates, and invented magnetic compasses, chronometers, radar, and other tools for navigation. They did so with an intellectuality, flexibility, and with techniques that no bird can emulate – that is, with amazing skillfulness, since skill involves more than physical reactions to natural forces and stimuli.

When Eckersley places the largely tropistic reactions of birds on a par with human thought, she diminishes the human mind and its extraordinary abilities. One might as well say that plants have skills that are on a par with human intellectuality because plants can engage in photosynthesis, a complex series of biochemical reactions to sunlight. Are such reactions really commensurate with the ability of physicists to understand how solar fusion occurs and of biochemists to understand how photosynthesis occurs? If so, then corals 'invented' techniques for producing islands and plants 'invented' techniques for reaching to the sun in heavily forested areas. In short, placing human intellectual foresight, logical processes, and innovations on a par with tropistic reactions to external stimuli is to create a stupendous intellectual muddle, not to evoke the 'deep' insights that deep ecologists claim to bring to our understanding of humanity's interaction with the natural world.

Eckersley's crude level of argumentation is no accident; Devall and Sessions prepare us for it by approvingly citing Warwick Fox to the effect that we can make 'no firm ontological divide in the field of existence: That there is no bifurcation in reality between the human and the non-human realms ... to the extent that we perceive boundaries, we fall short of deep ecological consciousness.'[23]

No one has quite told whales, I assume, about this new evolutionary dispensation. Still less are grizzly bears, wolves, entire rainforest ecosystems, mountains, rivers, 'and so on' aware of their community with human beings. Indeed, in this vast panoply of life-forms, ecosystems, mineral matter, and 'so on', no creature seems to be capable of *knowing* – irrespective of how they communicate with members of their own kind – about the existence or absence of this 'firm ontological divide' *except human beings*. If, as Devall and Sessions seem to believe, there is 'no firm ontological divide' between the human and non-human realms, it is unknown to every species in the biosphere, let alone entities in the abiotic world – except our own.

In fact, the ontological divide between the non-human and the human is *very* real. Human beings, to be sure, are primates, mammals, and vertebrates. They cannot, as yet, get out of their animal skins. As products of organic evolution, they are subject to the natural vicissitudes that bring enjoyment, pain, and death to complex life-forms generally. But it is a crucial fact that they alone *know* – indeed, *can* know – that there is a phenomenon called evolution; they *alone* know that death is a reality; they *alone* can even formulate such notions as self-realization, biocentric equality, and a 'self-in-Self'; they *alone* can generalize about their existence – past, present, and future – and produce complex technologies, create cities, communicate in a complex syllabic form, 'and so on'! To call these stupendous attributes and achievements mere differences in degree between human beings and non-human life-forms – and to equate human consciousness with the navigational skills of migratory birds – is so preposterously naive that one might expect such absurdities from children, not professors.

What apparently worries deep ecologists about this 'divide', with all its bifurcations and boundaries, is not so much that its existence is obvious as that it is inconvenient. Beclouding their simplistic monism, we may suppose, is a fear of the dualism of René Descartes, which they feel obliged to dispel. Ironically, they seem incapable of coping with this dualism without taking recourse to a Bambi-style anthropomorphism that effectively transforms *all* non-human beings into precisely what they profess to abhor – namely, anthropomorphisms. If they cannot make human beings into non-human animals, they make non-human animals into human beings. Accordingly, animals are said to have 'skills' in much the same sense that human beings do. The earth has its own 'wisdom', wilderness is equated with 'freedom', and all life-forms exhibit 'moral' qualities that are entirely the product of human intellectual, emotional, and social development.

Put bluntly: if human beings are 'equal in intrinsic worth' to non-human beings, then boundaries between human and non-human are erased, and either human beings are merely one of a variety of animals, or else non-human beings are human.

But then, why should they not be in the Disneyland world of deep ecology?

Having entangled the reader with extravagant claims for a set of unsupported personal beliefs, Devall and Sessions proceed in the name of an exclusively human 'active deep questioning and meditative process' to reduce readers to the status of ' "plain citizens" of the biotic community, not lord or master over all other species.'[24]

Devall and Sessions use words with multiple meanings to give the most alienating interpretation to people. Whatever a democracy could possibly mean in the animal world, human beings are not mere 'plain citizens' in a biospheric democracy. They are immensely superior to any other animal species, although deep ecologists equate *superiority* with being the 'lord and master of all other species', hence an authoritarian concept. But *superior* may mean not only higher in rank, status, and authority but 'of great value, excellence; extraordinary', if my dictionary is correct. That superiority can simply mean 'having more *knowledge, foresight,* and *wisdom*' – attributes we might expect to find in a teacher or even a Zen master – seems to disappear from the highly selective deep ecological lexicon.

Deep ecology's contradictory presuppositions, intuitions, anthropomorphisms, and naive assertions leave us spinning like tops. We are enjoined to engage in 'deep questioning' in order to decide on *intuitive* grounds that we are *intrinsically* no different in 'worth' or 'value' from any 'entity' in the 'ecosphere'. Yet the deep questioning so prized by Devall, Sessions, Naess, *et al.*, is something that *no other life-form can do* – besides us. In the vastness of the ecosphere, nothing apart from human beings is capable of even voicing the notion of 'biocentric egalitarianism', much less *understanding* any notion of 'rights', 'intrinsic worth', or 'superiority' and 'inferiority'. It is the ultimate in anthropomorphism to impute a moral sense to animals that lack the conceptual material of abstract thought provided by language and the rich generalizations we form in our minds from our vast repertoire of words.

Strictly speaking, if we were nothing but 'plain citizens' in the ecosphere, we should be as furiously *anthropo-centric* in our behavior, just as a bear is *Urso-centric* or a wolf *Cano-centric*. That is to say, as plain citizens of the ecosphere – and nothing more – we should, like every other animal, be occupied *exclusively* with our own survival, comfort, and safety. As Richard Watson has so astutely noted: '[i]f we are to treat man as part of nature on egalitarian terms with other species, then man's behavior must be treated as morally neutral true' – that is, as amoral. In which case, Watson continues, 'we should not think there is something morally or ecosophically wrong with the human species dispossessing and causing the extinction of other species.'[25]

Yet deep ecologists ask us precisely in the name of a biospheric 'citizenship' not to be occupied exclusively with our survival. Put simply: deep ecologists ask us to be plain citizens and at the same time expect – even oblige – us to think and behave as very uncommon, indeed quite extraordinary ones! In a perceptive article, critic Harold Fromm states this contradiction with remarkable pithiness:

> The 'intrinsic worth' that biocentrists connect with animals, plants, and minerals is projected by the desiring human psyche in the same way that 'the will of God' is projected by human vanity upon a silent universe that never says anything. ... The 'biocentric' notion of 'intrinsic worth' is even more narcissistically 'anthropocentric' than ordinary self-interest because it

hopes to achieve its ends by denying that oneself is the puppeteer–ventril-oquist behind the world one perceives as valuable.[26]

As biocentrists, deep ecologists ask us take the role of the invisible puppeteer – pulling the strings and ignoring the fact that we are pulling them.

If human beings are to regard themselves merely as plain citizens or equals to all other species in the biosphere, they must be invisible puppeteers: they must be guided by ethical canons that exist nowhere in the animal world and, at the same time, deny that they differ in their rights and intrinsic worth from the amoral world of nature, in short, bereft of ethics. Indeed, deep ecologists urge us to do this because we will aesthetically, materially, and spiritually 'benefit' from holding such an attitude toward the natural world – a crassly anthropocentric argument. That only human beings in the entire biosphere can confer 'rights' upon non-human beings precisely because as humans they are so radically different from other life-forms seems to elude most deep ecologists.

Where deep ecologists try to resolve this conundrum, their solutions are sophistic at best and circular at worst. 'Employing ethics and values, which are cultural objects,' observes Christopher Manes, one of the most misanthropic of the deep ecologists 'may appear to contradict the content of biocentrism, and it is undoubtedly incongruous to talk about the rights of nature when the concept of legal rights is traditionally associated with the triumph of culture over nature, or, in Kantian terms, duty over instinct.'[27] Despite the pejorative characterization of rights as the '*triumph* of culture over nature', 'legal rights' are not necessarily or often commonly equatable with 'ethics' and 'values', which may often stand in flat opposition to a culture's laws. In the absence of human beings, moreover, Nature cannot of itself generate any system of rights – which still leaves us in a puzzle. To resolve it, Manes invokes Naess's point that 'our self includes not only our ego and our social self, on which the imperatives of ethics play, but also a broader identification with ecology itself.' Speaking bluntly: this is pure rhetoric, not a 'deep' reply. Indeed, broadening our 'ego and our social self' does not necessarily bring about 'a broader identification with ecology', that is with other life-forms, mountains, rivers, and so on. There are many examples of selfhood in which the self is formed in contrast to other *human* selves, not necessarily in contrast to an encompassing natural world.

In another ideological strategy, Manes asserts that 'in the concept of the Ecological Self, human *interests* and natural *interests* become fused and there is no need to appeal to the *traditional* discourse of rights and values.

The *integrity* of the biosphere is *seen* as the *integrity of our own persons;* the *right*s of the natural world are implied in *our right to be human and humane.*'[28]

This amounts to a white flag of surrender. What 'interests' can be imputed to 'Nature' that are even definable in ethical terms? How do they become 'fused' with the 'interests' of humans, those 'plain citizens' whose 'intrinsic worth' is equal to that of all other life-forms? What constitutes the 'integrity' of the biosphere? Why are the 'rights' of the natural world 'implied in our right to be human and humane'? Where did ideas of 'interests' and 'integrity' come from, if not from human morality and an anthropomorphic conceptualization of 'human interests'?

To mechanically transfer the complex repertoire of rights, moral strictures, wisdom, and philosophy that exists in society to the biosphere, as though this repertoire could arise, let alone exist, without human beings is to grossly mystify humanity's interaction with the natural world and neutralize the rich content of these distinctly humanistic terms. Divested of their historical, social, and cultural moorings, these social ideas and practices are cheapened into slogans. This divestiture renders it impossible to formulate a serious ethics that can be used in humanity's relations with the natural world, as well as between human and human in the social world. Reduced to abstractions that float in an intuitional cloud, 'values', 'rights', and 'humane' behavior, are more transcendental than real, in a *de facto* dualism that simply bypasses their human origins – and actually becomes captive to the very origins it seeks to avoid. As Manes writes, invoking Warwick Fox, the real goal of this ecological ethics is 'the decentering of humankind' – as though it were not human beings alone and only alone who could follow ethical injunctions in relation to the natural world.[29]

While deep ecology trivializes the human spirit, it depends immensely on humanistic appeals to support its most basic tenets. Moreover, its absorption of human individuality into a mystical self-in-Self of cosmic proportions advances a reactionary message. In a mass society, where selfhood is atrophying under the assault of social forces and institutions over which the individual has virtually no control; when disempowerment has become an epochal social pathology; when women, people of color, the poor, and the underprivileged are asked to surrender what fragments of autonomy and freedom they still possess to the power of multinational corporations, impersonal bureaucracies, and the state – the 'decentering of humankind' opens the way for a cultural and social barbarism of frightening proportions.

Equally troubling is the outright misanthropy that many deep ecologists advance. To Christopher Manes, for example, humanity is a *'relatively expendable part'* of the environment.[30] Such derogatory views of humanity are matched by the icy indifference to human life and suffering in the writing of deep ecology's most important theorists. Consider the following dilemma: an active rattlesnake takes up residence under a family house, posing a grave danger to the child who lives there. The father must decide whether to kill the snake or risk the death of his child. For most people, this would not be a difficult decision; but for deep ecologists, the vital needs of the child and the snake – for life – are equal. Bill Devall, who actually cites such a case in his book, *Simple in Means, Rich in Ends* (1990), advances a principle of 'species impartiality' by which such decisions can be made. Devall's principle reads: '[f]airness in resolution of real conflicts can only occur when humans are not given any special privileges because they are humans.' By this principle, that is, humans should allow themselves no 'special privileges' in coping with such problems merely because 'they are humans'.[31] The child's father, who has already survived several bites from rattlesnakes, opts for killing the snake, earning Devall's reproval: 'I urged [the father] to make peace with the rattlesnake the way St. Francis made peace between a wolf and villagers in northern Italy in the famous thirteen-century story.'[32] Alas, we are not all 'saints' like Francis with a special pipeline to God.

Lest we suspect that Devall is merely fatuous, arrant misanthropy emerges in the closing pages of his book: '[w]e lack compassion and seem [!] misanthropic if we turn our backs on hundreds of millions of humans who reside in megalopolises. However, when a choice must be made, it seems consistent with deep ecology principles to fight on the side of endangered species and animals'[33] – and presumably ignore the plight of congested urban dwellers, which is a concern of 'misplaced humanists'. What concerns Devall about cities is not only the absence of 'wild animals' [!] there but the extent to which 'urban elites' exercise power with their 'materialist ideology and nihilism'. This trend, too, is a concern only of 'misplaced humanists', who also would wrongheadedly – in Devall's view – justify 'large-scale in-migration to Western Europe and North America from Latin America and Africa'.[34] Such views are redolent of the reactionary ideology currently abounding in the First World against people of color from the Third World.

Finally, deep ecology is heir to the lingering legacy of Malthus, whose warning about population growth outstripping food production 'was ignored by the rising tide of industrial/technological optimism', according to Devall and Sessions.[35] Whereupon they extol William Catton, Jr, author of *Overshoot*, for applying 'the ecological concept of *carrying capacity*' and remind us that William Vogt, who 'articulated' the environmental crisis, 'anticipat[ed] the work of radical ecologist Paul Ehrlich in the 1960s'. Vogt's recipes for diminishing population by withholding antibiotics from Third World countries go unmentioned. (See Chapter 3.)[36]

The misanthropic orientation of deep ecology was taken to its logical conclusion by Earth First!'s founding thinkers who, unencumbered by academic peer pressures, were more outspoken than Naess, Devall, and Sessions.

An inglorious moment of truth occurred in an interview with David Foreman, Earth First!'s indubitable leader, conducted by Bill Devall and published in an Australian periodical, *Simply Living,* in 1986.[37] Devall's introduction to the interview was inimitable in its admiration of Foreman. 'One of [Foreman's] quotes,' Devall exudes, 'is from John Muir concerning the relations between bears and people. Muir wrote, over a hundred years ago, that if a war should come between bears and humans, he would be sorely tempted to fight on the side of bears. Says Foreman: "That day has arrived, and I am enlisting in service to the bears."'

Devall first asked Foreman, 'What is the relation between deep ecology and Earth First!?' To which Foreman replied: 'I think deep ecology is the philosophy of Earth First! They are pretty much the same thing [but] I think EF! is a *particular style* of deep ecology.' The moment of truth, however, followed Devall's pointed question: 'Do you think population is an important issue?' To which Foreman responded:

> When I tell people how the worst thing we could do in Ethiopia is to give aid – the best thing would be to just let nature seek its own balance, to let the people there just starve there, they think that is monstrous. But the alternative is that you go in and save these half-dead children who will never live a whole life. Their development will be stunted. And what's going to happen in ten years time is that twice as many people will suffer and die.

These charitable remarks were followed by an opinion on immigration by Latin Americans to the United States. 'Letting the USA be an overflow valve for problems in Latin America is not solving a thing. It's just putting more pressure on the resources we have in the USA. It is just causing more destruction of our wilderness, more poisoning of water and air, and it isn't helping the problems in Latin America.' Devall – a pillar in the triune propagators of deep ecology in the United States – found nothing to object to in these statements; indeed, he seemed to acknowledge the legitimacy of Foreman's concern by offering the helpful query: 'Why haven't mainstream environmental groups dealt with the population issue?'

Foreman's mentor, Edward Abbey, intruded ethnic chauvinism, indeed, elements of nativism, into the debate that followed this interview. Abbey wrote:

> There are a good many reasons to call a halt to further immigration ... into the United States. One seldom mentioned, however, is culture: the United States that we live in today, with its traditions and ideals, however imperfectly realized, is a product of northern European civilization. If we allow our country − our country − to become Latinized ... we will be forced to accept a more rigid class system, a patron style of politics ... and a greater reliance on crime and violence as normal instruments of social change.[38]

Elsewhere he repeated this theme:

> Perhaps ever-continuing industrial and population growth is not the true road to human happiness. ... In which case it might be wise for us as American citizens to consider calling a halt to the mass influx of ever more millions of hungry, ignorant, unskilled, and culturally-morally-genetically impoverished people.[39]

'Genetically impoverished', no less? One is prone to cry: really!

In fact, an article I wrote in response to these remarks and the Foreman–Devall interview, 'Social Ecology Versus "Deep Ecology": A Challenge for the Ecology Movement', was greeted with savage acrimony, sprinkled with a measure of red-baiting, over several issues of Earth First!.[40] To this day, I can only wonder if academic deep ecologists would ever have dissociated themselves from the misanthropic and nativistic views Foreman expressed in the Simply Living interview had I not criticized it.[41] Even after my intervention, it took a year, to the best of my knowledge, before Arne Naess, Bill Devall, George Sessions, and Warwick Fox renounced Foreman's position with varying degrees of emphasis.[42] Still later, Foreman in a debate with me seemed to withdraw his harsher misanthropic formulations. For some two years, the environmental press resounded with the criticism and countercriticisms between supporters of Foreman's Simply Living views and my own − nor have they entirely quieted down to this day.[43] Sessions' dissociation from Foreman's views, in fact, proved to be equivocal. Writing in Foreman's new magazine, Wild Earth, in 1992, Sessions declared:

> In 1987, Murray Bookchin and his Social Ecology group attacked Earth First! and the Deep Ecology Philosophy. Certain casual remarks by individual Earth Firsters (made, to some extent, for their shock value to drive home the message of how out of balance contemporary humans are on the

*planet) concerning allowing Ethiopians to starve, and AIDS as Nature's
population control device, provided Bookchin with the opportunity he
needed.*[44]

Sessions' expression of solidarity with Foreman's behavior, which he had
previously renounced, hardly merits comment. At the time the *Simply
Living* interview was published, to the best of my knowledge, neither
Foreman, Devall, or other luminaries in the deep ecology 'movement'
characterized Foreman's observations as 'casual', still less delivered simply
for their 'shock value'. Quite to the contrary, Foreman and many of his
supporters defended these remarks militantly.

Deep ecology and much of its literature is unnervingly redolent of the
reactionary views chronicled by Fritz Stern and George Mosse in
Germany prior to the rise of National Socialism.[45] Cries like 'Back to the
Pleistocene!' during Earth First!'s militant days contribute to a mentality
that denies human uniqueness even as it appeals to human beings to carry
out an ethics that no animal can possibly have. At the same time, deep
ecology views humanity rather cheaply. Its literature abounds with
denunciations of humanity as a 'cancer' on the planet and human intervention into the natural world as demonic. Hardly any connection is
shown between the social maladies that afflict our age and their role in
determining society's relationship to the natural world. It holds the basic
assumption of Lynn White, Jr, that our present environmental problems
stem from cultural origins – that is, Christianity's disdain for the natural
world.[46] This argument reduces society's relationship to the natural world
to simplistic psychological terms. If we merely remedy our thinking and
living habits, individual by individual, we shall presumably become 'plain
citizens' of the biosphere with agreeable ecological habits. The impact of
this personalistic view of the ecological crisis and its sources, has – like
sociobiology and ecomysticism – significantly shifted public attention
from the social roots of our ecological dislocations to a psychological
level of discussion, if not a religious view.

Arne Naess, perhaps the most socially concerned of the deep ecologists, merely collapses into extreme inconsistencies when he deals with
his social ideas. In his *Ecology, Community, and Lifestyle: Outline of an
Ecosophy*, Naess avers that deep ecologists 'seem to move more in the
direction of nonviolent anarchism than towards communism.
Contemporary nonviolent anarchists are clearly close to the green direction of the political triangle.' Whereupon Naess quickly catapults from
his seemingly gentle anarchism into claims that 'with the enormous and
exponentially increasing human population pressure and war or warlike

conditions in many places, it seems inevitable to maintain some *fairly strong central political institutions.*'[47] Indeed, lest this not seem demanding enough, he adds that 'the higher the level of local self-determination the *stronger the central authority* must be in order to override local sabotage of fundamental green policies.' Aside from the element of 'Newspeak' here, in which the 'higher the level of local self-determination', the greater is our need for a 'central authority', such calls for a strong central authority, let it be noted, have become the bedrock credo of extreme right-wing 'environmentalists' in Europe.[48]

In the light of Naess's commitment to a strong state, what happens to free choice, idiosyncratic behavior, personal talents, and individuality? Or, for that matter, to his 'nonviolent anarchism'? And, if the Cosmic 'Self' into which the 'self' should dissolve is a suprahuman organism, a 'whole' – a 'totality'? – that blots out personal identity in traditional families and communities structured around castes, deep ecology can easily become an ideology for a strong centralized state in the name of perpetuating the 'rights of Nature'.

Ecomysticism is part of a larger spectrum of mysticism that plagues the Anglo-American and German consciousness on a scale that seems very much like a throwback to medievalism. It is smug, indeed, to express worried concern about the rise of Islamic and Christian fundamentalism while ignoring phenomena like channeling, astrology, feng shui, tarot, Jungian archetypal psychology, infantilism, and angelology, to cite some of the more prominent ideologies on the ever-widening landscape of spiritualism and mysticism.

Despite two centuries of enlightened humanism and rationalism, the past few decades have seen an appalling regression by a sizable part of the public into supernatural and supranatural cults. More than 90 per cent of Americans, for example, believe in the existence of a supernatural deity. A comparable number believe in the immortality of their souls, and a few individuals have 'tested' this conviction with 'near-death' experiences, in an effluvium of recent books. Sixty-seven per cent of the American public claims to have experienced 'extrasensory perception' (ESP); 42 per cent allow that they have had (or have) contact with the dead; 31 per cent claim to possess clairvoyant powers; and 29 per cent have had visions of one kind or another.

Andrew Greeley, who conducted this survey with the University of Chicago's National Opinion Research Council in the late 1980s, observes: 'Our studies show that people who've tasted the paranormal, whether they accept it intellectually or not, are anything but religious nuts or psychiatric cases. They are, for the most part, ordinary

Americans, somewhat above the norm in education and intelligence and somewhat less than average in religious involvement.'[49] Nor should Europeans be consoled that this problem is strictly American: the scale in Western Europe may not be as great as in the United States, but there is prima facie evidence of mysticism's rapid growth on the continent.

Indeed, at a time when Nobel laureates in physics and other leading figures in high culture argue quite seriously about the existence of deities and spirits, we have reason to shudder about what is going on among the less educated, ordinary people surveyed by Greeley and his associates. Seekers in the realm of the paranormal who undertake a survey of the cults themselves are likely to suffer few disappointments about their grip on the public mind.

A veritable jungle of paranormal cults and nostrums abounds in the United States. Broadcast airwaves are filled with fundamentalist preachers, of often dubious theological credentials and even more dubious morals; the advertisements of psychics and astrologists (many of whom profess to possess a license to engage in their crafts by 'professional' societies!) are everywhere. These tele-'visionists' are prepared to offer their insights on life and destiny over the telephone for a suitable charge, characteristically at $3.95 a minute (a bargain compared with a $4 charge!). Such sums are likely to chill the ardor of the most parsimonious mystics, who have to make do with the advice and predictions they glean from the astrology columns of the daily newspaper or from periodicals with names like *Miracles*. The airwaves are cluttered with the shrieks of strident 'opinion makers' who variously bark their views on God and interview people who claim to have communicated with extraterrestrials. Tabloid newspapers in supermarkets celebrate everything from the revival of Egyptian mummies to parents whose youngest child is half-fish and half-human.

To be sure, mystical cults are as much a part of Euro-American life as apple pie in the United States, fish and chips in Britain, knockwurst in Germany – or perhaps McDonald's hamburgers everywhere. We need not look to ancient Rome, the medieval world, or the Reformation to find evidence of how readily cults have turned into sedate, even universalist religions or demonologies. The explosive growth of the Church of Latter-Day Saints (Mormons) beyond its home terrain in Utah to all parts of the United States and to numerous countries abroad attests to the growing gullibility of people who live in an era that has actually unearthed the 'secrets' of life and matter. The influence of Mary Eddy Baker's gospel of Christian Science, with its rejection of modern medicine in favor of the therapeutic powers of biblical precept, by far exceeds the influence of Mark Twain's scathing books on Mormonism and

Christian Science alike. Yet Christian Science has been only a century or so in the making, while Mormonism began to surface on a worldwide scale only in the past two generations.

What makes the present-day cults a unique phenomenon is that they are appearing at a time when there is no *lack* of secular knowledge, such as characterized past ages, but rather when there is a *surfeit* of such knowledge.

Mystical and particularly *anti*rational and *anti*humanistic cults are becoming prevalent because more and more people know too much, even if vaguely, about the nature of reality – and they are frightened by what they know. Science and reason have 'told' them that they are on their own – with enormous powers to change the world around them, for better or worse. Lest we exaggerate the impact of metaphysics and high culture, their problem is not that Hegel and Nietzsche have told them that 'God is dead', or that Max Weber has told them that the world is 'disenchanted', however much these notions have been played up by academics.

Few of the modern cultists have ever read Nietzsche, still fewer Hegel, nor are they likely to be familiar with Weber. It is a vanity that academics entertain that their own interests correspond to those of the non-academic public. Moreover, as history has shown, people can behave quite frightfully or carry the burden of terrible afflictions, from famine to war, on their shoulders in the full belief that 'God is alive' and the world is 'enchanted'. Far more important than the archaic beliefs they hold or have discarded are the contradictions in the human condition itself. The enormous promise of technology to provide a world of material abundance, security, and freedom from toil has not been fulfilled for most of humanity, and it is largely the mystification of social reality, not the power of ideological hyperreality, that has produced a desire to escape from the existing state of affairs.

Put simply: modern people adhere to traditional beliefs with the same devotion that filled the hearts of their ancestors of earlier times. The enormous revival of religion in Russia, following the breakdown of a militantly atheistic Communist state, together with the growth of a bourgeois mean-spiritedness and anti-Semitism after two generations of 'socialist' re-education between 1917 and the 1980s, attests to the tenuous hold of belief systems when they are *merely* systems of belief. A good deal more than beliefs account for human behavior, even for the beliefs people profess to hold.

For most people, what truly counts is whether their beliefs are consistent with the reality around them. If they are not, people may shift their beliefs, adopting either an enlightened humanism that explains reality, or superstitions that allow them to escape from reality. In our own time, belief systems are particularly tenuous because the social world is changing too rapidly to support any ideology for a great length of time. An ideology that seems acceptable today quickly becomes obsolete tomorrow, even before it can be elaborated and become deeply entrenched in the popular mind.

The consequence of these rapid social transformations is that we live in a world of cults rather than entrenched traditional ideologies, of lightly held myths rather than seriously considered convictions – and, above all, of easily adopted absurdities that are only half-believed and discarded as easily as garments. Psychic instability reflects, in great measure, modern-day social and technological instability. The sillier a given craze, the more likely it is that it will be adopted as an ideological plaything and then let go as a passing absurdity. Its future depends upon whether it provides people with respite from the demands of a changing world that is very much in need of rational control and whose management seems to be clouded in mystery. Thus present-day cults, from ecomysticism to various theisms, 'reenchant' nothing, despite their extravagant claims to do so. In a broad sense, they are merely means to avoid an extravagantly mobile reality that must sooner or later be engaged by using candor and secular understanding, if its potentialities for a rational way of life are not to be aborted – be it by an ecological, social, or military disaster.

The process of psychologically eluding reality has been very much under way since the early 1970s. Its roots can be found in the 1960s counterculture, which, once it lost its political direction, rapidly disintegrated into privatism, an ever-changing collection of nostrums for personal development, and a mysticism inherited from the beatniks. An 'omnibook of personal development', published in 1977 with the imprimatur of *Psychology Today,* lists more than a hundred strategies for variously finding, sedating, and/or improving oneself.[50] Some of these strategies have gone out of fashion, after only a fairly short lifespan; others persist marginally, almost by sheer psychic and social inertia; quite a few are now 'established' techniques; and still others are quasi-religious and religious belief systems in their entirety. Their greatest merit, in most cases, is that they are 'usable', 'practical', and possibly 'interchangeable', each adding synergistically to the other for enhanced 're-enchantment' or therapy.

Acupuncture, of course, enjoys the prestige of antiquity. Just as the ancient Greeks thought Egypt was the font of wisdom because of its long history, so acupuncture, to which we can also add shamanism, tantra, and yoga, shares the pedigree of ancient Oriental origins. But much of the omnibook is filled with techniques and belief systems popular in the

1970s whose heyday has long since passed, supplanted by what I can best call 'old–new' mysticisms and theisms – the recycled products of traditional, even long-discarded, beliefs leveraged into usage for the end of the century and the beginning of the new one. They are marked by juvenility, by a steady retreat into a world of fairy tales and childhood phases of life. They are the stuff of primality, closed to critical examination and intellectual growth, with all its phases, pains, and demands.

An exemplary primal fad is the pursuit of the 'inner child', a psycho-mystique that was born decades ago when a cult shaped by the notion of a 'fall' from innocence in private life focused on an 'inner nature' of the individual that adulthood had tainted with experience, rationality, and responsibility. Synergized by neo-Freudian notions of infantile polymorphousness, Jungian archetypes, and the like, it can even be traced back to a Christian precept, which gives childhood innocence and sheeplike meekness a high degree of valuation over maturity and its overly civilized doubts about the world.

Like the new popularity of *The Simpsons,* a television cartoon series for adult audiences, the new infantilism seems to appeal to a still surviving sucking instinct in the psyche that is beyond the constraints of age and experience. As *Newsweek* reports, 'With grown baby boomers acting like perpetual teens, real teens are acting like infants.' At a juice bar in a fashionable New York dance club, a man wears 'a pajamas top and a Donald Duck backpack', while in a corner, 'Dr. Seuss-style stocking caps flop madly. Nearly everyone at the dance hall is adorned with pacifiers, kiddie charms, doll-like figurines, and playing with toys. A sturdy construction worker in his early twenties declares: "We've got to be tots again. That life was so cool. You just sucked." '[51]

Infantilism persists in modish stores that sell toys and games expressly designed for adults of all ages. Not only juvenile amulets but giant Panda bears are available to any middle-class man or woman who may want to cuddle up with ersatz furry things in the journey to sleepland. Tapes can be bought that bring on a gradual dozing – if not nostalgia – with songs like 'London Bridge Is Falling Down'. *Batman* and *The Flintstones,* movies based on cartoons popular when the baby boomers were children, draw record adult audiences today.

If these juvenilisms do not improve our knowledge of the world, people who say they have had near-death experiences assure us all will end well in the next one. Everyone, it seems, will be well received in heaven. An increasing number of articles, books, and radio and television interviews describe the contours of the afterlife. For those who doubt the immortality of the soul, most near-death experiences describe a glowing light after life has temporarily ended that is iridescently inviting, which should cause us to wonder – given the sales figures these books rack up – why the reader desires to remain in this earthly vale of tears at all.

Ecomysticism may be for highbrows, but angelology is for everyone. This latest extension of biblical theology into modern Yuppie and plebeian culture alike has a number of clergymen worried – for if we all have angels with whom we may directly communicate, what need have we for clerics? In any case, the growing public fascination with 'the angels among us', to cite the title of a feature article by several writers in *Time* magazine, may be taken as an example of how the modern mystical Zeitgeist relies on materiality and tangibility, not merely on the invisible and metaphysical.[52]

Clerical trepidations aside, such prestigious institutions as Harvard Divinity School and Boston College, among others, offer courses on angels, and the potentiality for a growing audience of believers should not be sneezed at. A recent *Time*/CNN telephone survey reports that nearly 70 per cent of the American public believe that angels exist. Fifty-five per cent believe that they are higher spiritual beings created by the deity who has empowered them to act as his agents on earth. Another 15 per cent believe that they are the spirits of people who died. Only 7 per cent believe that angels are a figment of the imagination, while 18 per cent regard them as symbolically important.

Inasmuch as angels are annoyingly invisible, certain techniques are obviously important to force them to materialize. A veritable industry has grown up to give angels tangibility. A recent article in *Time* read:

> In their modern incarnation, these mighty messengers [angels] have been reduced to bite-size-beings, easily digested. The terrifying-cherubim have become Kewpie-doll cherubs. For those who choke too easily on God and his rules, theologians observe, angels are the handy compromise, all fluff and meringue, kind, nonjudgmental. And they are available to everyone, like aspirin. 'Each of us has a guardian angel', declares Eileen Feeman, who publishes a newsletter AngelWatch from her home in Mountainside, New Jersey. 'They are nonthreatening, wise and living beings. They offer help whether we ask for it or not. But mostly we ignore them.

If we do, we are ungenerous – and the closing years of the twentieth century suggest that we may soon be giving them more attention than our medieval ancestors in the thirteenth century gave them. Authors seriously speculate about their form and fallibility, the reasons that they intrigue us, the nature of angel encounters, and their functions. Theologians are now beginning to complain that the trivialization of 'angelology' has reached a point where 'popular authors who render angels into household pets, who invite readers to get in touch with their inner angel, or summon their own "angel psychotherapist" or view themselves as angels in training,' write the *Time* reporters on the subject, 'are trafficking in discount spirituality'.

Initiates to this fascinating field may acquire a 'practical guide to working with the messengers of heaven to empower and enrich [their] lives' by consulting *Ask Your Angels*. To gain so commanding a power for only $10 is a literary bargain by any current standard.[53] Indeed, as the book cover advertises: 'If you've picked up this book, the angels have already touched you', which may well obviate your need to buy it. But should you do so, you will find within a winsome, fair, light-brown female angel, with flowery wings sprouting from her shoulder blades. The sketches inside the book show angels blowing trumpets – whether to attune themselves to the 'music of the spheres' or avoid oncoming traffic is not clear.

Most of the book is loaded with practical details on how to 'ask your angels' or, more inspirationally, 'The Grace Process', which subdivides into 'Grounding', 'Releasing', 'Aligning', 'Conversing', and 'Enjoying'. You can learn how to work in 'partnership with the angels' by 'fine-tuning the angelic connection', 'writing letters and dreaming with the angels', 'working with the angels to advance your goals', 'working with the angels in recovery and healing', and if all the bases aren't covered, 'working with the angels in all your relationships'. Indeed, lest your burdens be too heavy for one angel to handle, the book closes with a chapter titled 'working with the angels in groups'. It will help, the writers advise, to use a tape recorder so you can listen to the way you address angels – thus does the technological age intrude upon the divine and its blessings.

This kind of mentality falls within the province of sympathetic magic, an outlook that Sir James Frazier's *The Golden Bough* explains and illustrates in considerable detail. Its primitive ancestry is fairly assured: angels were variously deities and, earlier, spirits that people created out of their own fertile imaginations with the aid of shamans and later of priests. If Christianity ranks people just below 'angels', they are, in all truth, below nothing; and if 're-enchanting' the world or rendering it 'sacred' means looking up to nothing and populating it with figments of its own imagination, enlightened humanism demands that humanity look to reality and try to understand its own place in the world.

Notes

1 Naess's lecture was published as 'The Shallow and the Deep, Long-Range Ecology Movement', *Inquiry,* vol. 16 (Spring 1973), pp. 95–100.

2 *Ibid.*, p. 95.

3 For my own part, I had made a distinction between *environmentalism,* which I respectfully regarded as single-issue but often socially unsophisticated and instrumentally oriented struggle against pollution, nuclear power plants, road-building, and the like, and *ecology,* which located environmental dislocations in 'the very constitution of society as we know it today'. I presented this distinction in a lecture at the University of Buffalo in 1971, which was published first in a small periodical called *Anarchos* in 1972 under the title 'Spontaneity and Organization' and republished in my collection *Toward an Ecological Society* (Montreal: Black Rose Books, 1980), pp. 270–2. In 1971, to the best of my knowledge, neither Arne Naess nor the phrase *deep ecology* was known to most environmentally oriented people. My own lecture and subsequent related articles like my 1973 'Toward an Ecological Society' (in the anthology of the same name) called for a radically different sensibility toward the natural world and the need for a total remaking of society, in which I rooted the environmental crisis.

4 *Our Synthetic Environment*, under the pseudonym Lewis Herber (New York: Alfred A. Knopf, 1962); and 'Towards a Liberatory Technology', republished in *Post-Scarcity Anarchism* (San Francisco: Ramparts Press, 1971).

5 Naess, 'Shallow and Deep', p. 95, emphasis added.

6 *Ibid.*, p. 96, emphasis added on the word *intuitively.*

7 *Ibid.*, p. 96.

8 Warwick Fox, *Toward a Transpersonal Ecology* (Boston: Shambhala Publications, 1990), p. 58, emphasis added.

9 *Ibid.*, p. 59.

10 *Ibid.*, p. 60. Fox's account of deep ecology and its development is among the most serious to appear in the 'movement' – regardless of whether he himself is a member in good standing.

11 Dave Foreman, *Confessions of an Eco-Warrior* (New York: Crown Trade Paperbacks; 1991), p. 26.

12 Fox, *Transpersonal,* p. 66.

13 *Ibid.*, pp. 66–7.

14 Michael Tobias, ed., *Deep Ecology* (San Diego: Avant Books, 1985). At the time, I protested the use of this title for an anthology containing my article, 'Toward a Philosophy of Nature', only to be reassured by Tobias that the anthology contained many people who were not deep ecologists, including Garrett Hardin!

15 Bill Devall and George Sessions, *Deep Ecology: Living As If Nature Mattered* (Layton, Utah: Gibbs M. Smith, 1985).

16 Devall and Sessions, *Deep Ecology*, p. 66, emphases in the original.

17 *Ibid.*, p. 66.

18 *Ibid.*, p. 66, emphasis added.

19 *Ibid.*, p. 67.

20 *Ibid.*, p. 67, emphasis added.

21 *Ibid.*, p. 67, emphases added.

22 Robyn Eckersley, 'Divining Evolution: The Ecological Ethics of Murray Bookchin', *Environmental Ethics*, vol. 11 (Summer 1989), p. 115.

23 Devall and Sessions, *Deep Ecology*, p. 66. Actually, this quotation from Fox comes from a criticism of deep ecology in *The Ecologist*, vol. 14, no. 5–6 (1984), pp. 194–200 and 201–4. Which does not prevent Devall and Sessions from bringing it to the service of deep ecology.

24 *Ibid.*, p. 68.

25 Richard Watson, 'Eco-Ethics: Challenging the Underlying Dogmas of Environmentalism', *Whole Earth Review* (March 1985), pp. 5–13.

26 Harold Fromm, 'Ecology and Ideology', *Hudson Review* (Spring 1992), p. 30.

27 Christopher Manes, *Green Rage: Radical Environmentalism and the Unmaking of Civilization* (Boston: Little, Brown & Co., 1990), pp. 147–8.

28 *Ibid.*, p. 148, emphasis added.

29 *Ibid.*, p. 147.

30 *Ibid.*, p. 71, emphasis in the original.

31 Bill Devall, *Simple in Means, Rich in Ends: Practicing Deep Ecology* (Salt Lake City: Peregrine Smith Books, 1990), p. 176.

32 *Ibid.*, p. 177.

33 *Ibid.*, p. 189.

34 *Ibid.*, p. 189.

35 Sessions and Devall, *Deep Ecology*, p. 46.

36 *Ibid.*

37 Bill Devall, 'A Spanner in the Woods', interview with David Foreman, in *Simply Living*, vol. 2, no. 12 (*c.* 1986–87), pp. 3–4. *Simply Living* is published in Australia.

38 Edward Abbey, letter to the editor, *Bloomsbury Review* (April–May 1986), p. 4.

39 Edward Abbey, 'Immigration and Liberal Taboos', in *One Life at a Time, Please* (New York: Henry Holt and Co., 1988), p. 43.

40 Murray Bookchin, 'Social Ecology Versus "Deep Ecology"', *Green Perspectives*, no. 4–5 (September 1987). *Earth First!* (1 November 1987), pp. 17–22. For an exchange between myself and Edward Abbey, see *Utne Reader* (January–February 1988), pp. 4–8, and (March–April 1988), p. 7.

41 George Bradford was another early critic of Foreman's interview, in 'How Deep is Deep Ecology?' initially published in *Fifth Estate* (Fall 1987) and republished under the same title as a pamphlet (Ojai, CA: Times Change Press, 1989), p. 49. But Bradford was by no means unsympathetic to deep ecology's wilderness cult.

More opposed to technological innovations than even most deep ecology theorists, he wrote: 'Deep ecology loves all that is wild and free, so I share an affinity with deep ecologists that has made this essay difficult to write.'

42 See Bill Devall, 'Deep Ecology and Its Critics'; George Sessions, 'Ecocentrism and the Greens: Deep Ecology and the Environmental Task'; and Arne Naess, 'A European Looks at the North American Branch of the Deep Ecology Movement', all in *Trumpeter*, vol. 5, no. 2 (Spring 1988). See also Warwock Fox, 'The Deep Ecology-Ecofeminism Debate and Its Parallels', *Environmental Ethics*, vol. 11 (Spring 1989), pp. 20–1, note 38.

43 My debate with Foreman was published in book form, entitled *Defending the Earth* (Boston: South End Press, 1990).

44 George Sessions, 'Radical Environmentalism in the 90s', *Wild Earth* (Fall 1992), p. 66, emphasis added.

45 See Fritz Stern, *The Politics of Cultural Despair: A Study in the Rise of the Germanic Ideology* (Berkeley and Los Angeles: University of California Press, 1961); and George L. Mosse, *The Crisis of German Ideology: Intellectual Origins of the Third Reich* (New York: Grosset and Dunlap, 1964).

46 Lynn White, Jr, 'The Historic Roots of Our Ecologic Crisis', *Science*, vol. 155 (10 March, 1967), pp. 1203–7.

47 Arne Naess, *Ecology, Community and Lifestyle* (Cambridge: Cambridge University Press, 1989), p. 157, emphasis added.

48 Naess, *Ecology, Community,* p. 157, emphasis added.

49 Andrew Greeley, 'Mysticism Goes Mainstream', *American Health* (January–February 1987), pp. 47–9.

50 Katinka Matson, *The Psychology Today Omnibook of Personal Development* (New York: William Morrow & Co., 1977).

51 Ned Zeman, 'Who Let the Inner Child Out?' *Newsweek*, 28 December 1992, p. 67.

52 Sam Ellis *et al.*, 'The Angels Among Us', *Time*, 27 December 1993, pp. 56–5.

53 Alma Daniel, Timothy Wyllie, and Andrew Ramer, *Ask Your Angels* (New York: Ballantine Books, 1992).

CHAPTER 5

The myth of the primitive

There is a perverse irony in the fact that, after a virtual consensus has been reached about the abuses that European colonialists inflicted on aboriginal peoples, the possibility of attaining a realistic and sympathetic view of 'the primitive' is being gutted by assorted ecomystics, anticivilizationists, and more generically, self-avowed primitivists who have made 'the primitive' into a postmodern parody of the noble savage.

Today Euro-American primitivists have grossly distorted our understanding of the lives and cultures of aboriginal peoples by attributing to them suprahuman, paradisiacal dimensions. By turning ostensibly primitive lifeways into models for 'simple living' and 'closeness to nature', they have not only made tribal cultures into romantic caricatures of social harmony and virtue but reared them up as a standard that privileged, urban white people should emulate.

Not only is this romanticization extremely naive, it imposes an ideological burden on aboriginal peoples that downplays their real problems, needs, and hopes for a better future. Worse still, the 'noble savage' myth obliges aboriginals to be superior beings, indeed almost angelically virtuous and exemplary in behavior and thought, if they are to enjoy the prestige of Euro-American recognition and the rights to which they are entitled.

This conflict between the realities that aboriginal 'primitives' face and the taxing expectations that Euro-American primitivists impose upon them is eminently tangible. In the mid-1970s Northwest Indian communities were beginning to use technologically sophisticated methods to breed and harvest salmon. After years of neglect and poverty, the pride they took in their achievements was as moving as it was admirable. During a conference I attended in Bellingham, Washington, to my utter astonishment, some white ecomystics and primitivists reproached them for using modern technological, presumably 'non-ecological' methods. Having been degraded and exploited for centuries as 'savages', these Indians were now being told that they were being too civilized. By adopting advanced aquaculture techniques, they failed to qualify for their high estate in the ecomystical firmament. Having been defamed for being primitives in an earlier time, they were now being defamed for not being primitive enough.

Such ecomystical and primitivistic arrogance is epidemic today. Primitivism, to be sure, has many faces, ranging from a wholesale rejection of civilization (commonly designated as industrial and technocratic) to compromises with civilized practices guided by a 'primitive sensibility' or 'spirituality'. Thus the late Edward Abbey – whose writings were inspirational for Earth First! and are recited reverentially by self-styled 'radical' environmentalists – expressed his preference for 'the coming restoration of a higher civilization' than the present military-industrial one. This preference would certainly be laudable by any progressive standard. But Abbey's 'higher civilization', as it turns out, is one in which 'scattered human populations modest in numbers [would] live by fishing, hunting, food-gathering, small-scale farming and ranching' – a curious mix of occupations that would seem to stand at odds with each other ('small-scale ranching' mingled with 'food-gathering'?). The new 'primitives' would 'assemble once a year in the ruins of abandoned cities for great festivals of moral, spiritual and intellectual renewal – a people for whom wilderness is not a playground but their natural and native home.'[1] The 'ruins of abandoned cities' would become at one and the same time the despised playground for a 'moral, spiritual and intellectual renewal' and, oddly enough, the theater for the 'higher civilization's' festivals – which should put city life in any shape or form in its place!

For all its incongruities and its total failure to appreciate the universalizing historical role of the city, Abbey's vision is by no means the most extreme example of chic primitivism. Earth First!ers commonly sport bumper stickers with the slogan 'Back to the Pleistocene!' As John Davis, onetime editor of *Earth First!,* wrote, 'Many of us in the Earth First! movement would like to see human beings live much more like the way they did fifteen thousand years ago as opposed to what we see now', which, Christopher Manes soberly explains, means, 'the kind of hunter–gatherer, shifting agricultural economies of tribal peoples.'[2] Precisely why modern humanity should draw a straight line from Sunbelt cities directly back to the late Paleolithic is a problem I shall leave to the reader to resolve.

Judging from the examples usually given by ecomystics and primitivists, 'primal' sensibilities correspond to beliefs and practices imputed to American Indians. This identification of Indian peoples with archaic practices and 'Paleolithic' views has led to bitter conflicts between the expectations of Euro-American primitivists and the very peoples they extol.

Ecomystics, primitivists, and deep ecologists have challenged the rights of native Americans to divert water from rivers for irrigation purposes and harvest timber on their tribal lands. Their lands stolen by European settlers and their cultures subverted, victimized by genocidal attacks and denied free access to game and fertile soil, native peoples are now expected – if ecomystics have their way – to reject the 'technocratic-industrial' support systems that the privileged white world takes for granted.

I make no claim that a competitive 'free enterprise' economy, rendered even harsher by a highly sophisticated technology, is a desideratum – either for aboriginal peoples or for Euro-Americans. Quite to the contrary, I argue for a way of life that is not focused on capital accumulation and profit. Nor do I favor a 'technocratic-industrial' society that centers its concerns on the privileged few. Quite to the contrary: human life is meaningless if it is not enriched by art, ideals, and a spirituality that is ecological and humane.

But a way of life burdened by material insecurity and toil cannot nourish the kind of individual and social freedom that makes human life meaningful and creative – indeed, that is likely to foster a rich ecological sensibility. Materially deprived and socially underprivileged people whose bellies are empty are not likely to be much concerned with the integrity of wildlife and forests. What they need is food and a decent life before they can think of the welfare of other life-forms.

Nor can an ecological sensibility be found by trying to return to an idealized 'primitive' world. In the band and tribal societies of prehistory, humanity was almost completely at the mercy of uncontrollable natural forces and patently false and mystified visions of reality.

Like ecomystics, primitivists are shifting public attention away from the tasks of seriously remaking society along rational lines, toward dubious – and often contrived – arcadian cultural attitudes that are imputed to the long-lost past. For a humanistic vision of a future that has yet to be won, both for native and Euro-American peoples alike, they are trying to substitute mythic notions of a pristine and primitive past that probably never existed.

Understanding aboriginal life requires that we find a *balance* between the 'primitive' and the civilizational that corresponds to what we really know, based on evidence provided by paleoanthropology and anthropology. This problem cannot be sloughed off with dreamy accounts of what we would *like* to believe our Paleolithic ancestors did or thought. The evidence we have about ice age people and existing aboriginals must be examined seriously on their own terms, untainted by wishful thinking.

Whatever natural features we impute to the primitive world, and whatever synthetic features we impute to the civilized world, the old Victorian image of the demonic aboriginal savage and the contemporary ecomystical image of the angelic aboriginal saint are myths we can no longer entertain. Modern civilization is too dynamic to be dissolved into a largely mythic past. In the next generation or two humanity is likely to move ahead technologically, scientifically, and industrially even more rapidly than it did during the past three centuries.

But what *direction* will these changes take? Toward a rational future that creates a sensitive balance within society and between society and the natural world? Or toward a domineering and exploitative social order that makes earlier systems of domination seem benign?

If primitivists use the word *primitive* to refer to 'closeness to nature', the phrase *primitive culture* is simply an oxymoron, for culture – or society – is hardly a 'natural' phenomenon, a phenomenon of first nature.

Although animals may be more or less *sociable,* their sociability is not evidence of the existence of a *society*. Society is unique to human beings. There is a crucial difference between *society,* with its distinctly structured and mutable institutions, and *community,* with its simple, often undifferentiated relations between organisms. Societies, however well or poorly entrenched their institutions, can be *changed* by human action; animal communities are either the product of genetic factors, such as beehives, or they are relatively formless and unstable. Non-human animals can be very sociable indeed, as are wolves, African dogs, and baboons; but sociability does not make for a *society*, any more than the *ad hoc* use of stones by sea otters to open oyster shells or the use of twigs by chimpanzees to get at termites constitutes a technology (or what anthropologists call a tool-kit) with its carefully shaped permanent or semipermanent implements. In the absence of social institutions that can be modified or radically changed – a phenomenon that is distinctly human – non-human animals may form and dissolve groups, but apart from genetically induced aggregations, like those of 'social insects', they have minimal structure and permanence.

Hence no culture is 'natural' in a strictly biological sense. To be sure, a tribal culture may be 'close to nature' in that its environment is relatively pristine, but its members usually know of no other habitats than the ones in which they find themselves, formed by natural evolution. The forests, grasslands, and mountains that surround them may have been countless years, indeed aeons, in the making, together with the wildlife and plants on which they rely for food, clothing, and shelter, but it is a world seemingly unbroken by changes, apart from the few that they, as humans, have produced.

Such tribal cultures may base their social institutions on biological facts, such as age groups, gender relations, and kinship ties, which may seem natural because of their biological premises – age, gender, and kinship – but they are part of second nature, not first nature. No such institutional ensembles exist among non-human animals. Non-human animals have no gerontocracies, patriarchies, or systems of rights and duties based on a common ancestry – apart from mother-offspring relations, and even these relations tend to be unstable and tentative where they persist for any great length of time.

By contrast, the human societies of second nature are a qualitative departure from animal communities, an alienation from strictly biological phenomena, however much they initially rest on certain biological facts. A 'primitive' culture that is 'close to nature' is not in any way congruent with the natural world, or first nature. Once hominids and early humans fashioned, retained, and elaborated a tool-kit, established a division of labor (however rudimentary), shared food, acted altruistically, and organized their relationships into definable structures, they no longer merely adapted to their environment; they began to significantly change it with a distinct purposiveness. The second nature they created fundamentally separated them from their first nature as mere animals. Hence, however primitive a human culture may have been, it was not identical with purely biological lifeways – indeed, not even with the fairly sociable relations that exist among chimpanzees and baboons.

Humans were now engaged in doing things and using means that, nascent as they may be in other animals, sharply distinguished them from other life-forms. They began to *transform* their environment willfully, often with a clear idea of the means they required to create a more congenial habitat and way of life.

A 'primitive culture', then, is actually very 'unnatural'. It marks a decisive break with the largely passive and adaptive nature of animal behavior. To speak of a 'primitive culture' is to thoroughly mystify the 'primitive', not to speak of the concept of society. With the emergence of society, a qualitatively new realm of evolution, of subjectivity, and potentially, at least, of freedom developed *out* of a realm that was essentially biological, rooted in great part by genetically guided behavior.

Odd as it may seem, the fact that band and tribal cultures broke with first nature is most clearly seen in the appearance of what ecomystics and primitivists enthusiastically celebrate today – notably, 'primitive spirituality'.

Whether it is 'primitive' or not, spirituality is entirely *ideological*. That is, it is a process of thinking, of symbolizing, and of reflecting about experience. However clever or intelligent many animals may seem, they have no ideologies; by contrast, humans definitely do. They have systematic ways of trying to understand their environment in symbolic terms; they possess the complex form of expression that is language; they usually work collaboratively to gain the means of life and distribute goods according to certain accepted rules; they assume communal duties and demand certain rights. In short, they develop credos that render their activities intellectually and emotionally coherent.

Whether these forms of thinking are based on custom, or are enshrined in morals and guided by magico-religious beliefs, or are based on ethics and guided by canons of rationality, they clearly influence how people do things in the real world. Indeed, however mutable they may be, these influences often have the tenacity of animal instincts.

Precisely such belief systems, or forms of spirituality, markedly *alienate* humans from the natural world around them and distinguish them from the animal inhabitants that coexist with them in a shared natural environment. That is to say, the very *ideational* systems that ecomystics cite to distinguish 'primitive' sensibilities from civilized ones are already highly complex, and by acting according to precepts they formulated in their minds, band and tribal peoples transcend first nature; indeed, as social beings who act consciously upon the world, they manipulate their environments as best they can, indeed change them. In this respect, band and tribal peoples open a chasm between themselves and first nature for which there is no precedent in first nature, either in degree or in kind.

Even more disturbing for ecomystical and primitivistic notions of 'primitive' sensibilities, the spiritual views of aboriginal cultures often *pit* them against their environment. The exigencies of life in a demanding world usually throw aboriginals into competition with other life-forms, a conflict that may lead to severe environmental changes that render a given habitat unfit for other animals. These changes, in turn, may result in the complete extermination of food animals, indeed their wanton destruction on a large scale.

It insults the intelligence of aboriginal peoples to burden their lifeways and spirituality with New Age interpretations that make them more selfless and less opportunistic in satisfying their material needs than modern people. Although aboriginal methods of dealing with a given environment differ appreciably from modern ones, no human beings could survive if they fatuously sacrificed their own needs for food, shelter, and self-defense in favor of other species – unless, to be sure, they attained a modern level of technical development that left them sufficiently privileged and leisured to be concerned about the welfare of non-human creatures: that is, unless they were well-fed, well-housed, and affluent – like many ecomystics and primitivists today.

I do not wish to deprecate the good intentions of many ecomystics and primitivists who fervently urge us to develop a 'Paleolithic consciousness' out of a concern for protecting the biosphere. But certain troubling features of that 'consciousness' stand in the way of achieving so laudable an end.

To begin with, modern people certainly are not like Paleolithic or 'ice age' people. During the Euro-American ice ages, probably the great majority of Paleolithic people, as I have already noted, lived in the relatively warm or balmy climates of Africa and southern Asia. Nor do we know with any certainty how ice age people and warm-climate people really viewed the immensely different worlds in which they lived. Paleolithic people lived in such vastly diverse climatic and environmental conditions that they could hardly have shared a common sensibility – still less the unified set of values and beliefs that ecomystics and primitivists so eagerly impute to them.

Values and beliefs in today's aboriginal communities often do not conform to what ecomystics and primitivists think aboriginal peoples *should* think. Aboriginal sensibilities are generally more pragmatic and less 'spiritual' than Max Oelschlaeger in *The Idea of Wilderness* would have us believe.[3] As foragers, they have to know their enemies from their friends. They have to understand the behavior and habits of the animals they hunt, often in competition with animal predators. They have to develop practical techniques for coaxing herds into traps and develop systematic, carefully coordinated methods of hunting large, dangerous game lest they themselves become victims of the animals they hunt. In the uncertain and precarious world in which they live, these problems could be almost endless.

In the light of these realities, many of Oelschlaeger's notions of 'Paleolithic consciousness' are far-fetched. Some seem to rest on inferences made from modern aboriginal values, which may have little to do with 'Paleolithic values'. Indeed, many values held by aboriginal peoples today are likely to have been significantly shaped by their centuries-long contact with Western and Islamic cultures.

Oelschlaeger means to convey the idea that Paleolithic foragers spiritually viewed their world as pristine, and regarded first nature as 'feminine', 'alive', and 'sacred', a world in which time 'folded into an eternal mythical present' and 'ritual was essential to maintaining the natural and cyclical order of life and death.'[4]

Yet Oelschlaeger is looking back upon the Paleolithic world – which lasted some two million years and which including hominids and humans that ranged from Australopithecines through *Homo erectus,* Neanderthals, proto-*Homo sapiens sapiens,* and modern *Homo sapiens sapiens* – from a naively retrospective view. He infers from modern romanticizations of band and tribal peoples the 'consciousness' that a wide variety of hominid and human species held in a world that was extremely varied and notable for its different and fluctuating environments.

To begin with, the very concept of 'Nature' involves a long process of abstraction that reaches well into historical times. A duality between the natural and unnatural is necessary to bring the natural into clear relief conceptually. Paleolithic foragers, to be sure, were probably thoroughly informed about their habitat; indeed, a pragmatic and highly concrete knowledge of its features would have been indispensable for the survival and well-being of *any* foraging community. In this respect, our Paleolithic ancestors were no different from ourselves: they had, in effect, to be 'street wise', completely familiar with strategies to survive. But they would have been unable to distinguish contrasts between the natural and unnatural, or to call their own world natural, for what we blithely call 'Nature' was *all* that existed around them and all they could have possibly known – that is, their habitat. The concept of Nature, in effect, could have emerged only when human beings began to *transform* the natural world significantly enough to bring what was not Nature into relief against a notion of Nature.

Nor is it clear that Paleolithic foragers thought of the natural world as 'intrinsically feminine' – whatever Oelschlaeger means by this – unless we are referring to a Mother Earth Goddess or an all-pervasive, panthe-istic feminine principle associated with fertility. The very notion of a Mother Earth goddess is a blatantly anthropomorphic interpretation of ordinary natural facts of life. Such goddesses are usually embodied as dis-tinctly *human* deities with female breasts, buttocks, legs, and heads. We cannot even be sure that some female representations, like the goddess Astarte, signified a maternal principle in any general sense. In any case, goddesses like Astarte are not Paleolithic; they seem to have emerged for the first time in Neolithic and Bronze Age societies, which already approached the high civilizations of historical times.

The most widely cited evidence for the claims that ice age foragers 'regarded nature as intrinsically feminine' are the 'goddess' figurines – the 'Venuses' – found in upper Paleolithic caves and in early or middle Neolithic dwellings. The assumption that these remains are almost exclu-sively deities is a matter of pure faith rather than accurate knowledge; nor has much attention been given to the uses to which similar 'Venuses' have been put by aboriginal peoples in modern times.

Margaret Ehrenberg, in her splendid study, *Women in Prehistory*, warns us that these Stone Age figurines by no means support the notion that a

Mother Goddess religion – or, I would add, a view of Nature as 'intrinsically feminine' – pervaded prehistory. Such figurines may well have been used for pragmatic and magical ends rather than for reverential and religious ones. Ehrenberg writes:

> The use of figurines in sympathetic magic to aid fertility is attested in many ethnographic examples and may have been perceived as even more important in societies where the link between male impregnation and childbirth was not fully understood. A woman wishing for a child would make, or have made, a model either of herself pregnant, or – more commonly in known ethnographic examples – of the hoped-for child, perhaps shown as the adult they would eventually become. She might then carry the image around, perhaps sleep alongside it, or use it to perform other rituals.[5]

Such practices, Ehrenberg tells us, occur among a number of West African and American Indian tribes. Once the woman became pregnant, the figurine would be discarded, in much the same way that a sorcerer or shaman discards a representational figurine after completing a magical ritual. 'The fact that both Paleolithic and many Neolithic figurines are commonly found within houses and home bases, and often among debris, would strengthen this possibility, if the image could be cast aside once it had fulfilled its function, while the idea of discarding the image of a specific deity seems less likely.'

It is undeniable that goddesses existed in high civilizations throughout the world – at times as creative deities, at other times as destructive ones, at still other times both, but by no means always holding a supreme status in diverse pantheons. Goddesses, 'earth' or otherwise, abounded throughout the pagan world and, in the 'Mary' image, in Christian societies. But Ehrenberg's highly suggestive hypothesis that female figurines do not a 'Mother Earth goddess' religion make – indeed, that the figurines were merely magical and highly personal fertility symbols – is far more plausible than the belief that they enjoyed pantheistic supremacy in the Paleolithic world.

What casts even more doubt on the existence of an upper Paleolithic Mother Earth goddess religion is evidence that many upper Paleolithic figurines are not exclusively female. As Richard E. Leakey observes, citing fifty-seven engravings of isolated human heads on the walls of the La Marche cave in Western France: 'the so-called Venuses, statuettes with bulbous buttocks and breasts ... supposedly embody a fertility or mother-god image. Statuettes of this type are certainly very striking in their emphatic sexuality.' But, Leakey warns,

Of the many hundreds of carved figures so far discovered throughout Europe, some can be identified as female, although most of these have natural rather than exaggerated proportions, some are clearly male, but most are, to our eyes at least, sexless. The idea of a continent-wide cult of the mother-god, symbolized by the bulbous 'Venuses', appears to have been greatly overstated.[6]

Perhaps the earliest known Paleolithic figurine, at this writing, is that of a male, found in a cave some 32,000 years ago at Hohlenstein, Germany. He seems to be wearing a lion's mask or have a lion's head and a male body, not unlike ancient Egyptian deities that were part human and part animal. It is impossible to say whether the figurine signifies a deity, a shaman, or a 'big man' endowed with community respect, but it was decidedly not female.

No less dramatic are the full-face carvings and wall-sketched profiles of male individuals who are remarkably individuated. Staring in fascinating detail and with arresting strength of character – a distinct personality and a dignified mein – is the head of a man, carefully sculpted from the ivory of a mammoth tusk, found near Dolni Vestonice in Czechoslovakia. The head dates back to some 26,000 years ago.

Upper Paleolithic sketches show men in profile whose appearance is very individuated, indeed, who seem like playful caricatures, as witness the engraved (largely male) human faces from La Marche.[7] In fact, upper Paleolithic peoples may have created artistic works for purposes no more magical than artists have today – notably portraiture and head carvings that were meant to delight or to record an image of an individual for posterity – or simply as graffiti. We can only guess at what they were meant to convey: in some cases probably magical figures, in others fertility figures, and still others strictly personal sketches, including caricatures. To lump all of these figures together as 'feminine' symbols of all-living Nature is to read back, over a span of 30,000 years, a vision that all too many mystics *want* Paleolithic people to have believed – not what is revealed by the evidence at hand.

If it is true that, for Paleolithic foragers, 'the entire world of plants and animals, even the land itself, was sacred,' as Oelschlaeger asserts,[8] this assumption would hardly make them unique, even by comparison with much-maligned Judeo-Christian religious beliefs. In his very influential 'The Historical Roots of Our Ecologic Crisis', Lynn White, Jr, gave a warped image of the Christian tradition as inherently antinaturalistic.[9] Although by no means alone in this line of thinking, White's overwhelming subjectivist and ideological explanation of the present ecological crisis greatly contributed to the ecomystical and New Age accounts of ecological problems that are so pervasive today.

However much ecomystics and primitivists may quote biblical scriptures that assign to man 'lordship' – more properly, *stewardship* – over the biosphere, the fact is that Yahweh in Genesis is no less fecund and creative than any Mother Earth goddess. In scripture, the Judeo-Christian deity created the universe, light, and all manner of living beings. He created a 'garden in Eden in the east', causing 'every kind of tree that is pleasing to see and good to eat' to 'grow from the ground' (Genesis 2:8–9). He is an aesthetic as well as a functional deity. He is also an adoring biologist who causes 'the water [to] teem with an abundance of living creatures, and [lets] birds fly above the earth under the ceiling of the sky.' Apparently biocentric in His outlook, despite assigning the role of stewardship to 'man', He even creates 'the great monsters of the sea and all living animals, those that teem in the waters, according to their kind, and every winged bird, according to its kind'. He blesses them and enjoins them to be 'fruitful and increase in number, fill the waters of the sea, and let the birds increase on the earth' (Genesis 1:20–23).

Indeed, Ecclesiastes informs us that 'God wants to test [humans] and let them see that *they themselves* are animals. For the destiny of humanity and animal is identical: death for one as for the other. Both have the *same spirit;* humans have *no superiority* over animals for all passes away like wind. Both go to the same place, both come from dust and return to dust' (Genesis 3:18–20, emphasis added). Could biocentrists ask more of the most generous Mother Earth goddess in religious literature, east or west?

The 'sacredness' of the world would have not been specific to Paleolithic foragers, then, assuming with Oeschlaeger that they held such a view, or for that matter, to contemporary Judaism and Christianity, which are consistently disdained by ecomystics and primitivists as 'anti-naturalistic'. The attempt to impute to Paleolithic foragers a uniquely naturalistic spirituality to which we must somehow return – despite all we actually know today about the causes of phenomena that were complete mysteries to them – reflects not only bad anthropology but disquieting naivety.

Any religion that included a creator deity, male or female, treated the creator's work as divine or 'sacred'. Indeed, far more problematical today is whether Paleolithic foragers were actually religious in the sense that we ordinarily define that word, or whether their belief systems, to the extent that we can guess what they were, were mainly pragmatic and instrumental.

What 'primitives' really believed may be very different from what is generally supposed. Nearly all foraging societies known to modern anthropologists had already been affected by Western cultural mores and religions before trained Euro-American investigators reached them. Artifacts from Paleolithic foragers allow us to make *guesses* about what they thought, but in an era awash with mysticism like our own, it is necessary to show great prudence in making inferences about the figurines, sketches, paintings, and other materials from late Paleolithic caves – and not to leap from these remains to mystical notions about the psychological 'archetypes' and 'innate' gender sensibilities, so much in vogue today.

Aside from their aesthetic value, these Paleolithic remains seem to be primarily magical in function, particularly those that depict animals.[10] Paintings, drawings, and sculptures that survive from the Aurignacian and Magdalenian foragers of some 30,000 years ago in the caves of southern France and the Spanish Pyrenees (the so-called classic area of the late Paleolithic remains) commonly depict animals, in some cases clearly being attacked by hunters. Are these depictions magical efforts to assure success in the hunt? Are they evidence of magical efforts to increase the dwindling population of overhunted game animals? Do they reveal a respectful attitude toward the animals pursued? These questions are impossible to answer – nor are there any Paleolithic hunters around to answer them for us.

In fact, the range of functions these paintings, sculptures, and drawings had may have been legion. Circular incised dots on an ivory plaque suggest that Paleolithic people may have developed some sort of calendar; a cave lion engraved on a stalagmite is pitted by marks that suggest it was used as a target for throwing stones. Many animals are depicted in such amazing and sensitive detail that it is hard to suppose some aesthetic intention was not as important as 'religious' ones. Hunting scenes may have been painted to celebrate episodes of specific hunts rather than as magical and ritual symbols, or they may have been used to instruct the young in hunting techniques. Although most paintings and sketches portray animals, hundreds of them depict human beings – and of both sexes.

A multitude of possibilities could have led our late Paleolithic ancestors to produce the artifacts, figurines, and paintings in their caves and dwelling sites. The most likely common denominator that provides us with a plausible account of the animal figures and the scenes involving them is that they served the ends of sympathetic magic: the simulation by means of figurines, paintings, and drawings of successful events, like hunts and pregnancies. They are hardly evidence of 'reverence' either for animals or for a Nature that presides over human welfare and destiny. Such concepts are strikingly historical, as distinguished from prehistorical, more the products of civilization than we would like to think. Again, a concept like Nature has meaning only to people who have already created 'unnatural' environments like villages, towns, and cities, pushing forests and wildlife back to ever more secluded areas where they did not interfere with such 'unnatural' activities as agriculture and urban life.

It is eminently reasonable to suppose that the paintings and sculpture we find in Paleolithic caves and dwelling places had basically pragmatic functions. They were most likely meant to assure success in pregnancies and hunts and help people acquire the material means of life. Magic and the implements used to deploy it were ultimately guided by an everyday means–ends or instrumental rationality – not simply by a mysterious 'wisdom' about an incomprehensible Nature – to acquire meat, skins, bones for implements, and the like. We cannot fault Paleolithic foragers for employing specious magical techniques that, apart from the confidence they gave them, in no way enhanced their success. The figures painted on cave walls were *not* the living animals they hunted, and the images that they or their shamans depicted were strictly analogies. As such, they were no more effective in luring game into the range of their weapons than a board game of Monopoly makes its players wealthy or poor.

Whether these magical practices enhanced their respect for animals or wilderness is doubtful. The attitudes of modern band and tribal peoples toward the game they kill, even toward their domesticated animals like dogs, are anything but gentle. Suffice it to say that respect is a vague word, with multiple meanings. To ecomystics and primitivists it might mean love, awe, reverence, a religious intuition, or 'biophilia' – some allegedly instinctive longing for wilderness and wildlife. All of these possibilities actually presuppose a host of unstated beliefs or beg the questions they are meant to answer.

If anything meaningful can be said about Paleolithic paintings and carvings, it is that the foragers who produced them held a pragmatic belief in the power of magic, or what Sir James Frazier regarded as primitive man's science.[11] That our prehistoric ancestors held such belief systems is completely understandable in view of how little they knew about the often frightening natural forces that determined their well-being. What is incomprehensible is that millions of ostensibly civilized people today, even educated urban dwellers, firmly believe that Paleolithic and modern aboriginal beliefs provide a more valid, insightful, and superior account of the natural world than the brilliant explanations given by modern science.

That magic was not the sole component of Paleolithic ideologies is suggested by basic belief systems found among aboriginal peoples almost everywhere: the belief in spirits, in visions, and in spectral powers that were either beneficent or harmful and in one way or another had to be propitiated – a belief, alas, that is only too present today, in our chrome-plated techno-industrial-cybernetic society.[12]

Judging from what we know about existing band and tribal peoples, probably all Paleolithic people believed in the existence of 'spirits', a 'spirit world', and later some kind of spiritism. What is the source of their beliefs, how did they develop, and what attitudes toward wildlife and wilderness did they reflect?

The most likely source of primitive spiritism seems to be dreams, a night-world sort of wisdom that is still practiced among ecomystics today. Among aboriginal believers, spiritism gives supernatural explanations for phenomena that we can now explain in strictly naturalistic and scientific terms.[13] Aboriginals who lack an understanding of dream images (a vexing problem even until well into modern times) would take recourse to spirits to explain the reappearance of the dead in dreams, or the occurrence of bizarre events in sequences that were out of the ordinary.

Dreaming itself would have suggested the existence of another world, possibly more potent one than the waking world, a *spirit* world that presides over human welfare and to which the individual and the community held some sort of obligation. This sense of obligation may have been induced by outright fear – not necessarily by 'reverence'. Shamans embroidered this spirit world into a complex universe in its own right, embellishing dream materials in ways that gave these often cynical practitioners considerable personal power and many material privileges. Since dreams can be very complex, bizarre, and frightening, people who could not account for them would be vulnerable to the claims of any canny individual who professed to be able to interpret them, as is the case even in a secular society like our own that minimizes the importance of the supernatural. Shamans have always been available to give interpretations of inexplicable occurrences for suitable rewards.

The shamanistic imagination should not be underestimated: it can be a formidable power in elaborating myths as well as magical practices. Figures on late Paleolithic cave walls suggest that they were present very early on in foraging cultures. They probably provided increasingly complex magical techniques, devised assorted myths and rituals, explained the meaning of individual dreams, and preyed on collective fears, especially those engendered by lightning, thunder, and earthquakes. Much to their material advantage, shamans would have exploited these inexplicable phenomena and given interpretations of portents and dangers in dreams, as well as more mysterious phenomena like storms, meteorites, comets.

Actually, we probably tend to overstate the simplicity of late

Paleolithic cultures and their resemblance in this respect to band or tribelike cultures today. There is ample evidence, as I have suggested that in the great Pyrenees mountain passes, late Paleolithic hunters were creating hierarchical forms of social organization, mainly gerontocracies, and fabricating tools on a markedly industrial basis – not unlike hand-worked assembly lines of present-day vintage. Mass manufacture was not restricted to modern times by any means.

Late Paleolithic foragers, to be sure, knew very well how to survive under extremely inhospitable conditions. They were familiar with animal behavior and developed superb techniques for harvesting game. They knew how to select nutritious food plants and avoid toxic ones. Their knowledge of their habitats and their ability to gain subsistence from them was exceptional in every degree.

But their knowledge about the real sources of climatic, geological, and stellar events – would have been minimal. Their spiritism was in large measure a compensation for their ignorance, an attempt to explain the unknown and all that which was clouded in mystery. In the absence of authentic knowledge about dreams and seemingly cosmic phenomena, their shamans contrived a highly imaginative corpus of explanations structured around analogies and fancies, often blatantly serving social interests that involved power relationships within and between their communities.

Much of this knowledge was patently anthropomorphic, filled as it was with talking animals, mysterious omens, and a multitude of human-like myths and analogical magical techniques designed to give order, meaning, and stability to the world. Accordingly, myth, magic, and cosmic narratives made the puzzling and mysterious facts of life comprehensible to human minds. More commonly than not, they were probably contrived not simply to explain phenomena but to legitimate the authority of emerging hierarchical strata.

To show how the dream and spirit worlds are rendered anthropomorphic and subject to shamanistic control, the belief system of the Makuna Indians of Colombia is a valuable example. As Kaj Århem, who spent two years with these people, observes:

> When Makuna men go hunting and fishing they also, in their conception, carry out an exchange with the animal world. They believe that in another dimension of reality, all animals are people; they have houses and gardens, musical instruments and ritual ornaments, chants and dances, as people do. They are grouped into communities inhabiting particular territories and also have their headmen, or 'masters of the animals'. Before major

*hunting and fishing expeditions – such as those preceding the [commu-
nity's] Spirit Dance – a shaman must visit the long houses of the fish and
game animals and negotiate with their headmen. The shaman offers them
spirit foods, coca and snuff, and is promised fish and game in exchange.*[14]

What is intriguing about the Makuna cosmology is not only the reci-
procity between humans and animals and the active role shamans play in
negotiating the interactions between the two; this can be expected in
most animistic views of reality. But the 'spirit world' in Makuna cosmology mirrors in every detail all the features of Makuna society and culture.
That is to say, Makuna society is completely extrapolated into a spirit
world.

What is reality here, and what is not? Do the Makuna regard the animal world as sacred, or have they merely recreated animals as spirits that
institutionally and culturally suit their own needs? Indeed, where does
the patent anthropomorphism of the Makuna turn into a *de facto* anthropocentrism that transmutes all animals into human beings – socially as
well as individually – thereby rendering them objects of human manipulation in shamanistic 'negotiations'? The fact that the Makuna 'animals'
behave like human beings and are organized into distinctly human social
institutions with headmen is a patently anthropomorphic view of the
'spirit world' that clearly belies the popular myth that aboriginal peoples
identify with non-human life-forms. It is not humans who ostensibly
become or even co-exist with animals; it is animals who apparently
become human.

Nor does it follow that, because the Makuna have turned animals and
their communities into exact replicas of their societies, they believe that
the entire world is 'alive,' as many ecomystics and primitivists claim.
'Animism', as the nineteenth-century anthropologist Edward Tylor
called the view that *everything* in the world is living, by no means leads to
seeing life everywhere in one's surroundings. Tylor's assertion that an
American Indian would 'reason with a horse as if rational' should not be
taken to mean that an Indian regarded inanimate things *as such* as alive.[15]
Aboriginal peoples are not so absurd as to view stones and horses, for
example, as equally alive. However 'animistically' they regard the natural
world in theory, in practice they apply their animistic views with considerable discretion. In everyday life, as Bronislaw Malinowski has shown,
they dealt with rocks and animals on very different terms, just as many
religiously inclined people today separate their belief systems from the
practical demands of survival in the mundane world.[16] When A. Irving
Hallowell asked an old Ojibwa Indian if '*all* the stones we see about us
here [are] alive', he received a very shrewd response. 'No!' replied the

old Ojibwa emphatically, 'But *some* are.' Perhaps he meant those that were useful in one way or another to his people.[17]

None of these observations are meant to claim that techniques discovered by band and tribal peoples are lacking in practical value. Quite to the contrary: if anyone today wanted to hunt mammoths, mastodons, giant sloths, and longhorn bison with spears and with bows and arrows, the lore about animal behavior accumulated by our late Paleolithic ancestors might indeed be invaluable. Should a time come when society returns to a world of 'scattered human population that lives by fishing, hunting, and food-gathering', as Edward Abbey suggests, we might want to invoke their 'wisdom'.[18] Perhaps we could 're-enchant' the world with the fables that they believed in – assuming we could empty our heads of all the scientific and technical knowledge that presumably burdens our civilization. Whether such a return or revival is possible in a culture that knows a great deal about phenomena that were complete mysteries to men and women of the remote Paleolithic period, the reader will have to decide.

The notion that their 'Paleolithic spirituality' fostered in our distant ancestors a conservationist and respectful attitude toward wildlife, forests, and the various ecosystems they inhabited is perhaps the main reason that the virtues of a revived 'Paleolithic spirituality' are promoted today by ecomystics and primitivists, few of whom are themselves likely to really believe that animals live under headmen in a 'spirit world' or that the dream world is as real as the objective world around them.

How 'Paleolithic' or 'primitive' are modern aborigines, who seem to live like our Paleolithic ancestors and presumably provide us with evidence of the prehistoric world? Most anthropologists now agree that the foraging communities they encounter have already been profoundly altered by earlier Euro-American contact, particularly by missionaries, traders, and soldiers. As the eminent social anthropologist Clifford Geertz warns: the remote ' "out-of-the-way" peoples' whom cultural anthropologists in the past studied as 'natural communities' were not relics of the distant past. Geertz writes:

> *The realization, grudging and belated, that this is not so, not even with the Pygmies, not even with the Eskimos, and that these people are in fact products of larger-scale processes of social change which have made them and continue to make them what they are – has come as something of a shock that has induced a virtual crisis in the field [of anthropology].*[19]

The 15,000 or 20,000 years that have passed since the late Paleolithic were not a cultural and social vacuum but deeply affected even the most isolated aboriginal peoples today. Today's 'primitives' – and they are disappearing like snowflakes in a summer heat wave – underwent complex developments that separate them from the late Paleolithic peoples whose remains are the objects of extravagant fantasies.

In the 1960s many anthropologists adopted idealized visions of 'primitive' innocence and well-being. A 'Man the Hunter' symposium, held at the University of Chicago in April 1969, promulgated a myth of 'affluent' foraging cultures and the existence of pristine 'primitive' communities.[20] It gave the mystical 'counterculture' and later New Age children an idea that they wanted to hear: namely, that civilization is bad, and that neo-primitives (an oxymoron) adorned with flowers and beads are deliriously good. Various 'Pleistocene', 'Paleolithic', and 'early Neolithic' spiritualities sprouted up like mushrooms after a rain.

Careful research done since the 'Man the Hunter' conference indicates that people in foraging cultures suffered and suffer from considerable material insecurity. Monographic material reviewing aborigines at various levels of 'primitivity' are at odds with 1960s myths that our ancestors enjoyed 'affluence' and lived enviably pacific or untroubled lives. Many of the modern-day foragers whom anthropologists once described as enjoying 'affluent', even leisurely lives actually suffered serious material deprivations, and their lives were often quite short.

Nor should we be under any illusions that aboriginal foragers are a direct continuation of Paleolithic foragers; rather, they were driven from stable, largely horticultural ways of life into inhospitable deserts and forests. The Kalahari desert San people, or Bushmen, are a striking case in point, as Edwin N. Wilmsen and his colleagues have shown.[21] These hunter–gatherers, so widely celebrated in the pop anthropology literature of the past few decades as a leisurely and materially secure people, seem to have undergone several transitions from food cultivators and pastoralists to hunter–gatherers. To call them Paleolithic, let alone idealize their lifeways as 'affluent', is arguable to say the least. Their much-lauded cooperative outlook and tendency to share things was easily undermined in recent decades, and they now seem to be as acquisitive as the Europeans with whom they have been favorably contrasted.

Reasonable speculations based on similar facts can be made about many other present-day bands that were probably pushed back into inhospitable areas by competing tribes as well as by Europeans, and who were obliged to use very simple, often attenuated tool-kits by comparison with the more advanced techniques they had developed earlier. Some were forced to adopt simpler and less satisfactory ways of life because of invaders and competitors for resources. Thus the Yuqui Indians, 'discovered' in the 1950s, initially seemed free of European influence and 'blessed' with tools that were even more primitive than those of late Paleolithic peoples of some 30,000 years ago.[22] The Yuqui had never seen Europeans until their lands were invaded by missionaries (whom they initially killed) and the Amazon jungle near their community domain was deforested. They wore no clothing, and their weapons consisted exclusively of bows and arrows. They had no tools apart from the clawed legs of animals.

But significantly, their society had a slave caste, and after further study, anthropologists have good reason to believe that their ancestors had once had a fairly complex horticultural society with pottery and social hierarchies. They became foragers because centuries earlier they were obliged to flee farther and farther into the Amazon forest to escape predatory European colonists, until they lost all memory of their past.

Present-day band and tribal peoples must have undergone considerable cultural changes since the late Paleolithic. Indeed, due not only to their contact with other cultures, as well as Euro-American ones, they probably differ considerably from their own ancestors of only a few centuries ago.

Our early ancestors were probably not hunters, despite many claims by primitivists and sociobiologists that human beings are genetically predisposed to hunt or have an inborn love of wildlife. As I have noted ealier, archaeological artifacts and a growing body of anthropological opinion now support the view that, until the middle Paleolithic, about a million years ago, early hominids were more likely to be the prey than the predator. Using stone implements to crack open the long bones of herbivores for marrow, they were more likely scavengers than predators.

This way of acquiring protein-rich foods countervails the present-day image of 'man the hunter'. As Robert J. Blumenschine and John A. Cavallo observe: 'This question [of Man the Hunter] matters perhaps as much as any in evolutionary studies because it touches on the definition of human nature. Unfortunately, the answer given by the theory of Man the Hunter is based more on sexual and other prejudices than on the fossil record and the ecology of finding food.'[23] The literature on this subject has grown so considerably that the conclusion of 'man the scavenger' is now becoming the conventional wisdom of paleoanthropologists.

After tracing the 'Man the Hunter' notion from the 1969 conference, Blumenschine and Cavallo show that closer studies in the late 1970s and the 1980s produced increasing evidence that our hominid and even *Homo* ancestors were sophisticated scavengers, gaining an edge on other scavengers by developing increasingly effective crushing and cutting tools. Although the opportunistic hunting of small animals probably always existed among hominids and humans, it is likely that until human beings developed projectile weapons like spears and later bows and arrows, they scavenged on the prey of powerful predators, particularly leopards, who often leave their partly eaten kill in trees. Their sharp cutting tools and hand axes may have given them key advantages over other scavengers: they could quickly butcher animal remains before they were driven away by large predators, and they could crush open long bones that contained nutritious marrow and that even hyenas, with their powerful jaws, could not crack open. This scavenger position has been supported most recently by the detailed studies of Donald Johanson, the discoverer of the Lucy fossil, and his colleagues.[24]

In what paleoanthropologists increasingly call the 'Human Revolution' – reflected in changes in the technological and artistic evidence of *Homo sapiens sapiens* in Europe some 40,000 years ago – a rich repertoire of implements was developed, as well as art, with a rapidity and on a scale that has no precedent in earlier times. In part, this revolution can be attributed to the development of syllabic languages; partly, too, the revolution can be attributed to a very rich cultural evolution, the elaboration of human communal ties into fairly complex social institutions like clans and probably tribal forms of organization.

In a sense, human beings as we know them had arrived. They were rich in potentialities for self-consciousness, complex communication, rationality, cooperation, and social organization, marked by innovative abilities and a capacity to know, intervene, and change the natural world purposefully to a degree unknown to any other life-form.

How did these people deal with the world *practically,* whatever their spiritual equipment may have been? What can we tell from the archaeological and ethnographic evidence about Paleolithic attitudes toward conservation and wildlife? How ecological were they in dealing with other life-forms *existentially,* not only spiritually?

We have every reason to believe that as far back as the times of *Homo erectus,* our ancestors were prepared to alter their 'wild' environment in every way that served their advantage. Having gained the ability to use fire, *erectus* probably burned away forests to create grasslands on which game were to subsist for millions of years. Moreover, we have every reason to suspect that *erectus* cunningly used torches to stampede game animals over cliffs and chase off predators to gain access to their kills.

If *Homo erectus* altered the environment over time with fire, it is certain that more evolved forms of the human genus did so on a sweeping scale. Much of what seems like original grassland in Eurasia, Africa, and the Americas might still be covered by dense forests were it not for the burnings our distant ancestors systematically practiced over many thousands of years. Indeed, large parts of pre-Columbian America looked more like parkland than forest at the time of European contact, because of the repeated fires native peoples lit to provide open spaces for large herbivores, for the removal of brush that could conceal their enemies, and for gardening.

As Stephen J. Pyne observes in his detailed study, *Fire in America,* 'the virgin forest was not encountered in the sixteenth and seventeenth century; it was invented in the late eighteenth and early nineteenth centuries. For this condition, Indian fire practices were largely responsible.'[25] Evidence of human activities in dense forest areas appear to be sufficiently widespread for modern anthropologists and botanists to question how 'original' many tropical forests actually were, even in the Amazon and certainly in tropical Africa.

Our Paleolithic ancestors, like any other life-form, almost certainly used their habitats to the full. In North America, the retreat of the last glaciers about 11,000 years ago was marked by the rapid extinction of more than 80 per cent of the great Pleistocene mammals – an immensely higher percentage of extinctions than those that occurred in the immediate postglacial period on other continents. As Paul S. Martin has put it, the last retreat of the glaciers in America was probably marked by 'overkill' of large mammals, primarily by peoples with increasingly sophisticated weapons and hunting techniques.[26] Long before Europeans landed on American shores, fauna like the mammoth, mastodon, giant ground sloth, huge armadillos, saber-toothed tigers, dire wolves, large beavers, and various bear species, as well as camels and horses – which had evolved on the continent and survived only because they had migrated to Eurasia – were completely gone.

Some have tried to explain the disappearance of these species as a result of the ecological changes that followed the retreat of the glaciers. Perhaps, but many of these mammals had survived previous glacial and interglacial alterations, giving us little reason to suppose they could not survive the last of the postglacial climatic and ecological changes. What makes it difficult to accept an explanation based entirely on climatic change is the fairly recent discovery of a remarkably well-preserved mastodon, an animal presumably dependent upon the widely prevalent spruce-tree environments of the glacial period. The stomach remains of this extinct animal indicate that it had adapted quite satisfactorily to the bog-type environment favored by animals like the moose, which was widespread in the immediate postglacial world.

Significantly, the many ecological niches opened by these extinctions of Pleistocene fauna in North America were subsequently occupied by the Old World animals, which gave North America its celebrated character as a biotic 'paradise': short-horned bison, elk, moose, caribou, bighorn sheep, and the like. Unlike camels and horses, these animals did not evolve on the American continent but rather migrated to it from Eurasia.

Still, we are not obliged to accept the 'overkill' argument to agree that many now-extinct fauna were hunted down by proto-Indian foragers and ultimately exterminated, without any 'spiritual' restrictions on their ways. Whatever their 'Paleolithic spirituality' may have been, they were prepared to hunt game with few 'spiritual' constraints. Deep layers of bison bones have been found at the foot of cliffs, over which Indians stampeded thousands of animals for centuries, probably in numbers that far exceeded the uses to which their carcasses could have been put. Accumulations of bones at one site examined by Brian Reeves of the University of California reached a depth of thirty-five feet. At still another site, Jack Brink of the Archaeological Survey of Alberta estimates that, over the centuries, 123,000 bison were stampeded over a single 'jump site' by Indian hunters. As Brian Fagan observes in his survey of such cliff sites, 'the Blackfoot practiced bison hunting and butchering on a near-industrial scale for many centuries', settling down nearby in semi-permanent camps, 'trading the spoils of the chase to people living long distances away.'[27]

Native Americans were by no means the only foraging peoples who engaged in the massive and systematic killing of animals. Late Paleolithic hunters in Syria, for example, seem to have learned how to 'funnel' gazelles into killing and butchering sites during their seasonal migrations until they were completely exterminated.[28] In Pyrenean passes and other mountain areas, such practices occurred until game was virtually or completely wiped out. Indeed, fertility rituals may have been a very practical response to the decline of the great faunal herd animals that had fallen prey to late Paleolithic foragers. The disappearance of these game animals can hardly be attributed to climatic changes alone. The domestication of animals may even have preserved certain species whose extinction was at risk, as the hunting prowess of late Paleolithic peoples became increasingly sophisticated and deadly.

No native American hunting practices, to be sure, exculpate the massive extermination of wildlife that followed the settlement of the Americas by Europeans. The destruction of the great bison herds on the plains – possibly exceeding forty million in two or three decades – by white hunters in the nineteenth century has no equal among native peoples. I wish only to emphasize that the American Indian, Pyrenean, and Syrian hunters of thousands of years ago did no more than what any animal would have done: they tried to find ample quantities of food and good shelter – in short, to survive and to use their intelligence to make their lives as comfortable as possible.

Nor is there any reason to believe that quasi-religious scruples about the 'sacredness' of life made our prehistoric ancestors necessarily kinder or gentler in their treatment of wildlife than people are today.

Modern aborigines notoriously mistreated the animals they caught, often inflicting needless pain upon them. For generations, gardening peoples in Borneo made a practice of killing pigs by furiously beating them to death, on the theory that their roasted flesh was particularly tender after these practices. Eskimos were extremely harsh in dealing with their huskies, often kicking and striking them with little or no compunction, as were many Plains Indians in their treatment of their own dogs. Colin Turnbull, in his generous and appreciative account of the Ituri forest pygmies of Central Africa, was shocked to see how a sindula, a tasty doglike creature, was tormented after it was caught in a net following a collective hunt. Repeatedly speared to the laughter of the pygmies, observes a shocked Turnbull, the animal 'still writhed and fought' until 'a third spear pierced its heart', and it was finally put out of its misery. Turnbull reports:

> At other times I have seen Pygmies singeing feathers off birds that were still alive, explaining that the meat is more tender if death comes slowly. And the hunting dogs, valuable as they are, get kicked around mercilessly from the day they are born to the day they die. ... When I talked to the Pygmies about their treatment of animals, they laughed at me and said, 'The forest has given us animals for food – should we refuse this gift and starve?' I thought of turkey farms and Thanksgiving, and of the millions of animals reared by our own society with the sole intention of slaughtering them for food.[29]

These are the remarks not of an arrogant European but of an anthropologist whose affection for the pygmies is attested in every line of his writings.

My point is not to exculpate abuses of animals today by adducing abusive attitudes among 'primitive' peoples – cruelty to animals is inhuman and insupportable wherever and whenever it is practiced. But it is the height of naivety to suppose that because Paleolithic or modern foragers occasionally exercised a pragmatic restraint on killing certain species or tabooed them altogether, they regarded them or their lives as 'sacred'. Often a wide gulf existed between what they seemed to believe (generally for very utilitarian reasons) and what they actually practiced.

Seemingly uplifting exclamations by certain *modern* native American shamans and spokespeople, for example – to the effect that the wolf, bison, bear, or eagle is 'our cousin' or 'our brother' – do not mean that their ancestors treated these animals with fervent consanguinity only a few generations earlier.

Rituals centering on food animals like bison or bears were often performed for very practical reasons: to 'coax' them into becoming prey during a hunt or to allay their 'spirits' after they were killed. The pragmatic core of these ceremonies rested on analogical premises that are no different in principle from childish fears of encountering werewolves or vampire bats. Their ceremonies took the form they did because they knew little about the biotic factors that produce game for hunts. To early peoples, spirits abounded everywhere, not because they thought everything was alive but because the dream world itself was a continual source of perplexity. These spirits were not necessarily benign; indeed, if anything, they were often malevolent. Disease, it was believed, was caused by spirits, as were births, be they of children, bison calves, or bear cubs. If our late Paleolithic ancestors probably knew little or nothing about human reproduction, why should they have known more about animal reproduction? If they believed that human children are created by spirits, why should they have had a different view of bison calves or bear cubs?

Superstition being superstition, aboriginal spirit-beliefs were not only wrong but often ecologically deleterious. Calvin Martin has recently opined that before European contact, boreal forest Algonkians were conservationists who hunted selectively, in a 'contractual' relationship with game animals by which both humans and animals agreed not to 'ruin' each other. After contact, when the Algonkians died of European diseases in great numbers, they regarded the animals as having violated the 'contract' and spread epidemics among the tribes. As a result of this alleged breach of faith, so Martin's thesis goes, the Algonkians slaughtered animals wantonly in the belief that they were malevolent disease agents.[30] This thesis has been strongly controverted; some anthropologists have found that the Cree, with whom Martin deals, may never have been conservationists at all.

Indeed, Crees seem to have believed 'that game animals killed by hunters spontaneously regenerate after death or reincarnate as fetal animals', as Robert A. Brightman observes in a fascinating review of the literature on their magico-religious concepts.

Manitoba Crees in the 1980s call this process akwanaham otoskana, *'[animal] covers its bones'. Such events are taken for granted by some*

> *Cree trappers. I was told on a number of occasions that an adult, trapped animal was 'the same one' that had been killed the previous winter. Modern Crees also state that ritual procedures for disposing of animal bones and blood prefigure and influence animal regeneration and reincarnation. This knowledge was present in the nineteenth and eighteenth centuries and probably derives from archaic strata of Algonquian culture.*[31]

Brightman's conclusion from Cree attitudes toward animals demonstrates that 'ecological wisdom' depends far more upon knowledge and rational behavior than upon the vagaries of spiritism. Brightman observes:

> *If hunters are unaware that animals can be managed, they may also be unaware that they can be hunted to depletion. It cannot be assumed that Crees and others involved in game depletions initially understood their own role as determinants. Rather than inhibiting overkill, religious definitions of the human-animal relationship encouraged it insofar as they premised an environment of primordial abundance in which game could not be destroyed but only temporarily displaced. Some contemporary Rock Crees reproduce this traditional understanding. Similarly, some Osnaburgh House Ojibwas stated in the 1960s that conservation was unnecessary because animals were 'given' to hunters when they were needed. These understandings are held also by subarctic Athapaskan groups.*[32]

The Ojibwa view that animals are 'given' to the hunters, presumably by beneficent spirits, is very similar to the Ituri forest pygmy's view, as it was presented to Turnbull. As we have seen, the pygmies frankly declared that they could torment animals mercilessly because the forest spirit gave captured game to their community for their own disposition. In fact, although there is a certain amount of evidence for conservation among the forest Indians of North America, far more evidence exists for *lack* of conservation among forest tribes such as the Montagnais and very strikingly among Iroquoians in the Great Lakes region, who believed that, 'for all kinds of animals, whether they need them or not, ... they must kill all they find, for fear, as they say, that if they do not take them the beasts would go and tell the others how they had been hunted and that then, in times of want, they would not find any more.'[33] There are as many, possibly more, reasons for believing that precontact Indian spiritism fostered overkill of game animals rather than for holding the ecomystical belief that they lived in 'fraternal' solidarity with them.

Again, these examples are not intended to defame native American or African foragers, still less exculpate the predatory behavior of Euro-

Americans for their wanton destruction of wildlife environments throughout the world. I simply wish to explode ecomystical and primitivistic myths that foragers were somehow less pragmatic in dealing with their environment than any other life-form. In fact, they used it to the hilt, all their spiritism to the contrary notwithstanding. Moreover, the relationships of foragers to animals were very tenuous. The fact that late Paleolithic hunters painted animals on their cave walls or sculpted them does not mean that they viewed them as 'brothers' any more than they would view a mushroom as kin. The notion that a particular species, or for that matter, all animals, had a Chief Spirit was no inducement for treating *individual* animals with any more 'respect' than the worship of God, in the Western world, has made individuals ooze with kindness for the less fortunate humans in their midst.

If foragers regarded the world as alive, as ecomystics claim, this view can be explained by the fact that much of it *was* alive. Their world was largely organic, and it was the *only* world they knew. If it was sacred in their eyes (assuming they conceived of the sacred in any modern Euro-American sense), it may very well be due to their strong and pragmatic need to 'communicate' with their environment – more realistically, to *control* it to some degree. Magic and rituals were seen as effective means of attaining very pragmatic ends and of explaining an unknown spirit world that appeared in their dreams. Unlike modern humans, they did not understand the real origins of disease, the causes of sudden changes in the weather, eclipses, earthquakes, even the full meaning of death.

To extol magico-religious attitudes irrespective of their truthfulness, simply because they have a superficial affinity with certain ecological sensibilities today is grossly misleading. If modern foragers hold an idyllic 'Paleolithic spirituality' as though time had not affected their thinking after 20,000 years, they hold such beliefs because of ignorance, not because of any archaic wisdom. Notions celebrated as 'Paleolithic' by modern ecomystics and primitivists rest more on analogy than on supportable ideas, and they are inspired more by a spirit world deriving from inexplicable dreams than by ecological understanding.

To call for the revival of 'Paleolithic spirituality' is to ask human beings to accept ignorance as a value, indeed, to 'disenchant' the fascinating world that has been opened to them by science, philosophy, social theory, and psychology. Humanity's hope, I wish to contend, lies not in a return to a mythopoeic past that was riddled by ignorance and superstition and naive awe; nor does it lie in a passive acceptance of the *status quo*, riddled by greed, competition, and domination. It lies in a future that will draw from the past whatever is worth retaining, including the highly cooperative spirit that existed within foraging but largely parochial 'primitive' communities on the one hand, as well as the universalism and sense of human commonality that movements for emancipation have advocated in the modern era.

If cooperation and universality can be melded together, there is a possibility that a truly rational society might emerge in which a 're-enchanted' humanity nourishes a spirituality informed by sharing, a society informed by cooperation, and by a sensibility that gives due recognition to the well-being of the natural as well as the social world.

Primitivism stands woefully at odds with any attempt to achieve such a sensibility. In one sense or another, it seeks to turn back the clock, to go back to a mythic Golden Age of intellectual and social innocence that never existed. In the best of cases, primitivism argues for a non-rational mentality based on contrived myths about 'primitive reverence' for a mystified Nature in which humans can intervene only for the most limited reasons. In the worst of cases, it offers a misanthropic view of humanity, an identification of Nature with pristine wilderness, and a hatred of rationality, science, and technology.

Both views are antihumanistic. Resting on deep ecology's biocentrism, and on a host of ideas developed by postmodernists, they deny the unique position of humanity in social evolution, or worse, they dissolve it in a mythic animal-human community that renders any distinctions between animals and humans impossible to make – ironically depriving human beings of any responsibility for non-human life and its welfare. Once again, Harold Fromm's 'invisible puppeteer' is at work, mistaking the seemingly autonomous antics of the puppets for the puppeteer's manipulation of them.

Notes

1 Edward Abbey, 'A Response to Schmookler on Anarchy', *Earth First!*, 1 August 1986, p. 22.

2 Christopher Manes, *Green Rage: Radical Environmentalism and the Unmaking of Civilization* (Boston: Little, Brown & Co., 1990), p. 237.

3 Max Oelschlaeger, *The Idea of Wilderness: From Prehistory to the Age of Ecology* (New Haven: Yale University Press, 1991).

4 Oelschlaeger, *Idea of Wilderness*, Table 1, 'Conjectures on a Paleolithic Idea of Wilderness', p. 12.

5 Margaret Ehrenberg, *Women in Prehistory* (Norman and London: University of Oklahoma Press, 1989), p. 75.

6 Richard E. Leakey, *The Making of Mankind* (London: Abacus Books, 1981), p. 180.

7 The very old sculptures of human heads can be seen vividly in *National Geographic*, vol. 174, no. 4 (October 1988). The engravings can be found in Michel Lorblanchet, 'From Man to Animal to Sign in Paleolithic Art', in Howard Morphy, ed., *Animals into Art* (London: Unwin Hyman, 1989), p. 136.

8 Max Oelschlager, *The Idea of Wilderness*, p. 12.

9 Lynn White, Jr, 'The Historical Roots of Our Ecologic Crisis', *Science*, vol. 155 (10 March 1967), pp. 1203–7.

10 It should be obvious that I am speaking, here, of late Paleolithic people – *Homo sapiens sapiens* – not Neanderthals, *Homo erectus, Homo hablis,* and any remaining Australopithecines, who can also be regarded as Paleolithic 'people', but who left no artistic remains behind.

11 Sir James Frazier, *The Golden Bough,* 1890 edition (New York: Avenue Books, 1981), p. 120.

12 A belief in the existence of spirits should not be equated with 'spirituality', a word that can mean anything from the shared features that make a particular culture distinctive to a belief in a variety of ineffable, indeed metaphysical phenomena, be they the product of philosophical speculation or religious vagary. My own use of this word is primarily philosophical and, to some degree, cultural; I never use it to denote 'spirits', 'spiritualism' (a belief in spirits of various kinds), or religion of any kind unless in quotation marks.

13 I use the word *supernatural* with reference to aboriginals advisedly. The spirit world – the dream world – may have seemed quite 'natural' to them, and the distinction between sleeping and waking would have been understandably problematical.

14 Kaj Århem, 'Dance of the Water People', *Natural History,* January 1992, p. 51.

15 Edward Tylor, *Primitive Cultures* (London: Murray, 1873); excerpted in V. F. Calverton, *The Making of Man: An Outline of Anthropology* (New York: Modern Library, 1931), p. 646.

16 See Bronislaw Malinowski, *Magic, Science and Religion and Other Essays* (Boston: Beacon Press, 1945).

17 A. Irving Hallowell, 'Ojibwa Ontology, Behavior, and World View', in Stanley Diamond, ed., *Culture in History: Essays in Honor of Paul Radin,* (New York: Columbia University Press, 1960), pp. 19–52.

18 Edward Abbey, 'A Response to Schmookler', *Earth First!,* 1 August 1986.

19 Clifford Geertz, 'Life on the Edge', *The New York Review of Books,* 7 April 1994, p. 3.

20 See Richard B. Lee and Irven Devore, ed., *Man the Hunter* (Chicago: Aldine Publishing Company, 1968).

21 See Edwin N. Wilmsen, *Land Filled With Flies* (Chicago: University of Chicago Press, 1989).

22 See Allyn Maclean Stearman, *Yuqui: Forest Nomads in a Changing World* (Fort Worth, TX: Holt, Rinehart and Winston, 1989).

23 Robert J. Blumenschine and John A. Cavallo, 'Scavenging and Human Evolution', *Scientific American* (October 1992), pp. 90–6.

24 See Donald Johanson *et al., Ancestors: In Search of Human Origins* (New York: Villard Books, 1994).

25 Stephen J. Pyne, *Fire in America* (Princeton, NJ: Princeton University Press, 1982), p. 71.

26 Paul S. Martin, 'Prehistoric Overkill', in P. S. Martin and H. E. Wright, Jr, ed. *Pleistocene Extinctions: The Search for a Cause,* (New Haven: Yale University Press, 1967), p. 75.

27 All cited in Brian Fagan, 'Bison Hunters of the Northern Plains', *Archeology* (May–June 1994), p. 38.

28 Anthony J. Legge and Peter A. Rowley-Conwy, 'Gazelle Killing in Stone Age Syria', *Scientific American,* vol. 257 (August 1987), pp. 88–95.

29 Colin M. Turnbull, *The Forest People: A Study of the Pygmies of the Congo* (New York: Clarion/Simon and Schuster, 1961), pp. 101–2.

30 Calvin Martin, *Keepers of the Game: Indian-Animal Relationships and the Fur Trade* (Berkeley and Los Angeles: University of California Press, 1978).

31 Robert A. Brightman, 'Conservation and Resource Depletion: The Case of the Boreal Forest Algonquians', in Bonnie J. McCay and James M. Acheson, ed., *The Question of the Commons: The Culture and Ecology of Communal Resources,* (Tucson: University of Arizona Press, 1987), p. 131.

32 *Ibid.,* p. 132, emphasis added.

33 C. LeClerq, *First Establishment of the Faith in New France* (1691), p. 125; cited in Brightman, 'Conservation'.

CHAPTER 6

Technophobia and its tribulations

From the eighteenth century onward, enlightened humanism advanced three basic ideals that it identified with progress.

The first and most important of these ideals was a renewed focus on reason: the use of logical thought in dealing with reality. Since the time of the classical cultures of ancient Greece and, to some extent, Rome, reason had been relegated, at best, to a handmaiden of theology. Since that time, social arrangements, not to speak of the natural world, had not been explained in rational terms. Feudal hierarchies and royal power were looked upon as God-given, while social inequities were seen as the unchallengeable dispensation of a deity whose judgment was taken on faith. This outlook was reinforced by the State as well as the Church, indeed by tradition as well as by biblical precept, however much radical heretics and popular uprisings disavowed them from time to time.

The eighteenth-century Enlightenment stridently and effectively challenged this theistic view of worldly affairs. It persistently counterposed rational understanding to unthinking belief in claims to knowledge and truth, be they in the realm of human relationships or in the natural world. In this respect, the Enlightenment surpassed the Renaissance of a century or two earlier, which invoked Greco-Roman canons of art and rhetoric, revering that highly idealized ancient past rather than an innovative present and a rational future.

Second, and following from its emphasis on reason, the Enlightenment advanced an increasingly secular view of social reality – of a new polity that enhanced individual freedom and legitimated social institutions rationally, be they part of responsive constitutional monarchies or republics. Voltaire's famous cry *'Ecrasez l'infame!'* meant not necessarily a denial of the Church doctrine and institutions but rather its infamous control over political, moral, and civil affairs on the strength of dogma, fear, and tradition. Many of the Enlighteners sought to separate Church from State, leaving the Church with the authority only of a moral force on society.

This demand, to be sure, was more than an attempt to obviate ecclesiastical meddling in the civil life of a polity. As rationalists, the Enlighteners were deeply concerned with the adverse role of superstition, mysticism, and mindless beliefs in determining human behavior. Superstition, in particular, they believed, had to be banished from the way human beings viewed each other, through scientific explanations of reality in strictly naturalistic terms. Even more than Enlightenment 'mechanists', whose influence has been deprecated and exaggerated by antihumanists these days, the subtler critical thinkers of the time, such as Denis Diderot, stressed the focal importance of the natural world as an arena of human inquiry, indeed, as a guide to human behavior. To equate the Enlightenment's naturalism with narrow-minded mechanism, without regard for the evolutionary and dialectical theories that were also very much in the air, is to caricature it in support of modern-day mystical and irrational ends.

Last, and very significant, the Enlightenment placed a strong premium on the need to control natural forces on behalf of human material well-being. The appalling disparities in wealth in eighteenth-century society; the persistent famines that plagued France; the dire misery of the under-classes in cities and villages (all bucolic images of rural society notwithstanding); the uncertainties of economic life; material scarcity and the necessity for arduous toil, which limited participation in public life – all contributed to the enthusiastic embrace of advances in science and technology, with their potential for extending human freedom and personal dignity.

This point cannot be emphasized too strongly. Although the Enlighteners did not challenge private ownership of land and the means of production – worked mainly by peasants and craftsmen – they were almost one in their commitment to support scientific and technological advances for social purposes – not ideological 'hubris' for the purpose of 'dominating nature'. As the lavish technical illustrations in Diderot's monumental *Encyclopedia* indicate, the Enlightenment celebrated human ingenuity and its promise to produce a sufficiency in the means of life, indeed, to ease labor – with its implicit message of a more participatory polity – not to 'subdue' natural forces out of a lust for domination.

If the Enlightenment saw Prometheus as the mythic agent for promoting human welfare, it was not because it no longer respected first nature; indeed, few centuries exhibited a greater devotion to the 'natural' than the eighteenth century – be it technologically, behaviorally, educationally, or morally. Rather, the Enlightenment directly associated the removal of want and toil from humanity with social improvement and a relatively free polity.

The great democratic revolutions of the eighteenth century – particularly the American and French – were predominantly political events, although they had widespread economic ramifications for the redistribution of property ownership. Their greatest long-range achievements were in the realm of personal liberty, upholding the autonomy of the individual in a volatile economic world. The cry of 'liberty, equality, fraternity' rang somewhat hollow, however, as the great majority of people who had made these revolutions continued to live in material want, toiling on the land and in newly emerging factories from dawn to dusk. 'Liberty', without the means of life and the free time to exercise it, seemed merely rhetorical. 'Equality', in turn, became a mockery of revolutionary ideals as old privileges based on status differences were replaced with new privileges based on differences in wealth.

In the nineteenth century the focus of radicalism shifted overwhelmingly from exclusively political egalitarianism to *material* egalitarianism, to a form of equality that allowed not only personal political freedom but also dignity and leisure to all laboring classes, be they on the land, in craft shops, or in factories. More specifically, the various socialisms of the early nineteenth century avowed the need for a cooperative society that would bring not only political but economic egalitarianism to humanity – a society based on the satisfaction of human material needs with minimal toil. If humanity were to achieve a truly democratic polity, working people had to acquire the means of life and sufficient free time to participate in it.

It was in *this* context that the underprivileged masses of Europe and the Americas viewed technological advances. Despite Luddite opposition to the use of machinery that subverted traditional crafts (a provisional opposition, let me add, that did not challenge technological advance as such, present-day distortions of Luddism to the contrary), the laboring classes viewed the potentialities for human betterment opened by the industrial world with considerable hope and incorporated them into their programs for social change.

Indeed, the resistance to industrialism came mainly from the romantic intellectuals, artists, and mystics who decried the loss of a rural society that they idealized, steeped it in quasi-feudal traditions and a mythopoeic mentality. Not only did these romantics damn the patently harmful effects of capitalist self-interest and exploitative methods of production, they decried reason and the Enlightenment itself. Whatever the benign intentions of the nineteenth-century romantic movement, their ideas later fed into a seemingly 'populist' movement that culminated in German fascism.

Significantly, Karl Marx, the most influential socialist theorist of the last century, identified the achievement of the material preconditions for a cooperative and free society with the spread of capitalism. He held this view not because he admired capitalist social relations but because he believed that a market economy based on competition would yield vast advances in technological development. Such advances, he contended, would eventually establish the technical basis for achieving the largely political and cultural goals of the Enlightenment as well as the material goals of the emerging socialist movement.

There is a tragic irony in the fact that Marx enshrined a class and exploitative social system – capitalism – as an 'historically necessary' stage for achieving an economically emancipated society. Even as capitalism corroded the hereditary ruling stratum of feudalism, it did not challenge domination as such – capitalists were no less domineering than their feudal predecessors. The bourgeois system of domination that they created, however, was harder to define – and hence all the more effective. By creating a myth of individual autonomy – and identifying it with the achievement of the great democratic revolutions – the emerging bourgeoisie could legitimate its *de facto* rule over society. It made capitalism seem like the result of gritty personal enterprise, parsimony, and ingenuity. Its precept of *formal equality* – be it before the law or in the name of 'equality of opportunity' – concealed the *substantive inequality* in wealth and influence in society. Indeed, capitalist apologists even denied that capitalism was, properly speaking, a class society at all, inasmuch as 'anyone' could become a capitalist if he or she so chose.

Marx was intensely aware of this obscurantist subterfuge and properly designated capitalist social relationships as the most mystified in history: a system whereby class rule was shrewdly concealed by the myth of 'equal opportunity'. This mystification of social relationships remains one of the most compelling facts of modern-day class rule. In the past two centuries, it has greatly conditioned ways of thinking generally toward mystification, from which current antihumanistic ideologies strongly benefit.

Marx's claim that capitalism provided the technological preconditions for socialism and hence was 'progressive', however, raised problems in transforming society that he never theoretically anticipated. How could a society structured around competition lead, even after a social upheaval, to one structured around cooperation? How could a society, sedimented by a long history of class rule, lead, even after a social upheaval, to one structured around substantive equality? These problems were not adequately resolved by the socialist movements of the nineteenth and early twentieth century – and they linger with us to this day.

Yet in many respects, Marx's emphasis on the impetus that capitalism gives to technological development was prescient.

The market economy that attained predominance in Europe and America during the past two centuries *did* innovate an industrial apparatus unprecedented in human history. It fostered a broad naturalistic and scientific understanding of the world, greater by far than the mythopoeic insights of the past, clouded as they were in naive illusions. At least on a strictly pragmatic and instrumental level, capitalism carried much of the world out of an illusory animism, religiosity, and parochialism – the 'enchanted' world so treasured by the romantics – and into a secular world that encouraged human activity and rational inquiry.

At the same time, the capitalist system was a class and exploitative society that was riddled by contradictions and that made for profound social and ultimately ecological instability. From the 1830s to the turn of the century, the 'progressive' dimensions often overshadowed its ugly and deeply antihumanistic aspects, although exploited classes waged desperate struggles against them throughout the Euro-American world.

Yet even these conflicts were eventually marginalized by reforms won by trade unions and labor parties of one kind or another. Inevitably, European socialist movements flirted with the idea of sufficiently improving the capitalist order so as to render it more equitable and ultimately more cooperative – perhaps even more socialistic. Even as European and American socialist parties were drenched in the radical rhetoric of the previous century, they made socialism in England, Germany, and France increasingly parliamentary rather than insurrectionary, and they themselves became loyal oppositions rather than revolutionary challenges.

The First World War exploded the myth of a slow, progressive social evolution from a capitalistic society to a cooperative society. Beaten down by four unrelenting years of trench warfare and horrifyingly lethal weapons, soldiers from the mass armies of Europe returned home either to topple an entrenched social order in the East or threaten it menacingly in the West.

It was during the interwar period, between 1918 and 1939, that European society faced its greatest moment of truth: either it would carry out the historically crucial task of replacing a market society with a cooperative one, or it would spin off into an ominous period of terrible reaction. The tragic failure of various socialist movements in this period to achieve the great goals they had elaborated over the nineteenth century served to nourish the epochal crisis opened in August 1914 – a crisis which even the Second World War, bloodier and more destructive than the First, has failed to resolve.

In fact, the Second World War formed a sharp boundary between one era of capitalist development and another. The preindustrial culture of the 1920s and 1930s in America and Europe had not yet been entirely absorbed by the economy; indeed, as dominant as capitalism had become by the end of the nineteenth century economically, it was far from all-pervasive socially. Its system of market relationships – what early twenti-eth-century social theorists called commodification – had not yet fully penetrated into the largely preindustrial everyday life of family relation-ships, personal associations, and community ties.

In the years following the Second World War, however, this disparity between culture and economics changed drastically. Starting in the early 1950s the capitalistic market expanded throughout the world, to a point where it is now ubiquitous and all-penetrating, even by comparison with the capitalism of merely a generation or two ago. It now permeates nearly every facet of ordinary life, from the bedroom to the schoolroom, from the kitchen to the church. This market *society*, with its defining values of production, consumption, profit, and growth, was only dimly anticipated by Marx in the 1850s, even as his major works unmasked the competitive imperatives of capitalist expansion and its accompanying culture of material acquisition. Consumption for the sake of consump-tion, or what we now call 'consumerism', which Marx could not have foreseen, became the counterpart of what he had denoted as 'production for the sake of production' – a driven form of general economic growth that has enveloped the consumer as well as the producer, and has become an end in itself, irrespective of social needs or consequences.

Capitalism, abetted by its 'progressive' technological achievements, has thereby acquired a *technological persona* – a projection of itself as the indus-trial 'logic' of science and technology as such. Thus, added to its self-mystification as a society of 'individual autonomy' and 'political freedom', it has acquired still *another layer of mystification* – the myth that science, technology, and even reason constitute its imperative for unre-lenting expansion.

This cunning mystification has beguiled nearly all ecomystics and has enhanced the 'mystery' surrounding capitalism's economic and market operations. Not only has the specious sobriquet *industrial society* become synonymous with *capitalism,* but today it has virtually replaced it, com-pounding the mystification that surrounded capitalism from its inception.

This mystification may be the most obstreperous of all, having gener-ated a sizable literature, even a tradition, that assigns uncanny powers to technology *apart* from the social context that determines its use. It becomes difficult for the ordinary person to see that it is not science and technology that threaten to turn the entire world into a huge market and factory; rather, it is the market and factory that threaten to 'technologize', to *objectify* or commodify the human spirit and reduce the natural world to mere raw materials for capital expansion.

Thus, the dazzling scientific leaps and technological innovations that have occurred since the Second World War *are the product of very distinct social relationships and an ever-growing market society.* The notion that science and technology are 'autonomous' of society, that they themselves are controlling factors in guiding society, is perhaps one of the most insidious illusions of our time. That science and technics conduct lines of research and open visions toward new developments is certainly true, but these developments are rigorously guided by the prevailing market society rather than the other way around.

Although society abets scientific and technological developments, society also *aborts* the exploration of new techniques, depending upon the needs that guide corporate research. These needs are overwhelmingly economic, centering on corporate profit and expansionary interests, as witness the stimuli given by large enterprises to lines of scientific research that promise to give them economic hegemony, while willfully ignoring others that, although interesting to scientists or engineers, are not considered sufficiently profitable from a business standpoint.

Thus it took years to arouse the interest of business in organic agriculture, solar and wind power, non-polluting fuels, recycling techniques, and many other inviting technologies. Indeed, with the rise of the environmental movement in the 1970s, it was often necessary for scientists and engineers to establish precarious and privately funded institutes in which they could devote themselves to developing 'environmentally friendly' technologies that industry obdurately ignored or even disavowed. Where large corporate enterprises and governmental agencies finally undertook research to explore the possibilities of what I have called 'ecotechnics', they commonly did so only after considerable public pressure. Even today, various technologies that would improve safety in transportation – alluring as they may be to engineers eager to sophisticate them – still lie woefully on drawing boards because they are either too costly or too unprofitable from a corporate standpoint. Notoriously, the profit-oriented approach guides research in a host of technical areas, including steel-making facilities that, were they put to use, would yield products that are lasting, unlike the 'planned obsolescence' worked into appliances, cars, homes, and even tools today.

The factory model around which capitalism is structured has given social relationships themselves a technological form, just as in the Middle Ages Christianity gave social relationships a religious form. In a sense, every factory is a 'megamachine', to use Lewis Mumford's word for ways of mobilizing labor. Nor are megamachines peculiar to modern societies based on high technology. They existed thousands of years ago, in the Near East and in the Roman world, when tools were hardly more advanced than in the Neolithic period. The pyramids of ancient Egypt, the temples of Mesopotamia, and the roads of Rome were constructed primarily by the brute labor of serfs and slaves. In the early modern period, capitalism simply mobilized labor more mechanically by making the rural cottage worker an appendage to the spinning wheel and hand loom. In time, the two were brought together in the form of a factory that now encompasses society as a whole, not only its economy.

Today, the unbridled expansion of the market transforms nearly all traditional personal relationships into commodity ties, fostering a belief in the merits of consumption and a highly synthetic image of 'the good life'. Technological innovation has merely made this commodification of everyday life easier to achieve. To be sure, modern technologies may be used, as in the case of television, to promote the sale of goods, to influence taste, and to create new 'wants'. Yet by the same token, advertising techniques were *always* in use, whether in medieval fairs, Renaissance markets, or large precapitalist commercial centers. For centuries, the churches and mosques of precapitalist society were immensely effective networks for promoting ecclesiastical, noble, and royal interests, preaching messages of quiet acceptance of duties, awe toward saints, and deference toward one's social 'betters'. Deep-seated social crises were necessary before the captives of clerics could dislodge ecclesiastical control over the minds of the oppressed – a process that is far from completed today, with or without televangelists.

Conversely, even the highly civilized societies of the ancient world regarded technological advances with astonishing indifference at best and active hostility at worst, primarily because servile human labor was cheap and readily available. Not that the steam engine and the paddle wheel were unknown, but they were never put to industrial uses. Ironically, well into the Middle Ages, when Christianity (which technophobes regard as one of the most antinaturalistic of ideologies) reached its height, the powers that be often saw technological advances as demonic, not as an inspiration for pursuing the 'domination of nature'.

While capitalism has turned to technology with a fervor unknown to any previous society and dressed it in the mystifying garb of an 'industrial society', capitalists have notoriously neglected very important technologies and chosen to develop precisely those techniques that benefit its unique imperative for growth and its inflated appetite for profit.

I have examined at some length the extent to which technology is a heteronomous or dependent phenomenon because ecomysticism tends to emphasize its autonomy from society and the mystique of a 'technological imperative', crudely obscuring the profoundly social factors that promote or inhibit technological innovation. Given this simplistic view, modern technology and a 'technological mentality' become the principal, often the exclusive causes of environmental ills, cultural malaise, and the loss of 'primal' innocence.

Moreover, contemporary critiques of technology often go hand-in-hand with primitivism and ecomysticism. The sophistication of technics, we are often told, has alienated us from 'nature' and our 'primal' roots, rendering us merely parts of a vast 'megamachine' that threatens not only to destroy the natural world but to diminish our awe before the 'sacred' in the biosphere, our 'feeling' for life, and our contact with the 'spiritual'. From the romantics of the last century, to German conservative writers early in the present one, an effluvium of books and periodicals has surfaced, stressing the 'autonomy' of technological development and either explicitly or implicitly calling for a return to technically simpler ways of life. The more primitivistic of the recent technophobic writers call for a return to the pristine lives of Paleolithic cave dwellers, Neolithic horticulturists, or medieval serfs and craftspeople.

Whether such views can be accepted at face value is, to put it gently, arguable. Owing to the massive inroads personal computers have made into the lives even of technophobes, who are usually unprepared to sacrifice this highly sophisticated device for the quill, one would think that they are as natural as fruit and thrive in Californian orange groves. Indeed, few of technophobia's outstanding spokespersons have abandoned the horrors of the civilization they decry to live hermetic lives free from technological subversion; nor do they desist from accepting fees for books and lectures that inveigh against the megamachine and its 'despiritizing' impact on the individual and society. Indeed, one primitivistic, technophobic periodical confessed, 'We got a computer – and we hate it!'[1] Which causes one to wonder: why acquire one at all when the great revolutions of the past were summoned to action by simple handpresses?

If this kind of cant and silliness were all that technophobia produced, it could easily be disregarded. But technophobia raises serious antihumanistic issues that require critical examination.

First, technophobia sets up a misleading enemy for committed environmentalists and culture critics, redirecting their attention away from patently social concerns. Well-meaning people are urged to focus on a problem that cannot be seriously fought – specifically, technology –

assuming they agree it is a problem in the first place.

Second, technophobes leave unanswered the strategic question of how a truly democratic society could be possible, if its members lacked the means of life and the free time to exercise their freedoms. Claims that a 'primitive' way of life would allow for 'banker's hours', to use Jerry Mander's expression, are simply fallacious.[2] Mander's sources, nourished on the 1960s and 1970s craze for the virtues of aboriginal ways of life, are now very questionable, if not completely specious, as we saw in Chapter 5. Unless people are prepared to give up literacy, books, modern music, physical comfort, and the great wealth of philosophical, scientific, and cultural ideas associated with civilization, the basic decision they face is *how* to use their vast fund of technological knowledge and devices, not *whether* to use them.

This decision is of momentous social proportions – and must not be based strictly on a subjective love or distaste for technological innovation. In a better world, humanity might choose to discard many components of its current technological equipment, possibly sophisticate others, and innovate ecologically more desirable ways of producing things. But without a technics that will free humanity from onerous toil – and without values that stress democratic forms of social organization in which *everyone* can participate – all hopes for a free society in the future are chimeras.

Technological innovation, in itself, will not increase the free time that is needed for a democratic political culture. Indeed, in class societies the use of technologies to displace labor by machines, to deforest vast areas of the planet, to exploit low-wage populations in the Third World – all raise precisely the social issue of the *ways* in which technology is used.

Nor are all technologies neutral in their impact on social and ecological well-being – or even necessarily desirable. Clearly some technologies, such as nuclear weapons and power plants, should be banned completely. The same can be said for agricultural and industrial biocides, surveillance devices, high-tech weaponry, and a host of other socially and ecologically harmful techniques.

But to glibly abstract technology from its social context, to let destructive current uses of technologies outweigh their potentially more rational application in a better society, would deny us the opportunity to choose what technologies *should* be used and the forms they will take. Various societies use a given technology in radically different ways: some for personally profitable and exploitative ends; others use it restrictively, owing to traditions of parsimony or fears of social instability; and still others might well use it rationally, to advance human freedom, self-development, and an ecological sensibility.

Modern technophobes, especially of the mystical persuasion, tend to confuse social with technological factors. Langdon Winner, one of the more informed critics of technology, indiscriminately intermingles social with technological factors, an approach that often makes the most specious defenses of technophobia seem almost plausible. Winner observes:

> If the experience of modern society shows us anything it is that technologies are not merely aids to human activity, but also powerful forces acting to reshape that activity and its meaning. The introduction of a robot to an industrial workplace not only increases productivity, but often radically changes the process of production, redefining what 'work' means in that setting. When a sophisticated new technique or instrument is adopted in medical practice, it transforms not only what doctors do, but also the ways people think about health, sickness, and medical care. Widespread alterations of this kind in techniques of communication, transportation, manufacturing, agriculture, and the like are largely what distinguishes our times from early periods of human history. The kinds of things we are apt to see as 'mere' technological entities become much more interesting and problematic if we begin to observe how broadly they are involved in conditions of social and moral life.[3]

But how a technology affects social context depends entirely on which new technologies are introduced and the reasons for introducing them. In a cooperative society – unlike the one in which we live today – a robot introduced into a factory environment might remove people from onerous toil and assembly-line drudgery, leaving them free to engage in pleasurable and creative activity. On the other hand, in a market, profit-oriented society like the one in which we live today, a robot would probably intensify the exploitation of workers whose tasks are orchestrated by the presence of a robot and increase the economic problems of those who are displaced by it. Winner's unitary statement about the impact of a robot on work, in effect, lacks sufficient social contextuality and tends to be more obfuscatory than illuminating.

Implicit in Winner's notion of 'technological somnambulism', in which 'we so willingly sleepwalk through the process of reconstituting the conditions of human existence', is his own *social* somnambulism.[4] For Winner, the existing society is a given, seemingly unalterable phenomenon, the background for existing and future technological innovation. That technology autonomously orchestrates rather than is orchestrated by the social context in which tools and machines exist is essentially assumed. That the reduction of work by a robot may, in fact, make life easier, indeed richer, that its effects could be minimal or even desirable, is not spelled out in his book, which is tilted toward theorists who see technology as shaping society.

Like many technophobes who are preoccupied with unexplained 'technological imperatives' and the psychic effects of technological change, Winner marginalizes the centrality of social issues. Thus, he calls upon his readers to be aware of the ramifications of technological change upon society and its values – a rather foggy request, since the nature of the present society, its conflicting interests, and rational alternatives to the present human condition remain unexplored and are as problematically intermeshed as ever with each other. So are questions about who controls the development of technology. In the harsh, real world, those who decide which new technologies are or are not to be introduced into workplaces, hospitals, offices, and factories are the proprietors of those operations. Not even managers, engineers, and scientists – or what has been loosely called the 'new class' – make long-range decisions about the use of technologies in the modern economy. Ultimately, it is the owners and directors of a particular concern – least of all ordinary citizens – who decide what kind of technology will be used in a given enterprise, as the formulation of recent 'down-sizing' policies by large corporations throughout the world so clearly reveal.

These owners and directors are concerned less with the social, psychological, and ideological impacts of a new technology than with the profit and competitive advantages it may yield. Less socially visible than the corporate 'bosses' of an earlier era, like the old John D. Rockefeller, contemporary 'bosses' are often highly professional and well trained in the more complex aspects of business management and engineering. And their authority stems ultimately from their power as owners and directors at the apex of the economic pyramid, not merely as knowledgeable technical personnel.

Winner's outlook tends to conceal the real issues of *social power*. Much as technology may enhance the operations of a given society, it is a distinct means deployed by self-serving owners and directors to exercise their power and increase their gains. By emphasizing the *effects* that new technologies have upon people and their values, Winner's book keeps us from clearly understanding that these effects are the results of manipulations by definable social elites whose behavior, in real life, is guided overwhelmingly by economic facts – not by the extent to which ordinary people suffer from 'technological somnambulism'.

Doubtless, as Winner argues, technological changes 'affect the texture of modern life', but social changes affect modern life far more drastically. Thus, a Renaissance banker of some four hundred years ago – say, a member of the Fugger banking family – held a view of the world, possessed an individualized sense of self, and had political values that were much more akin to those of a modern businessman than, say, of an Athenian citizen in Periclean times. Yet Greek and Renaissance technologies were remarkably similar by comparison with Renaissance and modern ones. Both the Fugger banker and the modern banker lived in a calculating, money-oriented, egoistic, and commercial world that for many Greeks would have seemed debasing and asocial. Athenians of the fifth century BC were expected to place the interests of the *polis* or so-called 'city state' before personal considerations and generally viewed commerce as a degrading activity, unfit for an authentic citizen, an attitude that stood in marked contrast to Fugger and modern bankers. Although the technological distance between commercially oriented Renaissance bankers and Athenians was relatively small, the psychological distance between the two was immense.

Winner's assertion of technological autonomy ultimately becomes technological determinism. If 'our instruments are institutions in the making', as he fatalistically declares, and *'techně* has at last become *politeia'*, then our behavior is determined by technological factors. Nor is there any real hope that the 'political wisdom of a democracy' can 'discipline' technological innovation, since 'it would require qualities of judiciousness in the populace that have rarely been applied to the judgement of instrumental/functional affairs.'[5] His book, *The Whale and the Reactor,* ends with a question: '[a]t present our society seems to prefer ... monuments to gigantism, war, and the overstepping of natural and cultural boundaries. Such are the accomplishments we support with our dollars and our votes. How long will it be until we are ready to do anything better?'[6] Which question sidesteps the issue of how effective voting can be in a political system that is an oligarchy of the powerful and wealthy – a fact that leaves the preferences of 'our society' very much in doubt and its exposure to radically fresh alternatives very limited, so say the least.

Among the less sophisticated technophobes, like Jerry Mander, the ambiguities that mark Winner's treatment of technology become wild sloganeering, laced with appeals to the 'sacred' and genuflections before 'primitives', whom Mander ecumenically calls 'Indians' whether they are native to the Americas or not.

Intellectually, Mander's *In the Absence of the Sacred* is a cacophony of wildly discordant arguments that intermingles the social and the technological with a degree of abandon that verges on the embarrassing.[7] Technology, we are told, is all-pervasive. It invades our consciousness and, with each generation of technical development, separates us from the natural world by enfolding us in a purely technological environment.

Again, the megamachine image rears its terrifying head: 'The web of interactions among machines becomes more complex and more invisible, while the total effect is more powerful and pervasive. We become ever more enclosed and ever less aware of that fact. Our environment is so much a product of our invention that it becomes a single worldwide machine. We live inside it, and are a piece of it.'[8] In Mander's view, this 'web of interactions' is almost entirely a product of technology as such and the mentality it breeds.

A director of the Berkeley-based Elmwood Institute, Mander delivers what Kirkpatrick Sale enthusiastically lauds as a 'skewering critique of modern technology, in which cars, telephones, computers, banks, biogenetics and television ... all are shown to be part of a mad "megatechnology" that is destroying the world's resources and robotizing its peoples.'[9] The reader cannot help but wonder which of these terrifying technological artifacts are actually used by the Elmwood Institute's members and associates. Indeed, Mander, who robustly celebrates the fact that he merely uses 'an old IBM Selectric', may well be an exception among his associates.[10] In any case, like personal computers, not even old, indeed ancient IBM Selectrics grow on trees.

In a heady passage, Mander celebrates his technologically simple childhood world in the Bronx of the 1930s and 1940s, during which time his mother's 'favorite activity was shopping' and a physician, whose principal pharmaceutical seems to have been aspirin, attended to his family's health needs. The Mander family of this blissful era had a television in the living room that featured Milton Berle, at a time when broadcasting was happily restricted to seven hours each day. Mander senior's prize possession was a Buick sedan that he rotated only every three years and the Manders were satisfied with annual family trips to Florida, plus a stay at summer camp for Mander junior.[11]

Yet how free of 'consumerism' and 'technology' was this halcyon era, forty or fifty years ago? Did Mrs Mander beat the dirt out of her family's clothing with a scrub board and squeeze out the water with rollers, while Mr Mander indulged his passion for new Buicks? Did she clean the floors on her knees? Did she carry heavy shopping bags, filled with food staples, or was she driven to and from market by Mander senior in a new Buick?

Mander junior does not enter into these trivial details. But having grown up in the same Bronx milieu a generation or so earlier, I feel obliged to protest that the Manders enjoyed eminently privileged middle-class comforts and technological goodies that were entirely unknown to me, my family, and my friends. From the very beginning of the 1920s to well into the 1930s, my own family did not even own even a radio, still less a car, television set, or telephone. Nor were they so privileged as to make trips to Florida or send me to summer camp. At the onset of the Depression, my mother and I did not even have a family physician. Instead, when we were sick, we sat for hours in the clinics of New York City's public hospitals, hoping to receive *any* kind of medical attention.

I am not trying to guilt Mander or trade experiences with him. His technophobia is premised on a fairly well-to-do way of life, as is the technophobia of so many baby boomers of late. His deprecation of antibiotics rings hollow at a time when children underwent dangerous mastoid-bone surgery for deadly ear infections and elderly people became seriously ill from even minor wounds. Without antibiotics, I would probably have died of a streptococcus infection in the early 1940s. There is a sickening arrogance in technophobes who, having enjoyed the fruits of middle-class, even wealthy life-styles, condemn appliances that freed women from considerable domestic drudgery, machines that freed workers from mentally debilitating tasks on assembly lines, and opened alternatives to starvation in lands that were once completely at the mercy of 'Mother Nature' and 'Her' many climatic vagaries.

In extolling the relative technological simplicity of his Bronx child-hood, Mander, in fact, is extolling a *culture* – the Jewish immigrant middle-class way of life – that was preindustrial in many respects, that had not yet been completely penetrated by the marketplace. Its language, values, family structure, and ideals were ultimately eroded not by tech-nology – which, in fact, its members generally prized as much as Mr Mander did his Buick – but by the socially invasive power of capitalism and its commodity orientation.

My own mother, an Eastern European immigrant, welcomed with almost sublime ecstasy her first 'Frigidaire' and her access to washing and drying machines. To own a motorized vehicle in my childhood and youth would have been regarded as an unimaginable luxury, indeed a mark of new social status. Summer vacations were hardly common among poor people who had to haggle for lower food prices. As an adult, I worked as a foundryman and auto worker; to be finally free from that toil was an occupational epiphany of a kind at least as intense as the one Mander himself seems to have experienced after he left his work with advertising agencies and drifted into the Elmwood Institute.

Mander's careless confusion of the preindustrial cultural roots of his fam-ily with the social uses of technology lead to the same ideological disarray that marks Winner's more sophisticated book. Despite their different levels of discussion, both writers repeatedly confuse the promise of technological innovation in a *rational* society with its abuses in the *present* irrational one. With considerable aplomb, we are shown that technology does not, after all, produce more leisure today – as though 'today' were somehow 'forever' – or that radicals of past generations did not know that technology can be used for exploitative ends under capitalism, as it can be for liberating ends in a cooperative society.

Worse still, *technology* creates more work, we are told – with minimal references to society, because people must now hold two jobs instead of one, as a result of the way an innovation currently yields partial employment and lowered income. That an avaricious class of proprietors and administrators must – and want to – gain a 'competitive edge' in the market with unseemly profits and that money leads to exploitation all but eludes Mander, who develops a serious case of social somnambulism. The vested economic interests that use technological innovations to exploit rather than diminish labor are not only freed of their odium, but scented by flamboyant denunciations of technics as such.

Thus, after conceding that medical technology 'on the whole, aids longer life and that is good', Mander, as a constrast, then mingles apples with oranges by reminding us that the murder rate in the United States has skyrocketed, that the prison population is bursting, that suicide and drug use have reached epidemic proportions, that 32 million Americans live in poverty, that 13 per cent of the population has no health insurance, that 3 million people are homeless, that 27 per cent are functionally illiterate, and that 28 million American adults suffer from one or another kind of mental disorder.[12] One is obliged to ask – is all this really because of *technology*?

Finally, having recited more statistics on the extent of environmental degradation, Mander might be expected to deliver a powerful rebuke against a society that permits, indeed fosters, these terrible, patently social, abuses. Instead, we are told: 'Given that technology was supposed to make life better, and given its *apparent* failure in both the social and the environmental spheres, shouldn't reason dictate that we sharply question the wild claims we have accepted about technology?'[13]

Permeated as his book is by social amnesia, the reader often has the feeling that if only people could all get together in a huge encounter group, possibly at the Elmwood Institute, all our problems could be happily resolved. We are, it appears, entranced by a 'pro-technology paradigm' that has dazzled us into a belief in the promise of 'technotopia'. If only we could remove its *inherent appeal* to our psyches, we might – guided by the 'sacred,' as defined by California's version of native American sensibilities – find our way to self and possibly social redemption.[14]

As to society, Mander's insights are sparse. The most seminal thought in *In the Absence of the Sacred* is that 'corporations are machines,' by which he means that corporations constitute a business technology and are the product of a 'technological mentality'.[15] That corporations are impersonal and amoral – hence, machinelike – might make this formulation a reasonably good metaphor, provided that Mander explored their function as sources of profit and capital accumulation. But these basic attributes of *any* capitalistic enterprise are given minimal attention. 'The Profit Imperative', one of his subheadings, receives four scant lines, and no analysis is given to back up his conclusion that 'profit is the ultimate measure of all corporate decisions'.[16] 'The Growth Imperative', which immediately follows Mander's impressively abbreviated discussion of profit, occupies less than half a page, and it too is notable for its lack of serious analysis of the impelling factors in capital expansion. Last, Mander sees 'Competition and Aggression' primarily as an internal problem within individual corporations, a form of personal agonistic activity comparable to the behavior of competing professional football players.[17]

Mander's interpretation of technology is basically obscurantist: conceived as a quasi-mystical 'web of interactions', technology not only takes on an almost psychic and self-generative life of its own, but it is given an over-powering presence in every dimension of human affairs. In Marx's concept of the 'fetishism of commodities', people who make the things they consume seem under capitalism to be mysteriously ruled by them; so for Mander, technology, which results from interactions between human beings and the natural world, becomes a mysterious 'autonomous' force that plays a formative and overriding role in the human condition. To understand the authentic reality of the human condition today, we are thus obliged to strip away not only the fetishism of commodities but also the fetishism of technology. Not only do we live far more within a very real web of commodity relationships than technological ones, but we are justifiably far more afflicted by a market-oriented mentality than by a technological one. We are far more concerned with securing a living than with assessing the extent to which technology affects our psyches. Our thinking is fashioned along quantified lines more because of our attempts to balance a dwindling domestic budget than because of the influence of Cartesian mechanism.

The social amnesia that afflicts technophobes and antihumanists generates an arrogance toward the seemingly mundane problems that people ordinarily face, a New Age arrogance much greater than the arrogance of so-called 'technotopians' (a category that seems to include almost everyone who is seriously concerned with human welfare and the achievement of a materially abundant society). Indeed, left to its own devices, the present society might well produce environmental dislocations so profound that humanity will be obliged to live in a 'technotopia', an artificially created environment, with no appeals whatever for a return to the 'sacred', least of all to a contrived 'Paleolithic spirituality', will be able to bring back the ozone layer, restore a breathable atmosphere, undo the damage to basic biogeochemical cycles, and cleanse a hopelessly poisoned water supply. If such a sweeping ecological regression were ever to occur, future generations might well have to build domes over their cities, create oxygen-making machines, and produce synthetic food.

Such a nightmarish future – with its despotic political consequences – would not be the product of technological innovation or thinking. It would be the product of a social system that, by its competitive nature – with or without technological innovations – is incapable of placing any limits on growth and limits on the acquisition of profit with which to grow. If the competitive market society continues to expand unopposed, it will be because the serious radical movements for social change of former decades have been supplanted in recent years by antihumanist, mystical, and technophobic cults for self-redemption and narcissistic epiphanies.

As to Mander's knowledge of the 'sacred', much of the anthropology in *In the Absence of the Sacred* is questionable, drawn largely from the native 'Man the Hunter' school of the 1960s and 1970s.

Mander is characteristic of the more widely read antitechnological writers around these days, and like many of his pop confrères, has nourished a great deal of today's rising technophobia. But other theorists deal philosophically with technology, in writings that have broad implications for the conflict between enlightened humanism and antihumanism. Jacques Ellul's *Technological Society*, one of the ancestral literary sources of present-day technophobia, criticizes not only technology as such but *technique*; indeed, he gives the term such a broad scope that it can essentially be defined as nearly *any* means for effectuating a goal today: 'The term *technique*, as I use it,' he writes, 'does not mean machines, technology, or this or that procedure for attaining an end. In our technological society, *technique* is the *totality of methods rationally arrived at and having absolute efficiency* (for a given stage of development) in *every* field of human activity.' It might well be supposed that Ellul is talking as much about human-generated causality in the modern world as he is about tools and machines.[18]

Although Ellul gives us no specific reason to believe that *technique* as such is good or bad, it clearly becomes degraded when reason and consciousness enter into technical operations. Inasmuch as every technical operation unavoidably involves reason and consciousness, it is hard to believe that *technique* can ever exclude thought. Thus the two words are functionally interchangeable. Indeed, if Ellul is to be taken seriously, humanity has always been living in a technological age insofar as thought and tools have been operationally interactive with each other.

Claiming that he does 'not deny the existence of individual action or of some inner sphere of freedom,' Ellul notes that 'these are not discernible at the most general level of analysis.'[19] This entrance into the 'inner sphere of freedom' necessarily renders his book into an interpretive, not merely a factual, work – which means that we can only ask whether his interpretations are true and his facts accurate. On both accounts, Ellul significantly fails us. In a work that grandly marches from the 'primitive' to the Industrial Revolution and 'reports' on the 'characterology of technique' in general – its 'modern characteristics', its influence on the economy, its interaction with the State, and so on through a host of highly nuanced issues and topics – interpretation, of course, is utterly unavoidable. Indeed, from the moment he enters into a discussion of 'primitive technique', he expresses views on magic that rest on uncertain and speculative grounds. So too in his discussion of the ancient Mediterranean, Asian, and Christian worlds, during which, apart from a tangential reference to Archimedes, he completely omits the extraordinary technological achievements of the Hellenistic age. But what is at issue, here, is not that Ellul is to be faulted for loading his book with interpretations. Quite to the contrary, the fault lies with his utterly bizarre insistence that he *doesn't* do so!

Although Ellul asserts that in his book he has 'deliberately not gone beyond description' and denies that he is 'a pessimist', the conclusions of his considerable tome flagrantly belie these disavowals.[20] In fact, he is a clumsy technological determinist – perhaps not a 'rigorous' one, as he puts it, but significantly so. And he is *immensely* pessimistic. What Ellul does is to formulate a ubiquitous 'dialectic' of technique that inexorably ends in a dictatorial 'megamachine'. His closing chapter, 'A Look at the Future', which ends with 'A Look at the Year 2000', describes

> the monolithic technical world that is coming to be. It is vanity to pretend it can be checked or guided. Indeed, the human race is beginning confusedly to understand at last that it is living in a new and unfamiliar universe. The new [technological] order was meant to be a buffer between man and nature. Unfortunately, it has evolved autonomously in such a way that man has lost all contact with his natural framework and has to do only with the organized technical intermediary which sustains relations both with the world of life and the world of brute matter.[21]

Anticipating Mander and others like him, Ellul declares: 'Enclosed within his artificial creation, man finds that there is "no exit"; that he cannot pierce the shell of technology to find again the ancient milieu to which he was adapted for hundreds of thousands of years.'[22]

This prelapsarian vision of an 'ancient milieu to which [man] was adapted for hundreds of thousands of years', the most ragged myth advanced by primitivists, ecomystics, and technophobes, collapses under critical scrutiny. Although the different hominid species were variously vegetarian food-gatherers, scavengers, and – perhaps only within the past 60,000 years – fairly sophisticated hunters, there is even evidence that they began to systematically cultivate food during certain seasons in the Nile valley some 30,000 years ago, when much of Europe was still glaciated and the famous Magdalenian culture was flourishing in southern France and the Pyrenees.

It is important to stress these variations not only because they controvert the fiction of a single 'Paleolithic sensibility' but because Ellul, like so many other technophobes, bases his account of 'why the first steps were taken' toward a 'technological society' exclusively on ideological and subjective factors. After rejecting the common notion that these 'steps' were the result of scientific progress, 'which prepared the way for technical progress, but it cannot explain it', and noting that it would 'exaggerate the force of [Enlightenment] philosophic ideas and systems' to give them 'the highest place in the history of techniques', Ellul settles upon 'the optimistic atmosphere of the eighteenth century, more than [Enlightenment] philosophy.'[23]

This explanation is extraordinary. Relying on Lewis Mumford's very uneven account of the development of technics – the descriptive vividness of Mumford's narrations and style can easily be mistaken for a causal account – Ellul concedes that the accretions of small technical advances finally laid the basis for a qualitative leap, together with population increases, a flexible economic life, and, most decisively, 'the plasticity of the social milieu.'[24]

But as to what *made* for this 'plasticity' and, presumably, the receptivity of 'people' to sweeping technological innovations, Ellul gives us a jumble of ideological reasons ranging from the impact of Christianity to the breakup of traditional social groups. To be sure, the bourgeoisie, Ellul concedes, *did* play a role in catapulting the preindustrial eighteenth century into the highly industrial nineteenth century, 'but it was not enough to carry the whole of society along with it.'[25] That the bourgeoisie did not need 'the whole of society' to go along with it owing to its economic power seems to elude Ellul. In fact, rather absurdly, Ellul tells us that 'Karl Marx rehabilitated technique in the eyes of the workers' by preaching that it 'can be liberating' – as though Marx were that influential in 'the middle of the nineteenth century', which Ellul regards as his golden moment – and the industrial proletariat sprang up like mushrooms after a vigorous rain following the publication (barely noticed) of the *Communist Manifesto* in 1848![26]

Philosophically sophisticated technophobes who find the likes of Mander particularly crude can always turn to the works of Martin Heidegger, who essentially elevates *technē* (and presumably technology) to a largely metaphysical category. The tortured complexities of Heidegger's ontology of Being are beyond the scope of this chapter, nor is it possible, here, to cope in any detail with a philosophy that notoriously followed so many different 'woodpaths' and engaged in so many 'turns' – to use Heidegger's own jargon. My account of Heidegger's 'ontology' is admittedly selective and focused on its unadorned essentials. I may add that Heidegger, not to speak of his many disciples, was very much at odds with himself from the 1920s to the last years of his life in the 1970s.

Insofar as Heidegger can be said to have had a project to shape human lifeways, it was as an endeavor to resist, or should I say, demur from, what he conceived to be an all-encroaching technocratic mentality and civilization that rendered human beings 'inauthentic' in their relationship to a presumably self-generative reality, 'isness', or more esoterically, 'Being' *(Sein)*. Not unlike many German reactionaries, Heidegger viewed 'modernity' with its democratic spirit, rationalism, respect for the individual, and technological advances as a 'falling' *(Gefallen)* from a primal and naive innocence in which humanity once 'dwelled', remnants of which he believed existed in the rustic world into which he was born a century ago.

'Authenticity', it can be said without any philosophical frills, lay in the pristine Teutonic world of the tribal Germans who retained their ties with 'the Gods', and with later peoples who still tried to nourish their past amidst the blighted traits of the modern world. Since some authors try to muddy Heidegger's prelapsarian message by focusing on his assumed belief in individual freedom and ignoring his hatred of the French Revolution and its egalitarian, 'herd'-like democracy of the 'They', it is worth emphasizing that such a view withers in the light of his denial of individuality. 'The individual by himself counts for nothing', he declared after becoming a member of the National Socialist party in 1933. 'The fate of our Volk in its state counts for everything.'[27]

As a member of the Nazi party, which he remained up to the defeat of Germany twelve years later, his antihumanism reached strident, often blatantly reactionary proportions. Newly appointed as the rector of the

University of Freiburg upon Hitler's ascent to power, he readily adopted the *Führer*-principle of German fascism and preferred the title *Rektor-Führer*, hailing the spirit of National Socialism as an antidote to 'the darkening of the world, the flight of the gods, the destruction of the earth [by technology], the transformation of men into a mass, the hatred and suspicion of everything free and creative.'[28] His most unsavory remarks were directed in the lectures, from which these lines are taken, 'from a metaphysical point of view', against 'the pincers' created by America and Russia that threaten to squeeze 'the farthermost corner of the globe ... by technology and ... economic exploitation.'[29]

Technology, as Heidegger construes it, is 'no mere means. Technology is a way of revealing. If we give heed to this, then another whole realm for the essence of technology will open itself up to us. It is the realm of revealing, i.e., of truth.'[30] After which Heidegger rolls out technology's transformations, indeed mutations, which give rise to a mood of anxiety and finally hubris, anthropocentricity, and the mechanical coercion of things into mere objects for human use and exploitation.

Heidegger's views on technology are part of a larger weltanschauung which is too multicolored to discuss here, and demands a degree of interpretive effort we must forgo for the present in the context of a criticism of technophobia. Suffice it to say that there is a good deal of primitivistic animism in Heidegger's treatment of the 'revealing' that occurs when *technē* is a 'clearing' for the 'expression' of a crafted material – not unlike the Eskimo sculptor who believes (quite wrongly, I may add) that he is 'bringing out' a hidden form that lies in the walrus ivory he is carving. But this issue must be seen more as a matter of metaphysics than of a spiritually charged technique. Thus, when Heidegger praises a windmill, in contrast to the 'challenge' to a tract of land from which the 'hauling out of coal and ore' is subjected, he is *not* being 'ecological'. Heidegger is concerned with a windmill, not as an ecological technology, but more metaphysically with the notion that 'its sails do indeed turn in the wind; they are left entirely to the wind's blowing'. The windmill 'does not unlock energy from the air currents in order to store it'.[31] Like man in relation to Being, it is a medium for the 'realization' of wind, not an artifact for acquiring power.

Basically, this interpretation of a technological interrelationship reflects a regression – socially and psychologically as well as metaphysically – into quietism. Heidegger advances a message of passivity or passivity conceived as a human activity, an endeavor to let things *be* and 'disclose' themselves. 'Letting things be' would be little more than a trite Taoist and Buddhist precept were it not that Heidegger as a National Socialist became all too ideologically engaged, rather than 'letting things be', when he was busily undoing 'intellectualism,' democracy, and techno-logical intervention into the 'world'.

Considering the time, the place, and the abstract way in which Heidegger treated humanity's 'Fall' into technological 'inauthenticity' – a 'Fall' that he, like Ellul, regarded as inevitable, albeit a metaphysical, nightmare – it is not hard to see why he could trivialize the Holocaust, when he deigned to notice it at all, as part of a techno-industrial 'condi-tion'. 'Agriculture is now a motorized *(motorisierte)* food industry, in essence the same as the manufacturing of corpses in the gas chambers and extermination camps,' he coldly observed, 'the same as the blockade and starvation of the countryside, the same as the production of the hydrogen bombs.'[32] In placing the industrial *means* by which many Jews were killed before the ideological ends that guided their Nazi exterminators, Heidegger essentially displaces the barbarism of a *specific* state apparatus, of which he was a part, by the technical proficiency he can attribute *to the world at large!* These immensely revealing offhanded remarks, drawn from a speech he gave in Bremen in 1949, are beneath contempt. But they point to a way of thinking that gave an autonomy to technique that has fearful moral consequences which we are living with these days in the name of the sacred, a phraseology that Heidegger would find very con-genial were he alive today.

Indeed, technophobia, followed to its logical and crudely primitivistic conclusions, finally devolves into a dark reactionism – and a paralyzing quietism. For if our confrontation with civilization turns on passivity before a 'disclosing of Being', a mere 'dwelling' on the earth, and a 'let-ting things be', to use Heidegger's verbiage – much of which has slipped into deep ecology's vocabulary as well – the choice between supporting barbarism and enlightened humanism has no ethical foundations to sustain it. Freed of values grounded in objectivity, we are lost in a quasi-religious antihumanism, a spirituality that can with the same equanimity hear the cry of a bird and ignore the anguish of six million once-living people who were put to death by the National Socialist state.

Notes

1 E. B. Maple, 'The Fifth Estate Enters the 20th Century. We Get a Computer and Hate It!' *Fifth Estate*, vol. 28, no. 2 (Summer 1993), pp. 6–7.

2 Jerry Mander, *In the Absence of the Sacred: The Failure of Technology and the Survival of the Indian Nations* (San Francisco: Sierra Club Books, 1991), p. 248.

3 Langdon Winner, *The Whale and the Reactor: A Search for Limits in an Age of High Technology* (Chicago and London: University of Chicago Press, 1986), p. 6.

4 *Ibid.*, p. 10.

5 *Ibid.*, pp. 54, 55.

6 *Ibid.*, pp. 177–8.

7 Mander, *Absence of the Sacred*.

8 *Ibid.*, p. 32.

9 *Ibid.*, back cover.

10 *Ibid.*, pp. 33.

11 *Ibid.*, pp. 11–24.

12 *Ibid.*, pp. 28–9.

13 *Ibid.*, p. 29, emphasis added.

14 *Ibid.*, p. 381.

15 *Ibid.*, p. 121. In fact, Chapter 7 of the book is entitled 'Corporations as Machines'.

16 *Ibid.*, p. 129.

17 *Ibid.*, pp. 129–30.

18 Jacques Ellul, *The Technological Society* (New York: Vintage Books, 1964), p. xxv.

19 *Ibid.*, emphases added, p. xxviii.

20 *Ibid.*, p. xxvii.

21 *Ibid.*, p. 428.

22 *Ibid.*, p. 428.

23 *Ibid.*, pp. 46, 47.

24 *Ibid.*, p. 48–9.

25 *Ibid.*, p. 54.

26 *Ibid.*, p. 54. The clumsiness of Ellul's argument has to be read to be fully appreciated.

27 Quoted in Richard Wolin, *The Politics of Being: The Political Thought of Martin Heidegger* (New York and Oxford: Columbia University Press, 1990), p. 4.

28 Martin Heidegger, *An Introduction to Metaphysics* (New Haven: Yale University Press, 1959), p. 38.

29 *Ibid.*, p. 39.

30 Martin Heidegger, 'The Question Concerning Technology', in David Farrell Krell, ed. *Basic Writings,* (New York: Harper & Row, 1977), p. 294.

31 Heidegger, 'Question Concerning Technology', p. 296.

32 Cited in Wolfgang Schirmacher, *Technik und Gelassenheit: Zeitkritik nach Heidegger* (Freiburg and Munich: Verlag Karl Alber, 1983), p. 25. This mean-spirited and unrepentant passage appears in English translation in Victor Farias's *Heidegger and Nazism* (Philadelphia: Temple University Press, 1989), p. 287. Farias's extraordinary, brilliantly researched study of Heidegger covers his repellent ideas, career, and attempts at subterfuge after Hitler's collapse–and the academic enterprise of his acolytes to see this self-anointed *Führer* of National Socialist philosophy as more than an ideological miscreant. No less is Farias's book an indictment of Heideggerian mandarins, big and small, in the academy today.

CHAPTER 7

Postmodernist nihilism

The most academically entrenched attack upon humanism, the Enlightenment, and reason are the highly influential philosophical tendencies that go under the name of postmodernism. It is arguable whether this name adequately encompasses such disparate, even idiosyncratic views as those of Friedrich Nietzsche, Martin Heidegger, Michel Foucault, Jacques Derrida and a constellation of former French leftists such as Jean-François Lyotard, Gilles Deleuze, and Jean Baudrillard, to cite the most well-known to an Anglo-American readership.

Yet certain basic commonalities, I believe, justly designate their work as postmodernist or poststructuralist (the two words are often used interchangeably). To be sure, Nietzsche and Heidegger belong to a time when anti-Enlightenment sentiments were still rooted in the romantic reaction to the effects of the French Revolution and the emergence of industrial capitalism. Although these two thinkers expressed their sentiments in very different tones and formulations, they were alike part of an antimodernist tradition that dates back to the nineteenth century and the early part of the twentieth. To many elite intellectuals of these generations, the mechanization of society by capitalism and the rise of a growing socialistic working-class movement seemed equally repellent alternatives to a vaguely 'heroic' and 'inspired' past.

Basically, however, Nietzsche and Heidegger advanced philosophies of disillusionment and disenchantment. The world to which Nietzsche spoke was undergoing the cultural transition from a seemingly colorful preindustrial society to a gray, deadening commercial one. Heidegger, although himself a product of south German Catholic reactionism, found an audience in Weimar-era disillusionment – not only with German imperial pretensions during the Great War but with the pretensions of the socialist movement, which had patently failed to fulfill the promise opened by the Bolshevik Revolution.

Despite their differences in style and their different social pedigrees, however, both Nietzsche and Heidegger addressed the fragmentation, anomie, and loss of belief in progress that increasingly troubled intellectuals of their respective times. Although a generation apart, they provided a common cultural field, so to speak, within which later thinkers and journalists found the resources for basically antimodernist sentiments, especially as additional disillusionments arose in the troubled postwar world of the mid-twentieth century.

The years following the Second World War produced a new sense of failure, particularly in France, which was not really one of the 'victors' in the conflict. Defeated by the Nazis in 1940, France had had to be liberated by mainly Anglo-American armies. Nor was France quite an 'occupied' power like most countries the German armies had taken over in Europe; indeed, given the degree of French co-existence and even collaboration with the Nazis in the early years of the war, many of its citizens joined the Resistance only when it became clear that Germany was destined to lose the war. After the liberation and a brief social honeymoon of national unity – in which leftists, moderates, and conservatives professed to join hands to achieve national rejuvenation – the country was wracked by the Cold War policies of its most prestigious party, the Communists; by the Third Republic's efforts to retain its holdings in Indochina; by its debacle in Algeria; and in the 1950s, by a Gaullist Fourth Republic that was determined to radically modernize the country, at least economically.

Culturally, French intellectuals tried to relive the hopeful mood of the liberation days for as long as possible, particularly in the form of Jean-Paul Sartre's existentialist philosophy, with its strong emphasis on individual autonomy and its professed commitment to humanism. But Sartre and his colleagues had badly misjudged the roots of their largely personalistic philosophy of 'existence' – namely Heidegger and even more absurdly, Søren Kierkegaard, whose angst-ridden personalistic theology never found a congenial home among liberal or radical French intellectuals.

Although Heidegger himself publicly renounced Sartre's humanistic thrust in his 'Letter on Humanism', the German thinker, largely discredited at home because of his Nazi affiliations, had now acquired a Gallic audience for his antimodernism and anti-rationalism – an audience that was to grow significantly and reach into the English-speaking world. Sartre, in turn, behaved with the notorious flippancy that was to be the ultimate undoing of his influence in French cultural life. Skipping from Russian Communism to Chinese Maoism and thence to various shades of anarchism (the latter, as he professed in the last years of his life, was the abiding basis for his views), he made somewhat of a political buffoon of himself, despite the influence of his humanism among young independent-minded French radicals.

No minor factor in shaping the direction of postwar French thinking was the Communist Party, which initially seemed to offer a viable foundation for many French intellectuals, who joined it, however temporarily, in considerable numbers. Its enormous influence with the working class – a class that was historically detached from, indeed hostile to France's seemingly effete intellectuals – appeared to offer an earthy alternative to Sartre's existentialist ambiguities.

Not that Sartre was oblivious to the social problems of France; quite to the contrary, he was the engaged intellectual *par excellence*, however naive and unstable his politics. But the Communists seemed like a pillar of strength beside the café intellectualism that Sartre seemed to embody. The morally 'rejuvenating' and earthy working class to which the Communists were tied offered a kind of social and personal therapy to all who fell within the party's orbit.

Examining the problems that besieged French intellectuals from the end of the war to the 1960s helps to understand how French postmodernism arose and, more importantly, how it acquired its enormous influence. So far as the 'leftist' postmodernists are concerned – such as Lyotard, Deleuze, and Baudrillard – the influence of postmodernism must be related to the aborted student uprising of May-June 1968, particularly in Paris, and the failure of the uprising to enlist the support of the Communist Party, which turned upon the students with what seemed to many like counterrevolutionary fury.

The student revolt and the working class general strike that erupted in May had nothing to do intellectually with postmodernism, which was still largely unknown even to many politically sophisticated student radicals. The emerging academic 'stars' of the 1960s like Michel Foucault did not directly influence the French student movement and its May-June uprising, or the *événements* as they have been called. It was mainly Sartre's humanism, the largely Parisian libertarian socialism of Cornelius Castoriadis's *Socialisme ou barbarie* group, Guy Debord's Situationists, Henri Lefebvre's critique of everyday life, and an indefinable cultural anarchism that nourished the views held by most of the radical students.[1]

But the failure of the uprising, together with the decline of the New Left generally in Europe and America, opened the way to a nihilistic reaction whose effects are still being felt to this very day. Postmodernism is not only a nihilistic reaction to the failures imputed to Enlightenment ideals of reason, science, and progress but more proximately a cultural reaction to the failures of various socialisms to achieve a rational society in France and elsewhere in our century. This historic failure reached its nadir in the defeat of the May-June events of 1968 – which is not to say that *all* major postmodern thinkers can be so situated in this historical framework and sequence.

It may well be that the immediate factors leading to the ascendancy of postmodernism will be forgotten in the future and that postmodernism itself will give way to an even more antihumanistic reaction in its academic strongholds. But the specific circumstances that catapulted Nietzsche, Heidegger, Foucault, Derrida, *et al.* to such prominence in the last two decades of the twentieth century can be located in the inability of revolutionary movements up to and including the 1960s, to eliminate the massive obstacles that an increasingly industrial and commercial society places in the way of achieving a rational society.

Not surprisingly, there is a certain symmetry between the emergence of postmodernism as a widely accepted ideology and the emergence of the social circumstances that have made it so widely acceptable. Various societies *do* foster ideologies that render their pathologies tolerable by mystifying the problems they raise. From the primitive world through the ancient to the medieval, world views concomitantly sought to uphold the hegemony of those in power and to explain the crises that unsettled those eras. But they also took on a cathartically rebellious form against the established social order. Early Christianity, like Mithraism before it and the Reformation later on, is a striking case in point.

Today's market society is no exception to this rule. The very tendency of mature capitalism to fragment traditional social and cultural relations by means of commodification yields reactionary cultural sequelae of its own: specifically, a consolidating ideology that holds the mind captive to the social order *in the very name of fragmentation and its alleged virtues.* If the social order cannot make a virtue out of hope, it can try to make a virtue out of despair. I am not claiming that postmodernists necessarily bear a personal intention of becoming ideological supports for any social system or that they are the mere creatures of capital. But what makes any given body of ideas acceptable or academically respectable more often has to do with the social functions it serves rather than with the quality of the insights it offers. Indeed, many of the insights that have made postmodernism so attractive are not very new and have been recycled, often unknowingly, from a warehouse of Western and even Eastern ideas that were available in various forms for several centuries, indeed several millennia.

The more one feels disempowered about the human condition and bereft of social commitment, the more one becomes cynical and thereby captive to the prevailing social order. To the extent that hope and belief in progress are lost, a disarming relativism, ahistoricism, and ultimately nihilism replace any belief in the objectivity of truth, the reality of history, and the power of reason to change the world. Beliefs that foster social quietism and a withdrawal into personal life, in turn, tend to neutralize an activist and interventionist mentality oriented toward the public sphere.

By contending that reason is questionable as a path to ascertaining truth, indeed that it is simply a social artifact and that truth is merely a social artifice, postmodernism advances this process, as does its denial that an objective history exists – a denial that divests the present of any ethical moorings and social meaning. Civilization ceases to be regarded as a realm of rational attainments; indeed the very idea of progress as a basis for hope and social foresight begins to fade, if not disappear completely.

Moreover, such sweeping claims tend to obscure the social factors that have created the 'postmodern condition' (to use Jean-François Lyotard's phrase); in fact, by rendering social analysis anemic, even bloodless, postmodernism tends to underpin the *status quo* precisely by challenging its effects rather than its underlying workings. Considerations of space make it impossible for me to explore postmodernism generally, still less provide an exposition of its ever-changing, even convoluted ideas. Rather, I shall confine myself to examining those aspects of postmodernism that are antihumanist in the sense I am using the word in this book – as subverting a belief in the power of reason, science, and technology to render society and the human experience rational and free.

Within this delimited scope, postmodernism can clearly be seen as a fragmenting and relativizing ideology *par excellence* that reflects the anomie and despair so widespread in the closing years of the century. In this respect postmodernism, precisely *because* it is a 'weary' and nihilistic body of ideas, may very well serve to validate the present society or even render it possible for its acolytes to 'dwell' rather innocuously within the existing set of social conditions, however much they regard themselves as social rebels, especially concerning issues that do not challenge the structure of the present society.

Its denigration of reason, coherence, and historicism, can hardly provide a sense of direction for popular restiveness or the intellectual means for contesting the anti-ecological and multinational capitalism of our time, still less provide the bases for a serious project for social change. Rather, it more often leads to a pervasive relativism and to a dismembering of the 'universalist' projects initiated by Enlightenment thinkers and their more radical descendants), so as to produce a form of social myopia. Put bluntly: it disarms all serious oppositional tendencies toward the prevailing society, apart from the narcissistic adventures of mere personal rebellion in dealing with the frustrations the society arouses in oppressed but marginal cultural groups.

To understand how this often socially deflective approach of postmodernism has emerged, we must look, if only cursorily, into the proximate ancestors of the postmodern outlook and the way they provided the premises for the *devaluation* of all values – rather than responding seriously to Friedrich Nietzsche's call for a 'transvaluation of all values'.

That Nietzsche's name appears in nearly every discussion of postmodernism is by no means accidental. Indeed, he has been embraced by otherwise opposing theorists across the philosophical and political spectrums, even before his death in 1900, with an enthusiasm that is little less than extraordinary. The extent of his influence today has few precedents, with the exception of Kant, Hegel, and Marx.

Until fairly recently, Nietzsche's name conjured up an elitist belief in a 'Superman', a hatred of Christianity, and corrosive attacks on socialism, democracy, and the slavish masses or 'herd'. Indeed, his philosophy was seen as ideological furniture for the various reactionary beliefs that flourished in his time and that came to terrifying fruition in our own century. The favorable recognition he received from rabid reactionaries, and even the imprimatur of the Nazis on his writings, as edited by his reactionary anti-Semitic sister, Elizabeth Förster-Nietzsche – together with a personal visit by Hitler to the Nietzsche archives – reinforced the belief that Nietzsche was a precursor of National Socialism.

Yet Nietzsche's proclivity for slapping the face of bourgeois philistines earned him encomiums from socialists and anarchists as well. Radicals of all kinds delighted in his militant individualism, with its kinship to the ideas of the alleged anarchist Max Stirner. He enjoyed great popularity among militant syndicalists, such as Salvador Seguí, a leader of the Spanish syndicalist union, the National Confederation of Labor (CNT), and the anarchist, Emma Goldman, who praised his vibrant iconoclasm and hatred of the German state, as did socialists like Jack London. Many Marxists solidarized with Nietzsche's biting criticisms of bourgeois mean-spiritedness and vulgarity, while the father of Zionism, Theodore Herzl, admired his strident contempt for anti-Semites and the praises he heaped on the Jews.

That Nietzsche was neither a German nationalist nor an anti-Semite, as so many supposed, no longer requires elucidation today. He was indeed individualist, and a biting critic of mass culture and the 'slave mentality' inculcated in the 'herd' by Christianity. His broader philosophical notions of the *Übermensch*, of eternal recurrence, of life as the 'will to power', and his personal values shall not concern us here.

Nietzsche's thinking provides a base for postmodernist thought in that, more brilliantly than any other writer of the last century, he made relativism a pivotal tenet of his outlook. By doing so, he called into question all the seeming certainties of traditional philosophies based on objective truth. Not that he denied the existence of an objective world, or, more properly, even cared very earnestly to discuss this traditional philosophical question; the most important conclusion he drew from his relativism was his reduction of facts to interpretations with no objective validity of their own. His views thereby seemed to permit the freedom to shuffle opinions around without concern for whether they are verifiable independently of the observer who formulates them. Nietzsche's agnosticism, if such it can be called, implied that it is meaningless to speak of an objective realm in which values, theories, and experience can be based.

This relativism or 'perspectivism', as Nietzsche called his view, is built on Gustav Teichmüller's notion that every body of ideas is a simple, partial, and incomplete perspective on a highly complex world. Each view of the world, for Teichmüller, was equally valid with any other – a pivotal contribution to postmodern thinking – although his views are rarely, if ever discussed these days. Yet his approach that any body of ideas is partial, indeed that it contributes to an increasingly broader understanding of reality – was hardly new: Hegel, and much earlier Aristotle, assumed such a 'perspectivist' approach to the philosophical views that preceded their own. Moreover, Teichmüller assumed that there is a reality, however complex and unfathomable, that is beyond mere interpretation, and that it can be known by reason as well as by experience.

Nietzsche questions this traditional conclusion. In a posthumously published fragment he asks:

> What then is truth? A mobile army of metaphors, metonymns, and anthropomorphisms – in short, a sum of human relations, which have been enhanced, transposed, and embellished poetically and rhetorically, and which after long use seem firm, canonical, and obligatory to a people: truths are illusions about which one has forgotten this is what they are; metaphors which are worn out and without sensuous power; coins which have lost their pictures and now matter only as metal, no longer as coins.[2]

By omitting the certainties of truth from his discussion, Nietzsche presents a radical relativism – a subjective, even linguistic relativism – that has entered into postmodernism with a vengeance. Thus:

> Against positivism, which halts at phenomena – 'There are only facts' – I would say: No, facts are precisely what there is not, only interpretations. We cannot establish any fact 'in itself'. . . 'Everything is subjective,' you

say; but even this is interpretation. The 'subject' is not something given,
it is something added and invented and projected behind what there is. –
Finally, is it necessary to posit an interpreter behind the interpretations?
Even this is invention, hypothesis.[3]

None of these statements prevent Nietzsche, in principle, from exercising the privilege of saying as much as he cares to say about ideas and reality, least of all within the very philosophical realm he professes to reject. He even has a full philosophy, by no means far removed from the metaphysics he denounces. Nietzsche presents his 'perspectives', such as his notion of eternal recurrence, as though they have objective validity or facticity. Notwithstanding recent attempts to render this notion a metaphoric quality, Nietzsche himself actually wanted to study the natural sciences to find ontological evidence for this cyclical belief.

Although a number of Nietzsche's failings – arguably – were criticized by Heidegger and later by postmodernists, his lasting imprint on postmodernist thought cannot be ignored. By reducing truth to linguistic traditions and facts to interpretations, he provides postmodernists with the means – as well as the stylistic brilliance and fervent militancy – to radically subjectivize truth and facts, and to deny the validity of any objective concept of history as universalistic, indeed as more than a disjointed, variable, and free-floating collection of narratives. The same fragmenting and seemingly subversive strategy could also be applied to science, reason, the subject, and social theory, all of which postmodernists were to cast as specific social or even personal creations.

In a harsh deprecation of 'man' and reason, Nietzsche regales us with the fable of an inconsequential 'star on which clever animals invented knowledge' during 'the haughtiest and most mendacious minute of "world history" – yet only a minute' in cosmic time, after which 'the star grew cold, and the clever animals had to die'. Nor does the fable sufficiently illustrate, as Nietzsche puts it, 'how wretched, how shadowy and flighty, how aimless and arbitrary, the human intellect appears in nature. There have been eternities when it did not exist; and when it is done for again, nothing will have happened. ... There is nothing in nature so despicable or insignificant that it cannot immediately be blown up like a bag by a slight breath of this power of knowledge.'[4]

Nietzsche's explicit depreciation of humanity, his denigration of reason, and his view of truth as little more than metaphor reverberated among many reactionaries who followed him, people whom he probably would have denounced as *Reichsmenschen,* as he was to designate Richard Wagner for surrendering to German nationalism. His idiosyncratic mind and his brilliant style lures us too easily into his literary orbit and mystifies us with pithy and colorful generalizations. Yet the misanthropic attitudes that underpin so much of his thought should not be ignored. Nietzsche was no angel, and to his credit, he would have despised anyone who called him one. His irascibility, at once coaxing and bullying, self-certain and contradictory, may account for the ability of his books to speak to a very broad spectrum of thinkers at different times.

As criticism of the late Victorian world whose philistinism infected Germany no less than England, his work is sparkling when it is not recklessly self-adulatory. Waves of metaphors and an unrelenting linguistic brilliance carry the reader away. That his works were taken seriously during a period of social reaction some seventy or eighty years after his death, and elicited a vast number of commentaries on him as one of the three most influential philosophers of our era, side by side with Marx and Freud, is not surprising. Social reaction breeds cultural decadence, and the most articulate academic critics of that decadence, drawn in great part from a disillusioned French left, came to be among the most compelling symptoms of decadence itself.

What filiations do postmodernists claim with Nietzsche, and what have they added to his putative insights?

Certainly, Nietzsche's immediate, indeed 'programmatic' contribution is his perspectivism, his radical if undertheorized relativism. To this we must add his candid anti-rationalism, his linguistic interpretation of facticity, his denial of objectivity, and his view of the subject as something 'invented and projected behind what there is' – even to the point where he challenges the existence of 'an interpreter behind the interpretation'. Not only are these paradoxes dizzying, but Nietzsche himself was hardly prone to deny that they existed unresolved.

In the Paris of the 1950s and early 1960s, however, poststructuralist and later postmodernist intellectuals were not disciplined readers of earlier philosophers and tended to glide over such paradoxes, which often verge on outright contradictions. In fact, they even celebrated, when it was opportune, the needed 'ambiguities' that challenge the so-called 'logocentric' thinking of modernity and humanism.

The most important of French postwar philosophers to claim the direct heritage of Nietzsche – and stylistically the most bewitching – was Michel Foucault. Eschewing labels like postmodernism, he simply declared, 'I am a Nietzschean', shortly before his death in 1984, and with wry humor he deprecated postmodernism as a fad. Although Foucault earned a growing audience with his early works and some distinction as a thinker inside France, he really catapulted into the public eye after the May–June events.[5]

Foucault's readership grew with the publication of *Madness and Civilization* in France in 1961 and its translation in an abridged form into English in 1963, followed by his best-selling *The Order of Things* in 1965. Yet his work seemed no more relevant to the radical culture of the time than Norman O. Brown's *Life Against Death*, to which it was compared in a *New York Times* book review. His reputation swelled with the publication of *Discipline and Punish* in 1975, followed by its translation into English within two years. In the nine years that remained to him, Foucault became one of the most lionized, sought-after, and acclaimed intellectuals on the academic scene, not only in France but in the United States. By the 1980s many critics hailed him as the greatest thinker of the late twentieth century.

Why this enormous acclaim for a historian whose work is often anecdotal and who as a speculative thinker is not very searching? Foucault owes a great deal of his immense reputation to the failure of 1968 and its aftermath, not to any role he played as an initiator of or even a major influence on the May–June events. His books unquestionably speak to an intellectual need associated with the *événements:* the critique of power, the ideology of the traditional left, and the celebration of marginalized life-styles. He is deeply concerned with the masked forms of domination in everyday life that rarely reach the level of ordinary consciousness. In this respect he often followed paths reconnoitered by Henri Lefebvre, who pioneered the study of everyday life (*le quotidien*) as far back as the 1940s. Moreover, many of his readers saw Foucault's books as critiques of civilization *as such* and of any belief in progress, a view that was to come very much into vogue in the seventies and the decades that followed.[6]

Foucault is above all a chronicler of domination, regarded by many of his readers, all his excursions into language and the 'human sciences' notwithstanding; indeed, many present-day Parisians see him primarily as a historian, not as a philosopher. In the early and mid-1970s, Foucault's critique of domination, if by no means original, seemed particularly appropriate. The 1968 student uprising in Paris had been not only a revolt against the myth that socialism existed in Stalinist Russia but evidence of a growing sensitivity on the part of French academics to youth subcultures that placed an expanded interpretation of selfhood on the agenda of social liberation. In this respect the New Left initially stood in marked contrast to the economistic doctrines of the Old Left, which, in France, at least, was still organized into powerful parties. Freedom and domination seemed to acquire a broader meaning than they had had in the past, especially when colored by a radical aestheticism steeped in

Dadaist and Surrealist traditions rather than in Marxist or Communist ones.

Understandably, the failure of the May–June revolt did not diminish the new fascination with largely cultural interpretations of social development. Quite to the contrary: radicals of nearly all kinds saw a need for studies of *concrete* forms of domination; for investigations into the oppressive dimensions of everyday life, whether in the past or the present; indeed, for accounts of subjugation and coercion that eschewed 'grand', seemingly abstract, and finalistic theories about history and the future of society.

Foucault's critique of domination and power now became increasingly popular: it managed to satisfy these needs in varying degrees, earning considerable, and in France, popular acclaim. Not only did his books, interviews, and lectures describe oppressions that ordinarily take the form of rational and humane dispensations, such as asylums that profess to 'treat' the insane and prisons that profess to 'rehabilitate' their inmates; his criticisms of domination and power were ubiquitous, extending from asylums and prisons to the most minute features of everyday life.

Moreover, whatever he intended his work to achieve, Foucault attacked *institutions* as such. In one of his most interesting dialogues – with a Maoist, Pierre Victor – he defends the 1792 September massacres during the French Revolution, in which seemingly uncontrolled crowds, fearing 'internal enemies' of the Revolution, brutally killed thousands of prisoners in the jails of the Paris area; most of the latter were not political prisoners but prostitutes, debtors, and minor malefactors. The massacres, Foucault declares, were 'a political act against the manipulation of those in power, and an act of vengeance against the oppressive classes.' He favorably contrasts this 'popular justice' executed by a crowd with the institutionalized 'authoritarian manner' in which the Paris Commune of 1792

> set about staging a court: judges behind a table, representing a third party standing between the people who were 'screaming for vengeance', and the accused who were either 'guilty' or 'innocent'; an investigation to establish the 'truth' or to obtain a 'confession'; deliberation in order to find out what was 'just'. ... Can we not see the embryonic, albeit fragile form of a state apparatus reappearing here?[7]

This passage is plainly directed against institutionalization in any form – as though the crowd's behavior were entirely spontaneous (which it probably was not) and the Commune's creation of an *ad hoc* 'court' constituted an 'embryonic ... state apparatus' (which it did not, under the circumstances). Lacking any searching theoretical or historical contextuality, Foucault's statements on the profoundly important issue of just treatment for criminal behavior are completely reckless and only seemingly radical. To see an 'embryonic' state power in institutionalized human interaction, even in its strictly functional and *ad hoc* forms, is as simplistic as it is misleading. Carried to its logical conclusion, Foucault's view essentially excludes the possibility that *any* kind of society can exist without domination, unless it is a free-wheeling mass of individuals who somehow congeal into 'functional' bodies like the September crowds. That the arbitrariness of crowd 'actions' may undermine the imperatives of organized and rational human behavior seems to have been under-theorized at best or barely reached the level of conscious formulation at worst. Foucault's anecdotal and almost microscopic treatment of power notwithstanding, his very endeavor to show its ubiquity in fact makes power too cosmic and elusive to grasp. We know the details of power – often quite marginal details – but we do not know the *premises* and the *structure* of power, notably, the crucial social relations that underpin it. Seen only as the exercise of coercion (which the crowds of September 1792 certainly exercised!), power becomes too ubiquitous to cope with. It is everywhere – and, functionally, beyond comprehension – however much it may vary in degrees or be concentrated by institutions. There is no good reason why the September massacre crowds that brutally slaughtered the prisoners were more 'free' or desirable than a court set up by the Paris Commune to sift enemies of the revolution from petty criminals.

More specifically, power itself is not something whose elimination is actually possible. Hierarchy, domination, and classes can and should be eliminated, as should the use of power to force people to act against their will. But the *liberatory* use of power, the empowerment of the disempowered, is indispensable for creating a society based on self-management and the need for social responsibility – in short, *free institutions*. It seems inconceivable that people could have a free society, both as social and personal beings, without claiming power, institutionalizing it for common and rationally guided ends, and intervening in the natural world to meet rational needs.

Foucault's opposition to institutions as such significantly impairs his critique of power. Not only does the substantial and formal exercise of power vex him; institutionalization in *all* forms is so integrally related to the exercise of power that his critique is completely reductionist, which is to say, vacuously abstract. Institutions are part of even the simplest of human affiliations, be they families, clans, tribes, or municipalities of one kind or another, not to speak of the multitude of 'establishments' human beings require simply to have a *society*. Thus, Foucault exhibits little or no concern about the *nature* of power. His pseudo-libertarian approach is ultimately so sweeping as to verge on extreme individualism. No distinction is made between power held by state institutions and power claimed by popular institutions or between institutions that lead to tyranny and those that lead to freedom. Not surprisingly, Foucault, a political activist in his own way, was committed to episodic events: to demonstrations, protests, battles with the police – in short, to discontinuous occurrences, local situations that are entirely ephemeral, that come and go in the flux of mere events and never lead to the formation of broad social movements. Advancing no constructive structural analysis of power as such, Foucault offers no remedies for social change beyond the impact of incidents – tumultuous at best and passive at worst.

Like a gnomic wanderer with a taste for the marginal, Foucault searches historical accounts with an eye for the cryptic episode – the mythic, the 'masked', indeed, the irrational, of which he is not a critic in principle, but a celebrant, living below the level of conscious, forthright exploration. If Nietzsche declared that God is dead, Foucault announces 'the end of man'; but where Nietzsche was militant in his pronouncement, Foucault is hazy and elliptical. The often convoluted prose of *The Order of Things,* with its emphasis on the ontogenetic role of language, tells us little more than what Nietzsche was to say in his affirmation of human ephemerality.

Indeed, using language mythopoeically with a sense of private mystery, Foucault announces humanity's burial:

> *Thus, the last man is at the same time older and yet younger than the death of God; since he has killed God, it is he himself who must answer for his own finitude; but since it is in the death of God that he speaks, thinks, and exists, his murder itself is doomed to die; new gods, the same gods, are already swelling the future Ocean; man will disappear. Rather than the death of God – or, rather, in the wake of that death and in profound correlation with it – what Nietzsche's thought heralds is the end of his murderer; it is the explosion of man's face in laughter, and the return of the masks.*[8]

This is a singularly reactionary statement. It heralds the coming of 'new gods, the same gods' in 'the future Ocean', and with its quasi-mystical and ambiguous prose, it epitomizes Foucault's rejection of the Enlightenment, which tried to eliminate God from the human condition and bring humanity face to face with itself and with reality by removing its mythic 'masks'. In the Nietzschean myth of eternal recurrence, as Foucault seems to see it, the 'death of God' prepares the way not only for 'the end of man', but for the return of other gods and atavistic 'masks' –

if not the physical destruction of humanity itself in a nuclear holocaust.

As for truth, Foucault declares that it

> isn't outside power, lacking in power contrary to a myth whose history and functions would repay further study, truth isn't the reward of free spirits, the child of protracted solitude, nor the privilege of those who have succeeded in liberating themselves. Truth is a thing of this world: it is produced only by virtue of multiple forms of constraint. And it induces regular effects of power. Each society has its régime of truth, its 'general politics' of truth: that is, the types of discourse which it accepts and makes function as true; the mechanisms and instances which enable one to distinguish true and false statements, the means by which each is sanctioned; the techniques and procedures accorded value in the acquisition of truth; the status of those who are charged with saying what counts as true.[9]

Foucault, in effect, escalates Nietzsche's own perspectivism without adding any dialectic of truth, of knowledge, of thought, and least of all of history. The reader is left with only the impoverished relativism of a fixed time and place, of power in all its 'masks'. History appears as 'data' organized into 'regimes of truth', each of which is essentially hermetic and self-enclosed. Given these specific 'regimes of truth', social freedom is essentially impossible because power, as exercised by these 'regimes', is *integral* to social life as such. The 'regimes of truth' do depend to one degree or another on each other, in the form of shredded 'hand-me-downs', not as a developing continuum, let alone a universalistic one.

There is enough in Foucault's often equivocal and cryptic writings to suggest that he denies the possibility that we can actually attain social liberation. We may resist the social order perhaps, but only in the defensive actions of 'local insurrections', as Foucault calls them. We can defy, protest, strike a blow against the all-embracing authority of 'regimes of truth', but a radical breach with the established order and its replacement with a truly liberated one is precluded by the premise that social life and its indispensable institutionalization is essentially a system of subordination and domination that we merely 'reinscribe' when we try to replace one social form with another.[10]

There can be little doubt that Foucault was a humane man, viscerally concerned about the injustices that existed in the world, and frequently prepared to act militantly in defense of human rights. But he offers no basic philosophy for his actions and in many ways vitiates the emergence of one. As a critic of power he in fact leaves us quite powerless to change our fate, and foresees, along with Nietzsche, not only the end of God but the end of man. His explicit antihumanism, his rejection of the potentialities opened by the Enlightenment, his ahistoricism, and his treatment of truth as a 'regime' of domination are too debilitating in their social effects to support the image of the engaged French intellectual. He drifted from Stalinism to Maoism to a life-style anarchism – more properly, nihilism – within a span of only two decades. It is as a defining thinker of poststructuralism and postmodernism that his basic ideas are of concern here.

A variety of thinkers who emerged along with Foucault in the early 1960s and flourished after the collapse of the 1968 events laid the basis for what is now generically called postmodernism. The most notable of this group are Jacques Derrida, Jean-François Lyotard, Gilles Deleuze and Félix Guattari, and Jean Baudrillard, several of whom made their careers in the United States as well as France. Not all of these writers accept a postmodernist label, but their work rarely justifies this disclaimer and all of them, without exception, can validly be regarded as bitter opponents of the ensemble of ideas I have called enlightened humanism.

Apart from Foucault, the most widely known of the group is Jacques Derrida, a French Algerian of Sephardic Jewish ancestry, whose books, articles, and lectures have had an enormous influence in Anglo-American universities. And it is with Derrida and his intellectual grounding that we will be principally concerned in most of the pages that follow.

If Foucault expressly placed himself in the tradition of Nietzsche, Derrida places himself in the tradition of the later Heidegger. The extent to which these two 'traditions' can in fact be clearly distinguished from each other is arguable: Nietzsche could have nourished both French thinkers in formulating their many common and defining views. As we have seen, he had already 'abolished' the subject (or 'interpretator'), the objectivity of truth, and the significance of humanity in the cosmic nature of things. These are major motifs in both Foucault and Derrida. But Derrida himself has insisted upon his filiations with – and transcendence of – Heidegger, particularly in the closing pages of the 'Ends of Man' and in his *Of Spirit,* and there is no reason why we should not take him at his word as well as acknowledge his reservations.[11]

Today's academic investment in Heidegger (as well as in Foucault and Derrida) is so immense that anyone who challenges Heidegger's status as the 'greatest philosopher' of the twentieth century risks garnering opprobrium verging on defamation. Yet the emperor, in fact, is wearing very few clothes indeed. Far from being a significant philosopher, Martin Heidegger is not only grossly overrated as a thinker but he is one of the most reactionary on the spectrum of *Weltanschauung* thought.

More pretentious and mystical than his acolytes are prone to acknowledge, Heidegger was a product of south German provincialism.[12] The trajectory of his ideas from the 1920s to his last works in the 1970s situates him in what Fritz Stern has called a *Kulturreligion* that

> embraced nationalism ... for it insisted on the identity of German ideal-
> ism and nationalism. The essence of the German nation was expressed in
> its spirit, revealed by its artists and thinkers, and at times still reflected in
> the life of the simple, unspoiled folk. ... Common were the lamentations
> about the decline of the German spirit, the defeat of idealism by the forces
> of realism in politics and of materialism in business.[13]

Although he was initially trained in theology, Heidegger's 1920s writings retain a secularity that probably stemmed from his training with Edmund Husserl, the distinguished 'father' of modern phenomenology, who called upon philosophers to remove the multitude of assumptions that overlie direct access to 'the facts' – an appeal that ended, oddly enough, in a variant of idealism rather than empiricism. As Husserl's assistant and his chosen successor at the University of Freiburg, Heidegger, far from 'going back to the facts', essentially mystified them. In his *Being and Time* (1927), the work that made his reputation in Germany and abroad and that he dedicated to Husserl 'in friendship and admiration', Heidegger's jargon freights psychological notions with an 'ontological' perspective that only superficially resembles ontology as an inquiry into the nature of reality. In fact, Heidegger essentially intellectualized his regional provincialism and reactionism into a metaphysical psychology – much more than a philosophy – and made intellectual history by transforming moods and sentiments into categories. The work for which he is still best known, *Being and Time,* published in 1927, found a ready audience in Germany, particularly among young people and academic mandarins afflicted by the alienation, cultural pessimism, and *Weltschmerz* of the Weimar era.

Heidegger professed to break, root and branch, with what he took to be 2,500 years of Western philosophical thought – that is to say, in fact, with traditional ontology itself. Far from producing a new ontology, he subverted ontology by using traditional categories like 'Being' and 'Time' to radically redefine its appropriate concerns. From Plato's time onward, Heidegger contended, ontology had steadily focused on an elaboration of the ultimate foundations of temporal phenomena, be those foundations Platonic 'forms', Aristotelian substance, the Cartesian subject, materialism's matter, or contemporary science's energy. Heidegger's complaint, let me emphasize, is not worth a pfennig as criticism, for these traditional foci were and still *should* be the real concerns of ontology, regardless of whether one agrees with a specific ontological view such as Plato's or Descartes's.

But for Heidegger, this line of thought has 'concealed' or lost contact with what it means for phenomena 'to be'. It straitjackets 'isness' or 'Being' *(Sein)* in rational categories, instead of letting specific beings or entities *(Seiende)* simply 'be' or 'manifest' themselves for what they 'really' are. In the course of this 'concealment', human beings become separated from 'Being', indeed, from 'things themselves', and they develop a productivist mentality that views entities as mere objects for human use. Heidegger reduces ontology to a form of cultural and psychological criticism, overlaid by a verbiage that restates the ontological concept of 'Being' as 'self-realization' rather than reality in all its forms and characteristics.

In our own time, according to Heidegger, we are totally enveloped by a manipulative and technocratic attitude toward things, such that, divested from our contact with 'Being', we are left on our own, leading 'inauthentic' lives in which we dread our own finiteness and mortality. Far from heroically affirming the certainty of death and becoming 'authentic' in our affirmation of our humanness, or *Dasein* (literally: Being-there), with its wealth of possibilities, we have disengaged ourselves from nature and retreated into the crude materialism and everyday trivialities that occupy the lives of what Heidegger calls the 'They' *(das Man)* or, equivalently, what Nietzsche called the 'herd'. We are permeated by *Angst,* 'thrown' into a world that is marked by 'ambiguity', 'idle talk', a 'falling' *(Verfallen)* of *Dasein* into the herdlike world that renders our 'Being-in-the-world' (which Heidegger designates as the basic state of *Dasein*) increasingly 'inauthentic' *(uneigentlich).*

Being and Time essentially borrows themes from Søren Kierkegaard, Nietzsche, and anti-Enlightenment ideas from German romantic conservatives to explicate our 'fall' or 'falling' from authenticity to inauthenticity, using a metaphysical terminology that transforms verbs into nouns. *To fall,* for example, is a verb, loaded with religious meaning, but it is hard to say what it signifies when it is turned into the metaphysical noun *falling,* as is the case with 'thrownness', which essentially deals with the fact that we do not create the world in which we find ourselves. It is clear from a reading of *Being and Time* that we have been 'falling' for some time, now, and yet Heidegger's use of the term suggests a quasi-religious descent that the Bible encapsulated into a single event. Be that as it may, it is hard to avoid the feeling that Heidegger's 'falling' is a secular version of the biblical 'fall' and includes the penalty, as we shall see, of a loss for which we are or have been paying a grave, almost apocalyptic penalty in his later works.

Nor does Heidegger always provide us with clear formulations that have, in fact, been stated more succinctly by other thinkers before him.

Consider the following dense statement in *Being and Time:* 'Even if Dasein is "assured" in its belief about its "whither"', we are told, 'all this counts for nothing as against the phenomenal facts of the case: for the mood brings Dasein before the "that-it-is" of its "there", which, as such, stares it in the face with the inexorability of an enigma.'[14] Allow me to suggest that this is overloaded verbiage for a condition that Marx, for example, noted more pithily when he wrote: 'Men make their own history, but they do not make it just as they please; they do not make it under circumstances chosen by themselves, but under circumstances directly encountered, given and transmitted by the past.'[15]

It is necessary to tear off Heidegger's linguistic mask – one that hides the 'authentic' face of postmodernism generally – if we are to get to the essentials of the Heidegger-Derrida connection. The ease with which Heidegger's language permits him to engage in circular reasoning; his typically mystical recourse to 'silence' as the mode of discourse for 'conscience'; his contradictory emphasis on personalism on the one hand and the subordination of individual inclinations to the collective 'destiny' of the 'Volk', on the other – all can be examined only in a book-length account of Heideggerian thought.

But Heidegger's observation on the relationship of the individual to what seems uncomfortably like a *Volksgemeinschaft* or ethnic 'people's community' – so central to German reactionary and National Socialist 'moods' – is too compelling to ignore. Destiny 'is how we designate the historicizing of the community, of a *Volk*,' Heidegger tells us in *Being and Time*, nor is destiny 'something that puts itself together out of individual fates, any more than Being-with-one-another can be conceived as the occurring together of several Subjects. Our fates have already been guided in advance, in our Being with one another in the same world and in our resoluteness for definite possibilities.' Indeed, as Heidegger adds a few paragraphs later, given the 'authentic repetition of a possibility that has been – the possibility that Dasein may choose its *hero* – is grounded existentially in anticipatory resoluteness.'[16]

In such passages Heidegger is already, as early as in *Being and Time*, insinuating a 'leadership principle' into his 'ontology'. What is unambiguous is that he is a reactionary elitist, for whom the 'They' – bluntly, the Nietzschean 'herd' – is the inauthentic raw material of the authentic few, most notably the German reactionary mandarins who are guided by conscience, guilt, care, and a heroic stance toward the certainty of death. In an outstanding study of the relationship of Heidegger's 'ontology' to his political philosophy, Richard Wolin observes that, following Heidegger's thought, the 'They', or *those who dwell in the public sphere of everydayness are viewed as essentially incapable of self-rule. Instead, the only viable political philosophy that follows from this standpoint would be brazenly elitist: since the majority of citizens remain incapable of leading meaningful lives when left to their own devices, their only hope for 'redemption' lies in the imposition of a 'higher spiritual mission' from above.*[17]

Notoriously, Heidegger became a fervent member of the National Socialist party in 1933 and remained one until the collapse of the Third Reich. Notoriously, too, whatever differences he may have had with more dogmatic approaches to Nazism, he tried to 'elevate' it by enlarging its 'spiritual mission', albeit still retaining much of its folk philosophy. To deny this part of Heidegger's life and philosophy is totally unjustified in the light of what is now known about his own cynical attempts to conceal his past.

Nor did he show any contrition after the war for his membership in the Nazi Party. His failure to confront the Shoah or 'Holocaust', or even to acknowledge its distinctiveness, is beneath contempt, as are his contrived excuses for removing his original dedication of *Being and Time* to Edmund Husserl – his former mentor was Jewish – and for his own silence upon Husserl's death in 1936. Indeed, during the thirties, after he entered the National Socialist Party, his 'philosophy' began to acquire an increasingly antihumanistic, abstract, and essentially suprahuman form.

Thus, in *Being and Time,* Being can only manifest itself through *man,* or *Dasein,* which, unlike all other 'entities', has a capacity to understand Being. By the 1930s, Heidegger's conception of *Dasein* as an individual phenomenon vaporizes into a collective and essentially *völkisch* concept, and Being acquires a quasi-mystical autonomy. In a pithy and insightful interpretation of Heidegger's 'turn' (*Kehre*) in the mid-1930s and the 1940s, Richard Wolin observes that the thought of the later Heidegger

appears at times to be a summary justification of human passivity and inaction (Gelassenheit). *... Being assumes the character of an omnipotent primal force, a 'first unmoved mover' [a function that Aristotle assigned to his ontological God], whose 'presencing' proves to be the determinative, ultimate instance for events in the lowly world of human affairs. In its other-worldly supremacy, this force both withdraws from the tribunal of human reason and defies the meager capacities of human description: 'A Being that not only surpasses all beings – and thus all men – but which like an unknown God rests and "essences" in its own truth, in that it is sometimes present and sometimes absent, can never be explained like a being in existence: instead it can only be "evoked".*[18]

The collapse of the Third Reich did not eliminate Heidegger's lingering loyalty to the 'spiritual mission' of the 'National Revolution', as Hitler's ascent to power was called by its adherents – and his emphasis on National Socialism's regenerative 'spiritual' potentialities, as distinguished from its very secular performance, gave Heidegger a great deal of legitimacy among his later French- and English-speaking sycophants. It is hard to tell whether Heidegger was a naif trapped in a misguided skein of fascist intrigue and betrayal or whether his French admirers decided to behave like naifs trapped in an unsavory admiration for the former rector of Freiburg University.

Rambunctiously fascistic and nationalistic in his speeches and lectures during the early 1930s, Heidegger's metaphysics now acquired a more 'restful', indeed fatalistic tone, turning to poetry, particularly Hölderlin's, the ontogenetic role of language, and philosophical allusions to a quietism that are redolent of Asian theisms. His postwar writings were permeated by mysticism, indeed by an apocalyptic theism. In an interview he gave to the German weekly *Der Spiegel* in September 1966 (on the condition that it be published posthumously), he confronted the threat of the 'technological state' and philosophy's role in resisting its encroachment with the following conclusions:

> *If I may answer quickly and perhaps somewhat* vehemently, *but from long reflection: Philosophy will not be able to bring about a direct change of the present state of the world. This is true not only of philosophy but of all merely human meditations and endeavors. Only a god can save us. I think the only possibility of salvation left to us is to prepare readiness, through thinking and poetry, for the appearance of the god or for the absence of the god during the decline; so that we do not, simply put, die meaningless deaths, but that when we decline, we decline in the face of the absent god.*[19]

In a sense, the interview was Heidegger's testament – and also a fascinating clarification of his views which can be traced back even to *Being and Time*. It is often safer to take Heidegger's statements at face value than to rely on his exegetists to adorn them with overloaded interpretations that remove us from the essential meaning of his words – a solution, to be sure, that would bankrupt many commentators on Heidegger who have managed to render his works and postmodernism a hermetic world accessible only to devout initiates.

The entry of French postwar philosophers into the murky waters of Heideggerian thought was a disaster to serious reflection – and we are still bearing the burden they imposed as this century nears its end.

Whatever Nietzsche and Heidegger wrote, their French admirers ratcheted up to even more obscure, and in many respects, more antimodern levels than the two Germans achieved, albeit short of turning to fascism and nationalism. One of the most vexing members of this crew is Jacques Derrida, whose use of Heidegger left a trail of wreckage in Anglo-American literary criticism that has also passed over into social thought.

An indefatigable writer and lecturer with an enormous following, Derrida has made paradox, contradiction, linguistic juggling, and inchoate thinking into virtues. Many of his verbal gymnastics derive from Heidegger, although he cannot be denied the responsibility for generating considerable confusion in his own right. To enter into the Derridean skein of criss-crossing ideas, assertions, inscriptions, and convoluted 'horizons', 'spaces', and self-indulgent queries that, in my view, muddle rather than clarify a viewpoint is beyond the scope of this book. Indeed, more than one book would be needed to give Derrida his due – and I do not mean this in any complimentary sense.

The relationship of Derrida to Heidegger has been meticulously chronicled, step by step and word by word, in an essay by Charles Spinosa.[20] Despite his rather easygoing style, Spinosa's comparison is demanding, and I shall do no more than take up the salient commonalities that he identifies.

The conventional belief has been that Derrida's filiations with Heidegger began with Heidegger's 'turn' from a more or less traditional ontology to explicit antihumanism after the war. Yet Spinosa shows quite inadvertently that *Being and Time* feeds as much into Derrida's thinking as does Heidegger's very influential postwar antihumanist essay, 'The Question Concerning Technology', as well as other essays of the late 1940s and 1950s.

This relationship is not simply an academic issue. Derrida has emphasized that in *Being and Time,* written in the late 1920s, and particularly in his 1930s writings, Heidegger was still tied to a 'metaphysics of presence' – that is, a metaphysics of underlying foundations that characterized the traditional ontologies of Western philosophy from Plato and Aristotle to Hegel and even including Nietzsche. For Derrida, this 'metaphysics of presence' constitutes the premises of humanism, anthropocentrism, science, and rationalism – which, yes, led ultimately to fascism! Indeed, if I read Derrida's analysis correctly, National Socialism is a result of humanism, possibly even its apogee.

Thus it is worth referring to one of Heidegger's more repulsive Nazi 'texts', most famously his 'Self-Assertion of the German University', the lecture he gave on assuming the rectorship of the University of Freiburg in 1933, to get a sense of what Derrideans regard as Heidegger's explicit or latent 'humanism'. Laced with references to 'spirit' and the 'spiritual leadership' that the university must undertake in serving the Third Reich, Heidegger's address actually pivots around a rejection of academic freedom as merely 'negative liberty' and appeals for the more 'substantive' claims of service by students that result from 'three bonds'. All three are largely Hitlerian: 'The three bonds *by* the people, *to* the destiny of the state, *in* spiritual mission – are *equally primordial* to the German essence. The three services that are from it – Labour Service, Military Service, and Knowledge Service – are equally necessary and of equal rank.'[21]

Nor was Heidegger free of the jingoistic and racist rhetoric of the time when he referred to 'Spirit'. He told his listeners:

> *Spirit is not empty cleverness, nor the noncommittal play of wit, nor the boundless drift of rational dissection, let alone world reason; spirit is the primordially attuned knowing resoluteness toward the essence of Being. And the* spiritual world *of a people* [Volk] *is not the superstructure of a culture any more than it is an armory filled with useful information and values; it is the power that most deeply preserves the people's earth- and blood-bound strengths as the power that most deeply aroused and most profoundly shakes the people's existence.*[22]

It requires enormous credulity – or naivety – to regard such passages from the rectoral address as spiritual, still less as being in accord with a traditional, presumably humanistic metaphysics of spirit; rather, it is an odious exercise in fascist rhetoric. In their devastating account of 'the "French Heideggerians" gathered around Jacques Derrida', Luc Ferry and Alain Renault observe that, confronted 'with the question of Heidegger's Nazism', they

> *have irrevocably chosen their side and found their concept through an extraordinary recommendation: if Heidegger was a Nazi, which no one now can dispute, it certainly was not because he condemned the world of democratic humanism and thus saw the appeal of a conservative revolution; and if, as one student of Derrida's [Philippe Lacoue-Labarthe] coolly asserts, 'Nazism is a humanism' (sic), we should judge that the Heidegger of 1933 was naturally led to Nazism because he was still in the grip of a humanistic and spiritualistic tradition he had not yet adequately deconstructed, Q.E.D.*[23]

In fact, Derrida's *Of Spirit: Heidegger and the Question* bears out that Ferry and Renault have taken aim with considerable accuracy.[24] Derrida's 'text' begins with a tangled series of questions on the meaning of 'Spirit' (*Geist*) that leads the reader into an increasingly abstract discussion of the rectoral address. It requires no intellectual astuteness to see that, however much

Heidegger used philosophical verbiage to give a high tone to his address, it was meant to serve the needs of the Nazi regime. This fact does not elude Derrida, but his comments on the address are marked by numerous equivocations, in which he seems to take Heidegger's manipulation of philosophical terms, particularly 'spirit', in a strictly philosophical sense. Accordingly, Derrida observes that 'one *could* say that [Heidegger] spiritualizes National Socialism. And one *could* reproach him for this, as he will later reproach Nietzsche for having exalted the spirit of vengeance into a "spirit of vengeance" spiritualized to the highest point' – as if Heidegger's words and Nietzsche's were of comparable significance in this connection and Heidegger were dealing essentially with philosophical issues in his rectoral address:

'But on the other [!] hand,' Derrida proceeds, treating both sides of the argument as if they were equally valid,

> by taking the risk of spiritualizing nazism, he might [!] have been trying to absolve or save it by marking it with this affirmation [!] (spirituality, science, questioning, etc.). By the same token, this sets apart Heidegger's commitment and breaks [!] an affiliation. This address seems no longer to belong simply [!] to the 'ideological' camp in which one appeals to obscure forces – forces which would not be spiritual, but natural, biological, racial, according to anything but spiritual interpretation of 'earth and blood.'[25]

This deconstruction of the address is all the more unsavory because Heidegger's address was *eminently* ideological and *did* appeal to these 'obscure forces', such as 'the people's earth- and blood-bound strengths', even dignifying them with sweeping references to Plato, Greek philosophy, Hegel – and General von Clausewitz, the theorist *par excellence* of German militarism.[26]

As to Heidegger's and Derrida's similarities: despite their different emphases – notably, Heidegger's on the rural craftsman in his shop and Derrida's on language – the distinctions between the two are not particularly significant. Heidegger's notion of 'equipment', the tools and techniques with which a craftsman works, corresponds to Derrida's notion of *différance*, or the way we linguistically understand definitions. Our understanding of phenomena depends on differences or contrasts in meaning such as true/false, real/imaginary, discovered/invented, and so forth. For Derrida, a 'signified concept is never present in and of itself'. Indeed, 'every concept is inscribed in a *chain* or in a system within which it refers to the other, to other concepts, by means of the *systematic play* of differences.'[27]

I will not belabor the way Heidegger's 'equipment' and Derrida's *différance* converge in practice except to note that Derrida is only too conscious of their similarities in the closing pages of his essay '*Différance*'; and that we are not examining a post-'turn' or postwar Heidegger but the author of *Being and Time* himself. Spinosa goes on to show that Derrida's *différance*

> comes very close to Heidegger's notion of revealing (being) once we make adjustments for seeing things in terms of systems of differences instead of practices or components. ... No person controls différance. That would be like thinking that someone controls language. We might as well say that [when] a new way of revealing is happening this amounts to putting Derrida's insight about différance into Heidegger's language.[28]

At times, in fact, Derrida seems to out-Heidegger Heidegger. For it is not 'persons' who 'control *différance*' – still less society – but, vaguely and impersonally, 'systems', thereby reifying beyond lived experience and history the way in which *différances* 'reveal' themselves. Aside from the similarities between the two men, the differences between them are advances and retreats, clarifications and obfuscations, around their respective degrees of antihumanism. Where Derrida (as of this writing) shares Heidegger's view that philosophy is the originating source of all our cultural achievements – and problems – he adds nothing to the basically idealistic claim that Heidegger made early in his career, when he saw metaphysics as the determining factor in human behavior.

Although a good deal more can be written about the correspondences between Heidegger and Derrida, the parallel ends in the way that the two men focus on 'the Other'. In Heidegger's case, the section on 'Every Being-one's-Self [as an individual – M.B.] and the "They"' or, shall we say, using Nietzschean language, 'the herd', addresses in *Being and Time* the leveling down process induced by the 'herd', with its later implications of an authentic elite and a 'hero'. In Derrida's case, the 'play of differences supposes ... syntheses and referrals which forbid at any moment, or in any sense, that a simple element be *present* in and of itself, referring only to itself', so that 'no element can function as a sign without referring to another element.'[29]

In both cases, there does seem to be a 'leveling' down process which, be it accommodation to the 'They' in Heidegger's case that leads to an elite or hero, or a link in the 'chain' of 'differences' in Derrida's case that are expanded into 'othernesses' by the 'play of *différance*' to include *all* that traditional philosophy tries to suppress by creating an ossifying 'metaphysics of presence' with its forms, a priori categories, prime movers. Viewed from this abstract philosophical perspective, Derrida, like Foucault, exhibits a concern for the 'Others' that literally constitute the 'margins of philosophy'.

From a literary standpoint, this suppressed 'Other' includes the hidden meanings within a 'text'; from a social standpoint, it includes the suppressed 'Other', such as women, non-Western peoples, marginals, and the like – in both cases the victims of Western 'logocentrism'. 'Deconstruction', to cite the practice that Derrida brings to textual analyses, undermines 'logocentrism' and an all-pervasive 'metaphysics of presence' by revealing the element of *différance* – the hidden referents – whose exposure subverts the seeming coherence of a particular work. In 'mankind', for example, deconstruction finds traces of the repressed other, 'womankind' – or perhaps *kind* as such, man or woman. Deconstruction decenters the privileged sign – say, man – that 'inscribes' itself on a 'text'. These privileged signs are continually undermined by radically unstable or marginal signs, ('undecidables') and very significantly by 'deferment', in which one sign always refers to other signs that are implicit in a given work, thereby destabilizing a 'text's' 'logocentric' claims to coherence. One can thus think of deconstruction as a sort of octopus whose arms are continually extending outward toward hidden or implicit 'others' that serve to undermine the centrality of a 'text's' structure and identity – indeed, a sort of free association, which allows the critic to wander unrestricted in any direction he or she chooses.

Deconstruction is thus a formula – and practice – for incoherence in the name of in-depth critique. Immanent critique, to be sure, is eminently desirable, as long as it is not arbitrary. But by virtue of its anti-'logocentrism', deconstruction can mean almost anything. In current usage it can range from the most flippant criticisms to almost incomprehensible 'metaphysical' analyses. In 1968, Derrida himself described it in apocalyptic terms, when apocalypses were highly fashionable, after which its meaning seems to have aged with time from a 'radical trembling' to a fatalistic recognition that Western rationalism is so completely with us, even in 'traces', that 'breaks are always, and fatally, reinscribed in an old cloth that must continually, interminably be undone'.[30] By privileging the written 'text' over speech, deconstruction removes the reader from the author of a work and places him or her completely in the hands of the interpreter – or at the mercy of Harold Fromm's 'invisible puppeteer'. (See Chapter 4.)

In fact, deconstruction so depersonalizes the 'text' that it safely removes the reader from heated issues that are often raised in a literary work. Freed of that existential content, these deracinated writings can be coolly manipulated into any configuration one chooses like checker pieces on a blank board. Arthur C. Danto observes:

> To treat philosophical texts after the manner of Derrida, simply as net-
> works of reciprocal relationships, is precisely to put them at a distance from
> its readers so intraversable as to make it impossible that they be about us
> in the way literature requires. They become simply artifacts made of
> words, with no references save internal ones or incidental external ones.
> And reading them becomes external, as though they had nothing to do
> with us, were merely there, intricately wrought composites of logical lace-
> work, puzzling and pretty and pointless.[31]

Danto, if anything, is too kind to the Derrideans and deconstructionists.
Often deconstructionists subject the reader to a barrage of elusive questions, so characteristic of Derrida's own 'texts', that they turn from hortatory queries into unrestrained free association. In a pointed illustration
of deconstruction at work, David Lehman shows how an eight-line ele-
giac poem expressing bereavement for the death of a girl, 'A Slumber
Did My Spirit Seal', from the 'Lucy' series by Wordsworth, was con-
torted by a prominent deconstructionist, J. Hillis Miller, into a drifting
jargon-laden interpretation. The poem is short enough to be cited in full:

> A slumber did my spirit seal;
> I had no human fears;
> She seem a thing that could not feel
> The touch of earthly years.
>
> No motion has she now, no force;
> She neither hears nor sees;
> Rolled round in earth's diurnal course
> With rocks, and stones, and trees.

Not only does Miller treat this simple, economical, and touching poem
as a 'play of tropes' that 'leads to a suspension of fully rationalizable
meaning in the experience of an aporia or boggling of the mind' (I shall
make no attempt to interpret this jargon), but as Lehman observes, Miller
avers

> that the poem presents 'mother as against daughter or sister, or perhaps
> any female family member as against some woman from outside the fam-
> ily, that is, mother, sister, or daughter as against mistress or wife, in short,
> incestuous desires against legitimate sexual feelings.' For Miller insists
> that the poem is 'odder' than it looks, stranger and more enigmatic than
> traditional interpretations allow. The poet's 'I' is absent in the poem's sec-
> ond stanza, Miller notes; perhaps 'the speaker has lost his selfhood' as a
> consequence of Lucy's death.[32]

Miller's free association continues, often quite arbitrarily, until we lose complete sight of the 'text' and find ourselves entangled in the etymological derivation of the name Lucy – it comes from the Latin root for 'light' which allows Miller 'to take one final leap'. The poem, he says, is an allegory of loss. But it is not a dead girl that Wordsworth mourns for; it is 'the lost source of light, the father sun as logos, as head power and fount of meaning.'[33] We may or may not be dealing any longer with what Wordsworth wrote, but it is clear that we are completely in the hands of the critic.

It remains to survey several other French leftist intellectuals who carved postmodernist niches for themselves after the failure of May–June 1968. Gilles Deleuze, an academic, and Félix Guattari, a leftist militant and practitioner of an experimental psychoanalytic clinic, bolted across the post-1968 firmament with a book they co-authored in 1972, *Anti-Oedipus: Capitalism and Schizophrenia.*[34] It essentially melded elements in the works of Wilhelm Reich, R. D. Laing, David Cooper, Norman O. Brown, and Michel Foucault into an exploration of uses of sexuality for coercion and liberation, a theme that was already common in the English-speaking world of the 1960s and 1970s. In France this theme seems to have been relatively new; hence the encomia that the book received for its 'originality'.

'The truth is that sexuality is everywhere', declaim Deleuze and Guattari, as though the statement were extraordinary, if not outrageous. Sexuality is not only physically polymorphous, it is socially polymorphous as well. Thus: 'Hitler got fascists sexually aroused', declare the two authors. 'Flags, nations, armies, banks get a lot of people aroused. A revolutionary machine is nothing if it does not acquire at least as much force as these coercive machines have for producing breaks and mobilizing flows.'[35] These concepts are as close to Wilhelm Reich's as one can get without quoting from him directly.

For Deleuze and Guattari, schizophrenia is more a social pathology than an intrafamilial one, an insight that, they claim, distinguishes them from Freud's 'mommy and daddy' approach. The job of radical intellectuals is to probe this social domain that encompasses seemingly individual pathologies, but to do so on a micropolitical level – indeed, one redolent of Henri Lefebvre's emphasis on *le quotidien*. A truly revolutionary movement must not be so preoccupied with larger social issues that it fails to release energy blockages in individual human 'desiring machines' – especially if it is to provide a radical alternative to the sexual arousal produced by fascism, 'flags, nations, armies', and so on. Thus, Deleuze and Guattari contend, 'a revolutionary group at the preconscious level remains a *sub-*

jugated group, even in seizing power, as long as this power itself refers to a form of force that continues to enslave and crush desiring-production.'[36] Having attained the conscious level of 'desiring-production', however, it remains unclear how a revolutionary 'machine' is to advance beyond a naive 'life-style' anarchism, raging with desire and a libidinal sexual politics, and try to change society as a whole.

This *Anti-Oedipus* badly needed another volume to address this problem. What its admirers got as a companion work, eight years later (1980), was *A Thousand Plateaus,* adorned with the same subtitle as the previous book, *Capitalism and Schizophrenia.* Far from confronting the issues of social change, Deleuze and Guattari in this work ran riot in a self-indulgent exercise in literary styles, intellectual caprices, excursions into fields of trivia such as 'ticks and quilts and fuzzy subsets and noology and political economy', wrote the English translator, Brian Massumi, who warned the reader, 'It is difficult to know how to approach' the book.[37] Leaving aside 'its complex technical vocabulary', as Massumi puts it with excessive civility, 'the authors recommend that you read it as you would listen to a record.'[38]

In short, the question of how to advance 'desiring machines' along socially revolutionary lines was not answered. Instead, immunized to critical scrutiny by their language, style, and disorder, Deleuze and Guattari launched a typical postmodernist attack upon rational thinking and its intellectual consequences. Comparing reason to a 'tree', they challenged this longstanding Western metaphor for knowledge that has roots (foundations), form (logic), and structure (coherence), opposing to it their own metaphor of the 'rhizome', which snakes along underground, putting out tendrils that evoke notions of multiplicity, heterogeneity, decenteredness, formlessness – in effect, incoherence. This 'rhizomatic' imagery and method brings us back to Foucault, whose microanalyses tend to dissolve history into episodes and discontinuous events. Not surprisingly, Foucault wrote a warmly approving introduction to *Anti-Oedipus.*

Around the same time that *Anti-Oedipus* was causing a stir in France, Jean-François Lyotard also began to shine in the postmodernist world. Even more dogmatic than Guattari as a leftist, who was an avowed 'autonomist', Lyotard migrated from the *Socialisme ou barbarie* group to the dogmatic Workers' Power during the 1968 *événements.* After his enthusiasm for the marginal in the left diminished, he decided to abandon the 'proletarian revolution' for academic postmodernism. Lyotard's positions in this new incarnation have undergone so many changes that the differences between him and Derrida are now minimal, in my view.

No less a deconstructionist than Derrida in fields that range beyond literature, Lyotard created his own 'grammatology' out of a combination of Nietzsche and Wittgenstein, laced with Paul Feyerabend's chaotic 'epistemological anarchism'. It is not very fruitful to examine how Lyotard's 'pragmatics of language' yield the not particularly startling conclusion that 'to speak is to fight.'[39]

More important, for our purposes, is that Lyotard exhibits a sturdy hostility to reason, objectivity, and truth. All events are really narratives; their 'objectivity' consists in whether we commit them to paper as a narrative or not. In one dialogue with himself, the voice I will call Lyotard-I declares: 'When I tell my story, I am not acting as a mouthpiece for some universal history. And I make no claim to being a professional theorist, or to be saving the world by reminding it of a lost meaning.' 'What!' the second voice, Lyotard-II, exclaims. 'So the [Paris] Commune, Cronstadt, and Budapest in '56 are just stories! And what about the people who died?'

Lyotard-I dismisses this complaint with the observation: 'The dead aren't dead until the living have recorded their deaths in narratives. Death is a matter of archives. You are dead when stories are told about you, and when only stories are told about you. And you are free to expand the archive as much as you like, by including in it even the most anodyne of documents.'[40] Events are simply stories; theories are merely 'concealed narratives' – 'narratives' that presumably require deconstruction; and we should 'not be taken by their claims to be valid for all time' – as though such claims are usually voiced. This Nietzschean-perspectivist view of events and theories is a commonplace in the postmodernist world and leads to 'agonistic' duels between various texts rather than explorations of reality.

Like Lyotard, Jean Baudrillard is an academic of the French left. He essentially expanded Marx's theory of commodity fetishism into a critique of the 'consumer society', with its psychologically overwhelming media imagery and 'spectacles'.

Capitalist commodities, according to Baudrillard, produce a 'hypercivilization' of signs, a symbolic realm of 'sign values', which supplements Marx's economically oriented realm of 'exchange values'. Indeed, 'sign values' may involve not only symbolic intangibles but 'the exchange of looks, the present which comes and goes, prodigality, festival – and also destruction (which returns to non-value what production has erected, valorized).'[41] By removing symbolic exchange, according to Baudrillard, society can undermine the strictly productivist logic of capitalism.

By the late 1970s, Baudrillard was describing our era as a time of 'simulations', in which signs acquire a life of their own and come to dominate social life. The real is replaced by its image or simulation, as in television dramas, where actors who play doctors and detectives are solicited for technical advice. Hyperreality replaces reality; indeed, borrowing a word from Marshall McLuhan, images are 'imploded' into collages, and advertising saturates the media to the point where images, racing one after the other on television programs, form a dazzling and deadening blur. In the face of simulations that take over their lives, people become enervated and apathetic, such that this 'implosion' contracts experience into imagery that renders once-prized mores and political ideas meaningless.

In the end, Baudrillard is so overtaken by his notion of the implosion of simulations that, as he claims, power itself 'undergoes a metamorphosis into signs and is *invented* on the basis of signs.'[42] It may well be that Baudrillard was being overtaken by his own discussion of simulations and was becoming absorbed into the implosion he explored. In any case, he calls for a decentering of power so radical that even the micropolitics of Deleuze and Guattari were insufficiently 'molecular'. Finally, in his later writings, his absorption into the world of simulations is really completed, with the result that his work is now part of the very constellation of images that bombard us today.

Having jettisoned even symbolic exchange as a social desideratum, Baudrillard ends up with an arid nihilism. 'If being a nihilist is to be obsessed with the mode of disappearance, and no longer with the mode of production, then I am a nihilist,' he declaimed in the mid-1980s. 'Disappearance, aphanisis, implosion, fury of the *Verschwinden* [the disappearing].'[43] But a radical nihilism that once challenged the social order, he observes, is 'utopia'. The system itself is also nihilist, in the sense that it has the power to reverse *everything* in indifferentiation, including that 'which denies it.'[44]

This passage, which Douglas Kellner has called a 'cul-de-sac', did not mark the end of Baudrillard's voyage into the 'hyperreal'.[45] But in my view this *cul-de-sac* tells us all we need to know about the frivolities of postmodernist philosophy – if we can dignify postmodernism by regarding it as a philosophy.

Notes

1 For an excellent account of the French thinkers who directly influenced the student movement of May–June, the reader should consult pages 139–56 of Arthur Hirsch, *The French New Left* (Boston: South End Press, 1981). Hirsch goes a long way in describing the ideological sources of the uprising–although he notably omits the influence of the *Noir et Rouge* group, with whom Daniel Cohn-Bendit was associated, and the Situationists.

2 Friedrich Nietzsche, 'On Truth and Lie in an Extra-Moral Sense', from *The Portable Nietzsche*, edited and translated by Walter Kaufmann (New York: Viking Portable Library, 1959), pp. 46–7.

3 Friedrich Nietzsche, *The Will to Power*, trans. Walter Kaufmann and R. J. Hollingdale (New York: Random House, 1967), p. 267.

4 Nietzsche, 'On Truth and Lie', p. 42.

5 I made two fairly lengthy visits to Paris in the autumn of 1967 and in mid-July 1968, when street fighting occurred throughout the capital on the evening before Bastille Day. During that time I interviewed several student activists in great detail, most of whom played leading roles in the March 22nd Movement, which spearheaded the student struggle. When I asked about their philosophical and political influences, they made frequent references to the *Socialisme ou Barbarie* group, the anarchist *Noir et Rouge* group, and even to the Situationists, whom they viewed with a certain measure of disdain because of their withdrawal from the movement. But no one I interviewed mentioned Foucault. Eager as I was to explore the ideological influences on the student movement, I did not even learn of Foucault's existence until he became fashionable in the United States years later.

6 On the multilayered 'genealogy' of Foucault's ideas and all their convolutions, see James Miller's superb *The Passion of Michel Foucault* (New York: Simon & Schuster, 1993), a respectful but critical account that in many respects contains an implicit criticism of our times and explores the philosophical milieu in which Foucault's views were developed.

7 Michel Foucault, *Power/Knowledge: Selected Interviews and Other Writings, 1972–77*, trans. Colin Gordon *et al.* (New York: Pantheon Books, 1980), pp. 1–2.

8 Michel Foucault, *The Order of Things* (New York: Vintage Books, 1973), p. 385. The editor of the series in which Foucault's work appeared was R. D. Laing.

9 Foucault, *Power/Knowledge*, p. 131.

10 In his last works, particularly the brief essay, 'Subject and Power', Foucault declared that 'it is not power, but the subject, which is the general themes of my [current] research.' For him this shift was meant 'to expand the dimensions of a definition of power if one wanted to use this definition in studying the objectivizing of the subject.' Did this change in focus denote any emancipatory intention? 'Maybe the target nowadays is not to discover what we are, but to refuse what we are. ... We have to promote new forms of subjectivity through the refusal of this [dominated and domineering] kind of individuality which has been imposed on us for several centuries.' These passages are cited in Hubert L. Dreyfus and Paul Rabinow, *Michel Foucault: Beyond Structuralism and Hermeneutics*, 2nd ed. (Chicago: University of Chicago Press, 1983), pp. 209, 216. Foucault's call for a 'refusal' to *be* what the system wants us to be and to resist its hold upon us while promoting 'new forms of subjectivity' arose early in the 1960s, only – alas – to be subsequently absorbed into the prevailing order as a cult of narcissism. Hence the crucial need for *changing* society, not ourselves alone.

11 Jacques Derrida, 'The Ends of Man', in *Margins of Philosophy* (Chicago: University of Chicago Press, 1982), pp. 123–34; and Jacques Derrida, *Of Spirit: Heidegger and the Question* (Chicago: University of Chicago Press, 1989).

12 Stefan Schimanski's description of the 'master' is all the more interesting because it is written by a swooning disciple. After celebrating the fact that Heidegger 'never left' Messkirch, in which he was born, even after receiving an invitation from the Führer to visit him in Berlin in 1935 (actu-

ally, he traveled widely, both on his own and for the Nazis), Schimanski tells us that to meet with Heidegger he had 'to drive for an hour to the small town of Todtnau in the Black Forest Mountains' and then to climb a path to the top of a mountain, where he lived under 'primitive conditions' with 'few books' and a 'stack of writing paper.' The philosopher was 'dressed in the costume of a Swabian peasant, a dress he often also used to wear when he was Rector of Freiburg University. His heavy, squarish skiing boots (it was summer) emphasized still more strongly his relationship to the soil … and his brother still farms in the region.' More than one writer has alluded to Heidegger as a peasant-philosopher–without stressing the provincialism this implies. As to whether wearing ski boots in the summertime was sheer affectation or evidence of Heidegger's 'relationship to the soil', the reader will have to decide. See Stefan Schimanski's foreword to Martin Heidegger, *Existence and Being* (Chicago: Henry Regnery Co., 1949), pp. ix–x.

13 Fritz Stern, *The Politics of Cultural Despair: A Study in the Rise of the Germanic Ideology* (Berkeley: University of California Press, 1974), p. xxvi. See also George L. Mosse, *The Crisis of German Ideology: Intellectual Origins of the Third Reich* (New York: Grosset and Dunlap, 1964).

14 Martin Heidegger, *Being and Time*, trans. John Macquarrie and Edward Robinson (New York: Harper & Row, 1962), p. 175.

15 Karl Marx: 'The Eighteenth Brumaire of Louis Napoleon', in *Selected Works,* vol. 1 (Moscow: Progress Publishers, 1969), p. 398.

16 Heidegger, *Being and Time*, pp. 436, 437, emphasis added. The Macquarrie and Robinson translation renders Heidegger's world *Volk* as 'people', which is usually how *Menschen* is translated. In view of the deeply ethnic implications of *Volk*, especially in the context of Heidegger's 'historicizing of the [German] community', the use of 'people' softens and neutralizes Heidegger's disturbing meaning.

17 Richard Wolin, *The Politics of Being: The Political Thought of Martin Heidegger* (New York: Columbia University Press, 1990), p. 46.

18 Wolin, *Politics of Being*, p. 147. Wolin's quotation is of an appraisal by Karl Löwith in *Heidegger: Denker in dürftiger Zeit* published in 1984. At the time of writing, Löwith's book has not been translated into English, but some of his important accounts of his former teacher are translated in an invaluable selection of Heidegger's texts and comments by critics and former students of the 'master', under the title: *The Heidegger Controversy: A Critical Reader,* ed. Richard Wolin (Cambridge, MA: MIT Press, 1993). Wolin's preface and introduction are compelling commentaries on Heidegger and one of his foremost French admirers, Jacques Derrida.

19 Martin Heidegger, '*Nur noch ein Gott kann uns retten*' ['Only a god can save us'], interview by Rudolf Augstein and Georg Wolff, 23 September 1966. The interview was published in *Der Spiegel* ten years later, on 11 May 1976, shortly after Heidegger's death. The English translation is in Günther Neske and Emil Kettering, *Martin Heidegger and National Socialism: Questions and Answers* (New York: Paragon House, 1990), pp. 56–7, emphasis added. The book is a collection of documents and comments by apologists and critics of Heidegger.

20 Charles Spinosa, 'Derrida and Heidegger: Iterability and *Ereignis*', in Hubert Dreyfus and Harrison Hall, eds. *Heidegger: A Critical Reader,* (Oxford: Basil Blackwell, 1992), pp. 270–97. Neither Spinosa's essay nor the book as a whole seems intended for the general reader; both presuppose a considerable familiarity with Heidegger and the topics that the various authors take up.

21 Martin Heidegger: 'The Self-Assertion of the German University', in Neske and Kettering, *Martin Heidegger*, p. 11.

22 *Ibid.*, p. 9.

23 Luc Ferry and Alain Renault, *Heidegger and Modernity*, trans. Franklin Philip (Chicago and London: University of Chicago Press, 1990), p. 2.

24 Jacques Derrida, *Of Spirit: Heidegger and the Question* (Chicago: University of Chicago Press, 1989), pp. 31–46.

25 *Ibid.*, p. 39, emphasis added.

26 Richard Wolin has examined the regressive implications of Derrida's interpretation of Heidegger's 'humanism' with detail that I cannot duplicate here. See Wolin, *Politics of Being,* pp. 156–60.

27 Jacques Derrida, '*Différance*' (1968), in *Margins of Philosophy* (Chicago: University of Chicago Press, 1982), p. 11, emphasis added.

28 Spinosa, 'Derrida and Heidegger', pp. 274, 275, emphasis added.

29 Heidegger, *Being and Time,* pp. 163–8; Jacques Derrida, 'Semiology and Grammatology: Interview with Julia Kristeva', in *Positions,* trans. Alan Bass (1972; Chicago: University of Chicago Press, 1981), p. 25.

30 Derrida, 'Semiology and Grammatology', p. 24.

31 Arthur C. Danto, *The Philosophical Disenfranchisement of Art* (New York: Columbia University Press, 1986), p. 160.

32 David Lehman, *Signs of the Times: Deconstruction and the Fall of Paul de Man* (New York: Poseidon Press, 1991), pp. 125–7.

33 *Ibid.*, pp. 125–7.

34 Gilles Deleuze and Félix Guattari, *Anti-Oedipus: Capitalism and Schizophrenia,* trans. Robert Hurley, Mark Seem, and Helen R. Lane (New York: Viking Press, 1977).

35 *Ibid.*, p. 293.

36 *Ibid.*, p. 348.

37 Gilles Deleuze and Félix Guattari, *A Thousand Plateaus: Capitalism and Schizophrenia,* trans. Brian Massumi (1980; Minneapolis: University of Minnesota Press, 1987), p. ix.

38 *Ibid.*

39 Jean-François Lyotard, *The Postmodern Condition: A Report on Knowledge,* trans. Geoff Bennington and Brian Massumi (Minneapolis: University of Minnesota Press, 1984), p. 10.

40 Jean-François Lyotard, 'Lessons in Paganism', in Andrew Benjamin, ed. *The Lyotard Reader,* (Oxford: Basil Blackwell, 1989), p. 126. *Cronstadt* is a reference to Kronstadt, the site of the Red sailors' revolt against the Bolsheviks in 1921.

41 Jean Baudrillard, *For a Critique of the Political Economy of the Sign* (St. Louis: Telos Press, 1981), p. 207.

42 Jean Baudrillard, *Forget Foucault* (New York: Semiotext[e], 1987), p. 58, emphasis added.

43 Jean Baudrillard: 'On Nihilism', *On the Beach,* no. 6 (Spring 1984); cited in Douglas Kellner, *Jean Baudrillard: From Marxism to Postmodernism and Beyond* (Stanford: Stanford University Press, 1989), pp. 118, 119.

44 Baudrillard, 'On Nihilism'.

45 Kellner, *Baudrillard,* p. 119.

CHAPTER 8

Science and anti-science: anything goes

Postmodernism is a concept that has been applied not only to philosophy but to architectural, literary, cultural, and behavioral styles as well. To be postmodern is to be 'hip' today, to an extent that the word has become part of the very contemporary culture it professes to criticize. This might render it quite harmless, indeed ludicrous, were it not for its impact on what has been called the sociology of science. In the scientific realm, relativistic moods nourished by postmodernism's antihumanism are corrosive not only of popular attitudes toward scientific research but, as we shall see shortly, toward reason itself.

By *science,* let me emphasize, I am referring to the real stuff: physics, chemistry, biology, physical anthropology, and their offspring, such as astrophysics, biochemistry, molecular biology, and archaeology. What minimally defines these disciplines as sciences is the fact that they presuppose that external reality is relatively orderly, and many of its facets or levels of development can be discovered and systematized into verifiable, testable, and predictable laws, which in turn may have a direct practical application to human needs and desires.

Studies of society, human behavior, economics, and the like, that deal more with the speculative uncertainties of theory than with the more tangible facts of the natural world, are so dependent upon vagaries of human volition and arbitrary human interactions that they can be called sciences only by undermining the integrity of sciences dependent upon lawful and predictable behavior. To regard 'social studies', including economics, sociology, and psychology as 'sciences' is to make the word and its criteria for truth meaningless.[1]

Nor should *science,* let me emphasize, be confused with *scientism.* Scientism is a state of mind or even a creed that claims that the scientific techniques and criteria used typically in physics can be applied to *all* domains of knowledge and human activity. Advancing the idea that the full wealth of experience can be encompassed by scientific analysis, with a view toward achieving the effective control (rationalization) of human beings as well as the natural world, it emphasizes efficiency and value-free 'objectivity' in social affairs. Although scientism has been prevalent over the past two centuries, it is a naive failing of the Enlightenment thinkers and of many nineteenth-century writers on social theory and politics, even utopians like Charles Fourier – a failing that persists in words like *social science* and *political science*.

The distinction between science and scientism should be strongly emphasized, since the two are very commonly confused, with the result that science as such is blamed for the harmful effects of scientism on social life, notably for fostering the dehumanization and mechanization of everyday life.

The distinctions between science and scientism bear directly on the 'sociologies of science' that are fashionable today. Postmodernists and antihumanists alike make a strong point when they criticize the 'scientization', more properly the *rationalization* of everyday life and work. Such criticisms have been made for generations – not exclusively by the romantics from whom antihumanists draw so much of their inspiration but also by humanistic social thinkers, from Marx and Max Weber to C. Wright Mills and Herbert Marcuse.

What gave a major impetus to postmodernist and antihumanist assaults on the objectivity of science was Thomas S. Kuhn's *The Structure of Scientific Revolutions,* initially published in 1962[2] – a work that Paul Hoyningen-Huene, in his survey of Kuhn's 'philosophy of science', has described as 'among the most influential academic books of the past quarter-century', one that 'has given rise to what is now an unmanageably vast secondary literature'.[3]

An essential thesis of Kuhn's book is that the scientific understanding of truth and its advances come in paradigms, by which he means certain 'universally recognized scientific achievements that for a time provide model problems and solutions to a community of practitioners'.[4] Major scientific 'revolutions' consist not simply of piecemeal accretions of theories and facts; rather, they are radical 'paradigm shifts' that are brought about when a prevailing scientific consensus changes. A new consensus may be caused by the appearance of more explanatory hypotheses and supportive data for them, or even by mere swings of opinion among scientists themselves.

After a sufficiently large number of 'anomalies' emerge in the 'normal science' that marks an established paradigm, a 'new paradigm' is called for that, in effect, constitutes an entirely new way of thinking about a specific field of science – after which a new 'normal science' consolidates itself within the newly accepted paradigm. Specifically, Kuhn's book examines the conservative *behavior* of scientific communities over history: their tendency to hold on to the prevailing 'paradigm'. Kuhn, whose definition of a paradigm is fairly restricted, can hardly be held responsible for the fact that the word has been expanded to mean a veritable world outlook by New Agers, deep ecologists, and other ideological children of the 1960s 'counterculture'.

But to what extent did Kuhn lay the basis for a 'sociology' or 'philosophy of science'?

The sizable literature that has grown up around Kuhn's writings variously characterizes his views as neo-Kantian, phenomenological, empirical, and in a broad sense postmodernist. But a closer look at *The Structure of Scientific Revolutions* suggests that it is largely a *psychological* account of how science undergoes 'revolutions' or 'paradigm shifts'. It is decidedly *not* a study in epistemology, still less an analysis or modification of 'scientific method'.

Kuhn himself has not been shy about citing the psychologists who inspired a good many of his reflections, notably 'Jean Piaget [who] has illuminated both the various worlds of the growing child and the process of transition from one to the next'; similarly, his reading of 'papers in the psychology of perception, particularly [those of] the Gestalt psychologists.' He also credits the influence of B. L. Whorl's 'speculations about the effect of language on world view' and W.V.O. Quine's 'philosophical puzzles of the analytic–synthetic distinction', which appear to have sensitized him to psychological behavior rather than a philosophical outlook.[5]

So far as the methodologies of science are concerned, Kuhn's contributions have largely been marginal and descriptive. Kuhn, in fact, did *not* write a book on 'scientific method', despite the general misconceptions on this score. Explorations about the merits of induction and deduction date back to Aristotle's day, some 2,300 years ago, and were formalized during the Middle Ages by Christian scholastics. The importance of experimentation (Francis Bacon), of combining speculative hypotheses with a deductive approach (William Whewell), and of using canons of agreement and difference to determine the causes of natural phenomena (John Stuart Mill) – all of these methodological points have a long pedigree. In recent times, even more sophisticated and abstruse views of scientific method were advanced by the logical positivist principle of verifiability and Karl Popper's method of falsification, which contends that a scientific hypothesis has to be capable of being proven false before it is worthy of consideration as possibly true.

Kuhn does not engage these methodological issues. Rather, he examines how scientists come to accept 'normal science' in their specific fields, how they conservatively try to integrate 'anomalies' into a dominant paradigm, how alternative paradigms that deal more adequately with troubling anomalies shake them into doubt, and finally how scientists undergo a kind of 'religious conversion' or 'political revolution' (Kuhn's own expressions) in achieving a 'shift' from an old paradigm to a new one.

Essentially what Kuhn shows is that scientists are like most people. Far from being omniscient and objective intellectual mandarins, they are typical human beings. Like most people, they tend to resist change when they have been schooled into a specific paradigm or outlook. They quarrel (sometimes quite unreasonably) over the validity and significance of obvious anomalies that challenge entrenched beliefs. They enter into 'crises' about the competing views they face; but in time they accept a new paradigm as 'normal science' – until they are obliged to undergo the agonies of another paradigm shift. They are subject to all the fiery passions, conditioned reflexes, entrenched customs, mental blocks, and agonistic compulsions that mark ordinary human behavior.

Yet after all is said and done – and Kuhn gives it little attention – they significantly *do* something else *that is not frivolous*. In contrast to religious fanatics, befogged mystics, and confirmed anti-rationalists, scientists are *obliged* to respond, sooner or later, to the imperatives of facts, logical inferences, and rational evaluation. They may not follow 'scientific method', in all of their experimental procedures; but minimally they have to *prove* their claims mathematically, experimentally, or both, without recourse to supernatural or mystical factors.

In this connection, the various specific scientific methods – inductive, deductive, or hypothetico-deductive – are not merely a set of *procedures* for arriving at the truth of a given hypothesis. Very significantly, they serve to support larger experimental *criteria* for establishing the validity of scientific hypotheses. That is to say, no matter *how* scientists *arrive* at their hypotheses – whether through intuition, chit-chat, dreams, fantasies, or systematic thinking – they must subject them to carefully formulated, experimental, and logical standards of *proof* before their hypotheses are acceptable in the scientific world.

Nor have these *criteria* – with their demanding naturalism, reality principle, and logical consistency – been surpassed by any of the criteria advanced by the supernatural and mystical critics of science, still less by gossipy postmodernist and antihumanist accounts of 'how' scientists behave in and out of their laboratories, libraries, class rooms, conference rooms, cafeterias, or bedrooms.

In short, what we often call *scientific method* – an ideal procedure at best – might more appropriately be called *scientific criteria* – namely, standards of proof that, however idiosyncratically scientists arrive at their conclusions, still oblige them to formulate them as verifiable – not intuitive or mystical – speculations and facts.

Kuhn, to be quite fair, was not so crude as to explore the private lives of scientists in *The Structure of Scientific Revolutions*. Rather, he examined how, as a community, scientists often confront anomalies in 'normal science', new paradigms, and paradigm shifts. Alas, his demonstration that scientists commonly do not follow step-by-step procedures based on icy canons of objectivity touched off a literature that was intended to subvert scientific methods of verification as such, indeed of the integrity of science as a source of knowledge about the real world.

The passionate endeavor of many antihumanists – particularly New Age mystics, anti-rationalists, self-styled 'counterculturalists', and postmodernists – to deny the capacity of science to explain even limited aspects of reality has generated a stormy debate that actually turns more on *how* scientists do science rather than the *criteria* for scientific verification. That is to say, the debate focuses on the 'idiosyncratic' way in which scientists engage in doing science instead of on the ultimate criteria that justify or disqualify their work. In an ideological leap that can be regarded as an amazing non-sequitur, antihumanists often use these scientific behavioural idiosyncrasies to reach the facile conclusion that science *itself* is a myth.

One would suppose that antihumanists who stake out this crassly illogical claim might thereafter welcome science into their fold, inasmuch as the procedure they impute to scientists closely resembles the intellectual chaos that marks their own fields, variously Taoism, Buddhism, and a pot-pourri of Californian and Stonehenge mysticisms.

This phenomenon, let me note, is not strictly American or British; it has found a rich spawning ground in Paris, the home of postmodernism and its 'discourse'. For its rising star, Bruno Latour, the confusion between how scientists behave and what they discover has generated a postmodernist uproar. Latour, a professor at the Ecole Nationale Supérieure des Mines in Paris, gained a measure of repute as an 'anthropologist' of science when, in collaboration with Steve Woolgar, a British 'sociologist', he produced a 'field study' – *Laboratory Life: The Construction of Scientific Facts* – that describes the behavior of scientists at the Salk Institute for Biological Studies at La Jolla, California.[6] Latour seems to have done most of the 'fieldwork', going into the jungles of a scientific laboratory with the mental outlook of a Franz Boas or a Claude Levi-

Strauss. At times he assisted in scientific research and interviewed the scientists and members of the Institute, as well as listening to them and observing their interactions.

Clearly influenced by Kuhn's book, Latour found precisely what he was looking for – namely, that scientists behave like human beings. Designating the Institute's scientists as a 'tribe', our fieldworker notes that every few minutes his subjects exchange remarks about a new scientific paper here, an old one there, and a new word-of-mouth scientific finding elsewhere; in short, how they interact with each other, not unlike gifted primates in a cage.

As the trivial observations of our worthy 'anthropologist' mount in number, he perceives descent from 'order to disorder', in which 'the routine work carried out' in the laboratory rests – surprise! – 'on the routinely occurring minutiae of scientific activity'.[7] We soon learn, based on observations of this nature, that 'scientists' statements ... systematically conceal the nature of the *activity* which typically gives rise to their research reports.'[8] The use of the word *activity* rather than *results* seems to assume the worst about the behavior of scientists, notably that they hide their behavioral waywardness in formal observations or analyses.

Having settled into his behavioral study of scientists at work, Latour makes a quantum leap to assert that scientists do not live up to their claims of practising an orderly methodology. Facts are 'socially constructed', not *discovered,* he concludes, as a consequence of the microrelational give-and-take that makes up laboratory routines; their *validity* seems to hinge more on subjective interplay in the social world than the realities (if any) of the natural world. This conclusion seems to support the postmodernist notion that reality is actually chaotic and is only organized by disorderly scientists into orderly schemes.

Thus we learn that

> *scientific activity [sic] is not 'about nature', it is a fierce fight to* construct *reality. The* laboratory *is the workplace and the set of productive forces, which makes construction possible. Every time a statement stabilises, it is reintroduced into the laboratory (in the guise of a machine, inscription device, skill, routine, prejudice, deduction, programme, and so on), and it is used to increase the difference between statements. The cost of challenging the reified statement is impossibly high. Reality is secreted.*[9]

Alas, very little in Latour and Woolgar's book supports so sweeping a conclusion, which is far more mystifying than the alleged 'reified statements' that scientists ostensibly fear to challenge. To the contrary, seemingly 'reified statements' are repeatedly subjected to enormous challenges these days, and furious debates are waged in scientific journals from issue to issue, obviously at odds with Latour's claim that reality 'is secreted'.

Indeed, I fail to see that Latour's fieldwork reveals more than the flow of gossip about the comings and goings, vagaries and interactions of scientists. Yet with 'philosophical' aplomb, Latour and Woolgar render a verdict of stunningly relativistic proportions:

> Our account of fact construction in a biology laboratory is neither superior nor inferior to those produced by scientists themselves. It is not superior because we do not claim to have any better access to 'reality', and we do not claim to be able to escape from our description of scientific activity: the construction of order out of disorder at a cost, and without recourse to any preexisting order. In a fundamental sense, our own account is no more than a fiction.[10]

Stripped of their postmodernist verbiage, Latour and Woolgar almost pride themselves in acknowledging that their work is merely a fiction. Inasmuch as they offer no criteria at all by which to judge our suppositions about the natural world, we are deprived of all 'preexisting order' as a basis for formulating truthful statements about reality. Thus we are condemned to an ongoing and unresolvable problem – one that apparently angered the book's original publishers, who rightly declared that 'they were not in the habit of publishing anything that "proclaimed its own worthlessness"'![11] Accordingly, in the revised edition the authors added a postscript that, after considerable wordplay, concludes that scientific 'interpretations do not so much inform as perform'. Having turned scientists into actors, with performance as their criterion, Latour and Woolgar dismissively declare that 'our scientists are obviously better equipped at performing the world we live in than we are at deconstructing it.'[12]

One might suppose that Latour would hereafter have found silence the better part of valor, but instead he undertook an even more ambitious work, *Science in Action*. Here he conceives the world of science as a war of all against all, wherein each white-coated participant parries one 'fiction' against all the others, until the battle of papers, alliances, and histrionics becomes too formidable to provide any reliable truths about the natural world. Hence: '[s]ince the settlement of a controversy is the *cause* of Nature's representation, not its consequence, we can never use this consequence, Nature, to explain how and why a controversy has been settled.'[13] Not only science but now the natural world itself is a social artifact. Trapped in a no-man's-land in the scientific battleground, we are at a loss as to how to determine the objective validity of any scientific conclusions whatever.

As Paul R. Gross and Norman Levitt have aptly observed, if we accept

Latour's notion of science as a form of conflict resolution rather than as the investigation of truth, 'we must believe that William Harvey's view of the circulation of the blood prevailed over that of his critics not because blood flows from the heart through the arteries and returns to the heart through the veins, but because Harvey was able to construct a "representation" and wheedle a place for it among the accepted conventions of the savants!'[14]

Beneath much of the 'analysis' in Latour's postmodernist engagement with science, he seems to be intent on trying to deny science's ability to understand the natural world but conceivably to a denial of the validity of reason itself. This deprecation of science can easily pass over into theism, a conclusion to which wandering minds at the end of the twentieth century seem to be particularly vulnerable.

The anti-scientific literature is almost too diverse to categorize with any subtlety. Given its mixed messages and its appeal to various constituencies, much of it is blissfully contradictory from book to book, chapter to chapter, even page to page. Some feminists have tried to genderize everything from algebra to biology, with results that verge on the hilarious. Spiritualists and mystics have tried to place science in the service of largely religious ends, even as their theistic brothers and sisters flatly condemn science as *the* source of the 'disenchantment' of humanity and the natural world. Still others confuse what science *is* with the fact that science is often *used* for ends that are patently destructive, such as weapons research and the exploitation of labor. Epistemological anarchists, too, have edged their way into this terrain, denying that science has any valid rational grounds and supporting an intellectual 'liberality' that verges on chaos – indeed, the more chaotic the better.

Among feminists who try to genderize science, rhetoric often seems to replace insight and intuition is often celebrated as a source of a chthonic wisdom to which males are more or less impervious. Maryanne Campbell and Randall K. Campbell-Wright have, for example, called for what they refer to as a 'feminist algebra', which involves no advance beyond existing algebraic studies but rather demands a restatement of problems in college algebra textbooks that presumably involve 'gender stereotypes' and where 'mathematics is portrayed as a woman whose nature desires to be the conquered Other'. As a corrective, students should be asked to calculate how 'Sue and Debbie', a lesbian couple, will finance their new home, rather than 'Tom and Debbie'. Whether rewriting textbook questions in this manner will induce female students to take a greater interest in algebra is arguable; but to assume that using female names can lure women into solving logical problems that they otherwise resent entertaining is not without aspects demeaning to women.[15]

The now-abundant literature on uniquely female ways of thinking, living, feeling, and understanding might well make women seem like the overly sensitive beings that Victorian males and patriarchs of old regarded them. Rather than segregate women into a ghetto, this traditionally patriarchal image of their capabilities must be dispensed with altogether. What is troubling is that far too many self-styled 'feminists' not only allow for these updated Victorian stereotypes but actually celebrate them!

The nine co-authors of the Biology and Gender Study Group, for example, regard scientific depictions of mammalian fertilization as gender-biased. Sperm, after all, are portrayed as active, while the egg is supine and passive. In such masculinized biology, the study group observes, 'the fertilizing sperm is a hero who survives while others perish, a soldier, a shard of steel, a successful suitor, and the cause of movement in the egg. The ovum is a passive victim, a whore, and finally, a proper lady whose fulfillment is attained.'[16] Such interpretations bring the quarrel between dogmatic feminists and the masculine world down to the cytological level, where epithets like *victim* and *whore* verge on the ridiculous – and are actually cheapened in meaning. Reductions of patriarchy to gynecology did indeed exist in earlier times, but such views have long since perished, and what fragments remain of them are under serious assault. Indeed, the majority of new students in American medical schools are now female. It is hard to imagine that women find any comfort in learning, as David Freeman puts it in the June 1992 issue of *Discover,* that there is an 'aggressive egg', one that, 'pins [a spermatazoon] down in spite of its efforts to escape', then 'yanks' it in, engaging in what some might compare to rape.

Equally silly are the attempts to genderize physics and chemistry – and in the process lessen their validity as serious disciplines. These attempts are often made on epistemological grounds. Women, some feminist ideologues argue, have a deeper, more organic, intuitional, and neurosensitive apparatus for understanding the cosmos, in contrast to males who are mechanistic, 'logocentric', and rather dull neurologically. Accordingly, women view physical reality with insights that are alien to their gender counterparts. Such views have nourished the revived appreciation of Hermetic and Gnostic 'wisdom', occult, magical, and mystical notions that date back to ancient times.

Carolyn Merchant's *Death of Nature: Women, Ecology, and the Scientific Revolution* has done more to stimulate this interest than any single book in recent memory.[17] Finding that the rise of science, industrial capitalism, and modern patriarchy was historically accompanied by a decline in a more female-oriented, nature-friendly culture, Merchant expresses strong affinities for prescientific cosmologies, which were among those more 'feminine' and 'ecological' outlooks. What we learn from Merchant is that 'the Scientific Revolution' is an 'ideology of "power over nature"', an ontology of interchangeable atomic and human parts, and a methodology of "penetration" into her [first nature's] innermost secrets.'[18] Thus to *know* first nature, to 'probe' the 'secrets' of the natural world, becomes an enterprise more like rape than discovery – let alone discoveries that could benefit humanity and the rest of first nature as well.

This drama has its villains and heroes – and the book gives precarious interpretations of their views, with considerable equivocation. Its most notorious villain is Francis Bacon, whose 'science' is basically demonical – fixated on technology and the 'rape of the Earth', to use the parlance of ecofeminism. Merchant 'deconstructs' Bacon from a late-twentieth-century vantage point as a brutal misogynist for seeking to 'wrest' the 'secrets' of a feminine 'Nature' as though 'She' were a witch subjected to the tortures of the Inquisition. If Bacon's call for scientific experimentation is entangled with the mechanical torture of witches, we have reasons to doubt that this view can really be supported; unlike witch prosecutors on the Continent, the English in Bacon's time did not subject women – or men – accused of witchcraft to mechanical torture, which has not prevented the sizable readership of Merchant's book from regarding Bacon as the archetypal scientist-misogynist.

That Bacon lived in an England riddled with hunger, superstition, brutality, an enormously high mortality rate, and the economic dispossession of its yeomanry; and that his *explicit* goal, so clearly revealed in his utopia, *The New Atlantis,* was the alleviation of poverty and the certainty of early death – problems which he hoped, with good reason, could be removed by technological advances and improved living conditions owing to the application of science to technics – all of this gains little, if any mention, in *The Death of Nature.* Nor does the fact that one of Merchant's heroes, Paracelsus, was an avowed misogynist who expressly disdained women.

Today, many key feminist voices deprecate science *qua* science, and indeed, 'masculine' forms of reason. Not only does this message echo traditional patriarchal images of women as brainless bundles of hormonally induced emotions who must invent uniquely female ways of knowing and innately possess 'organic wisdom', but these trends in feminism feed directly into anti-rationalism. Women who attend many American universities are being fed messages that divest them of the insights they need to deal with the uses – morally and social beneficent – to which scientific discoveries and rationality can be put. No less disturbing, antihumanist and postmodernist images of science are now associated with what remains of the Left, which in former years fervently heralded *scientific* as well as technological advances with the deep conviction that in a rational society they could be placed in the service of human freedom and used to diminish the impact of theism and superstition.

The general deprecation of science so rampant these days has not prevented many mystics from trying to bring twentieth-century science into conformity with various theisms or spiritualisms.

Perhaps among the most successful such effort, at least in terms of book sales, is Fritjof Capra's *Tao of Physics*.[19] Celebrating the extent to which modern physics conforms to mysticism, particularly the Eastern genres, the book has reached up to a million readers since its publication in 1975. Scientists – least of all Capra, who holds a doctorate from the University of Vienna and has done research in various highly regarded institutions around the world – should not be mistaken for science. As Latour has shown, they are people – and their heads may be filled with bizarre notions as well as sound truths. Thus it should not surprise us to learn that Niels Bohr, J. Robert Oppenheimer (the 'father' of the atom bomb), and Werner Heisenberg (whose relationship with Nazi military projects has yet to be clarified) believed that there were affinities between modern physics and Eastern religions. Einstein was a pantheist of a Spinozist variety – and quite a few Nobel prize winners were supporters of Nazi 'spirituality'. That brilliant scientists are sometimes ideological naifs tells us nothing about science as such.

Fritjof Capra, for example, is a mystic. The stated purpose of his work

> is to explore [the] relationship between concepts of modern physics and the basic ideas in the philosophical and religious traditions of the Far East. ... The two foundations of twentieth century physics – quantum theory and relatively theory – both force us to see the world very much in the way a Hindu, Buddhist or Taoist sees it, and how the similarity strengthens when we look at the recent attempts to combine these two theories in order to describe the phenomena of the submicroscopic world: the properties and interactions of the subatomic particles of which all matter is made.

Indeed, Capra finds wall-to-wall similarities between particle physics and mysticism: 'The parallels to modern physics appear not only in the *Vedas* of Hinduism, in the *I Ching,* or in the Buddhist *sutras,* but also in the fragments of Heraclitus, in the Sufism of Ibn Arabi, or in the teachings of the Yaqui sorcerer Don Juan.'[20]

If Capra had *failed* to meld quantum theory and relativity theory, given their sweeping generality, to such a sweeping array of mystical ideologies – with their many variations, nuances, and idiosyncrasies – it would have been a miracle. Modern physics does indeed defy commonsensical perception, and proponents of the mysticisms that Capra cites are all too ready to celebrate astonishing similarities. Like mystics, physicists are indeed 'now dealing with a nonsensory experience of reality' (although with sophisticated technical equipment).[21] And like mystics, physicists often do 'experience' the universe 'as a dynamic, inseparable whole which always includes the observer in an essential way' (although at different levels of organization).[22]

After parading his various Eastern religions – Hinduism, Buddhism, Chinese thought, Taoism, and Zen – Capra returns us to the 'Unity of All Things', 'Beyond the World of Opposites', and 'The Cosmic Dance', wherein he matches richly formulated truths or discoveries in particle and relativity physics with quotations from Eastern mystical texts, even when they read like metaphors rather than insights. In this eclectic jumble, the Eastern sages talk in vague phrases that often have multiple meanings, as befits most religious teachers, who normally hedge their statements lest a prophecy fail to materialize in reality. Meanwhile, Western physicists seem intent on providing *rational* explanations of their theories and discoveries with mathematical formulas and experiential evidence. It may help followers of the Tao to know that 'Man follows the laws of the earth; / Earth follows the laws of heaven; / Heaven follows the laws of *Tao;* / Tao follows the laws of its intrinsic nature,'[23] but it will hardly help them understand the insights of modern physics. In later years, Capra's *Turning Point: Science, Society and the Rising Culture*, published in 1982, went on to eclectically wed modern physics, Prigogine's systems theory of chemical dissipative structures, 'holistic' health, and solar energy – a bouquet of dubiously related areas of knowledge in which it would be hard to find at least *one* idea that did not constitute a palliative for our psychic discomforts.

One can, of course, try to reconcile modern science with a homemade theology that fits its advances. Thus: 'The breakdown of classical science and the rise of modern physics,' observes James W. Jones, 'provide resources for a new theology of nature.' And if Jones has his way, this will be theology with a vengeance.

> *The physical world is grounded in and arises out of the immaterial divine Spirit; events that make up the physical world are given their form by the free act of God; the universe is a unity in diversity. ... God's immanence is the presence of the Spirit within matter; his transcendence is his freedom to give the universe the form that it has (through the imposition of certain symmetries) and to constitute the events of the universe, not in a chaotic or arbitrary way, but as the product of free and careful choice by which one*

possibility among many is brought to fruition.[24]

On the whole, this Christological work with Spinozistic tendencies avowedly agrees with Capra's thesis on the oneness of the universe, although Jones seems eager to stress its diversity as well. More explicitly Christian and expressly antiscientific, Philip Sherrard warns us that 'man's sovereign faculty or organ of knowing it not the [sic] reason and ... his knowledge is not consequently confined to the sphere of the rational.' In addition to reason, he possesses a 'supra-rational faculty or organ, one through which he is capable of entering into direct communion with the divine, of experiencing directly spiritual or metaphysical realities, and so of knowing the truth or nature of each thing.'[25]

Where, then, have we gone wrong? Why have we failed to exercise our 'supra-rational faculty' for 'entering into direct communion with the divine' and experiencing reality directly? The snake in our garden is, of course, 'modern science', which 'presupposes a radical reshaping of our whole mental outlook. It involves a new approach to being, a new approach to nature, in short, a new philosophy.' We have been warped into believing that science 'represents a great break-through, a marvelous advance on the part of mankind, even a sign of our coming of age'.

But now that we are beginning 'to see the consequences of our capitulation to [science] – and we are only now beginning to see these consequences' – that is, our loss of direct communication with the divine and the natural, and – 'we are not so sure'. Among the 'fruits' of this misadventure, 'clear for all to see, and implicit in the philosophy on which it is based, is the dehumanization both of man and of the society that he has built in its name.'[26] Sherrard, let me emphasize, is no holy roller in a Chautauqua tent, nor a televangelist; more than half of his small book is based on lectures he gave at King's College, University of London, bespeaking respectability, authority, and intellectual probity.

No discussion of science and its travails would be complete, however, without taking into account Paul K. Feyerabend, whose anti-rationalism is so explicit and whose relativism is so extreme that his support for a methodological anarchism consists of little more than paeans to chaos in the realm of thought. Whether wittingly or not, Feyerabend establishes the premises for a universal ethical nihilism. Accordingly, his work, taken at its face value, would represent a hopeless dead end for 'scientific method' – or even scientific criteria.

The book that catapulted Feyerabend to public attention, *Against Method: Outline of an Anarchistic Theory of Knowledge,* published in 1975, advances a seemingly 'radical' critique of *any* method for determining scientific truth, and of any criteria for judging its validity.[27] Not that Feyerabend is against scientific method as such, any more than he is against scientific research. But he challenges its claim to exclusivity as a source of truth about the natural world.

In itself, this challenge would not be objectionable – or unusual – if Feyerabend had *seriously* explored other ways of pursuing knowledge in which scientific criteria may or may not have a place. E. A. Burtt's *The Metaphysical Foundations of Modern Science,* published in 1923, remains to this day an exemplary account of early science that unearths its metaphysical presuppositions with clarity and responsibility.[28] Similarly, various evolutionary schools of philosophy have explored approaches to the natural world that are more qualitative than the largely quantitative approach favored by most scientists – which is not to reject the enormous contributions that the physical sciences have made.

Nor do I wish to suggest that society does not exercise a major influence on the areas of research that scientists emphasize or the strategies they adopt in studying them. Quite to the contrary: scientists are not asocial beings, immunized from social life as a whole in their laboratories. The considerable attention given to mechanics as a field of investigation in sixteenth- and seventeenth-century Italy, for example, cannot be divorced from Mediterranean society's growing need for machinery, for artillery whose accuracy required a better knowledge of the trajectory of cannonballs, and for better fortification, as the notebooks and letters of Leonardo da Vinci reveal. Similarly, in the nineteenth century the development of theories of biological evolution stimulated a more developmental approach to phenomena that had been preceded not only by Lamarck and by Hegel. Nor can we ignore the social uses to which scientific theories have been put, as social Darwinism and all its wormy offspring attest.

Nor are scientists immune to dogmas of their own. But scientific criteria still require *experimentation and proof,* irrespective of the *way* in which scientists formulate hypotheses. *How* scientists arrive at their hypotheses is an interesting subject for psychological investigation, but it has no decisive bearing on whether their hypotheses can be validated, or on whether scientists are dealing with *facts* rather than chimerical illusions.

Feyerabend radically shifts the ground of these central issues. Although he tries to show that there is no fixed way to formulate a particular hypothesis – an issue that by itself is rather trite – his account of *why* one proof is accepted in preference to another is often arbitrary. Science becomes a playground for all kinds of ideas. This arena could be highly creative, but in the anarchic 'marketplace of ideas' that he celebrates, a crystal-gazer, a fortune-teller, and a shaman who offers occult explanations have no less standing in principle than a scientist who offers a carefully reasoned explanation of a phenomenon and proof of its soundness.

In the mundane world of everyday life, to substitute mystical numerology for trigonometry in constructing the steel frame of a building would lead to catastrophe. There is nothing like practice – and the results it yields – to decide the truth of an approach. Doubtless, broad areas of research and knowledge involve a great deal of speculation, like the origin and structure of the universe and problems in quantum mechanics. But if a crystal-gazer's intuitions and rational inquiry are equally valid 'methods', reason has no special claim over divination. The 'ecstatic trances' of Rabbi Akiba, according to Feyerabend, yield *'genuine observations* once we decide to accept his way of life as a measure of reality, and his mind is as independent of his body as the chosen observations tell him.'[29]

This is accepting a lot indeed, notably a Nietzschean perspectivism, which could validate any view once 'we decide' to accept *any* 'way of life as a measure of reality'. It is no caricature of this line of reasoning to say that once we accept Torquemada's 'way of life as a measure of reality', the Spanish Inquisition also yielded 'genuine observations' – and results. In fact, given Feyerabend's radical relativism, who is to say which observations are and which are not 'genuine'?

When advised that science 'works', Feyerabend anemically replies that 'it often fails and many success stories are rumours, not facts.'[30] This Feyerabendian legerdemain simply side-steps a problem with which he apparently cannot cope – namely, that a science that *does not work* is eventually, often quickly, discarded, which alas is not true of many other self-styled 'disciplines'.

Nor does Feyerabend clarify very much by asserting that 'the efficiency of science is determined by criteria that belong to the scientific tradition and thus cannot be regarded as objective judges' – a sheer sophism that tells us nothing about the fact that science, when it is correct, *must work in practice* if it is to retain its legitimacy. This observation should make us wonder why the Rabbi Akiba's visions should be regarded as reliable 'once we decide to accept his way of life as reality', to repeat Feyerabend's case for the venerable sage. If we accept Stalin or Hitler's 'way of life as reality', on what ground can one complain about the horrors of the gulag or the monstrosities of Auschwitz?

Cannily, Feyerabend immunizes himself to critical evaluation by avowedly refusing to take himself seriously. The guiding maxim of *Against Method* can be summed up as (in the author's phrase), 'anything goes'. This maxim is apparently meant to express militantly Feyerabend's judgment that 'the idea of a fixed method, or of a fixed theory of *rationality*, rests on too naive a view of man and his social surroundings.'[31]

Yet *Against Method* is not without a certain 'methodology' of its own: that of grossly overstating the views against which Feyerabend often directs his criticisms. The 'fixed' methods and 'fixed' theories of rationality that bother Feyerabend are by no means as 'fixed' in the minds of scientists and rationalists as Feyerabend would have us believe. Science and reason have been extraordinarily open to variation and change: they have been among the most liberating forces in a history plagued by fanatical dogmatism and superstition. Indeed, Feyerabend demolishes straw arguments when he deals with 'fixities' in scientific *method* that are ostensibly sacrosanct but are transgressed in actual research – which in no way challenges the scientific *criterion* that proof is the ultimate arbiter of truth.

Nor is Feyerabend's 'method' free of social influences in its own right. By the 1970s, in fact, almost anything *did* 'go' in Berkeley, California, Feyerabend's academic habitat in the United States, where the 'counterculture' carried idiosyncratic behavior and irrationalism to the point of absurdity – with a great deal of public approval. Today, in fact, 'anything goes' in epidemic proportions, as anyone who visits a bookstore or dials a 'telemystic's 900 number will quickly determine. Feyerabend's guiding maxim places superstition, Rabbi Akiba's 'ecstatic trances', and even outright shamanism – like Carlos Castanada's visions of 'reality' as expressed in *The Teachings of Don Juan* – on an equal footing with scientific criteria. Feyerabend's work, in effect, is a socially conditioned account of the 'deconstruction' of science and reason in a mystical milieu, demolishing simplistic 'fixities' by using Dadaesque rhetoric rather than intellectual firepower. This seemingly provocative endeavor – so very much attuned to sociocultural changes in the Californian 'scene' – is more sensationalistic than informative and, worse, is often misleading.

In the first place, Feyerabend is not an anarchist, as he observes in a rather confusing footnote. Anarchism 'as it has been practised in the past and as it is being practised today by an ever increasing number of people has features I am not prepared to support,' he explains uneasily. 'It cares little for human lives and human happiness (except for the lives and the happiness of those who belong to some special group); and it contains precisely the kind of Puritanical dedication and seriousness which I detest' – except, Feyerabend adds, for 'some exquisite exceptions such as [Daniel] Cohn-Bendit, but they are in the minority.'[32]

To anyone who lived in 1960s and 1970s Berkeley and was not confined to a hermetic ivory tower, this portrayal of the anarchic, often highly personalistic tendencies that wafted through New Left and the 'counterculture' in 1975, around the time *Against Method* was written, is a gross misconception. A sizable corps of lifestyle anarchists were abandoning the socialistic content that serious social anarchists like Michael Bakunin and Peter Kropotkin had claimed for their anti-authoritarian beliefs and were preoccupied with their own egos and desires. Feyerabend's view of Cohn-Bendit, moreover, is very naive. 'Red Danny's' commitment to anarchic ideas was always tenuous and he is currently fulfilling his new ideals as a *realo* or pragmatically oriented officeholder in the German Green Party. Finally, Feyerabend's observations reveal that too often his 'antimethodological' technique consists of tossing off irresponsible remarks and judgments *ex cathedra*, as though his own assertion of an idea were sufficient to give it validity.

In fact, the very essence of a Feyerabendian contention is its notable lack of seriousness and responsibility. Far from being an 'anarchist', Feyerabend, as it turns out, confesses he is *really* a Dadaist, who is 'utterly unimpressed by any serious enterprise', who 'smells a rat whenever people stop smiling and assume that attitude and those facial expressions which indicate that something important is about to be said. A Dadaist is convinced that a worthwhile life will arise only when we start taking things *lightly*. ... It is for these reasons that I now prefer to use the term *Dadaism*' to designate his beliefs.[33] Alas, we would do well to take many enterprises very seriously these days, and there is no reason why anyone should care a fig for the facial expressions with which they are undertaken. Feyerabend's own Dadaesque cuteness begins to wear thin, in fact, when he often delivers his harangues with extraordinary and labored seriousness, indeed, with a dense complexity that renders them very inaccessible to the general reader.

The paradox that suffuses Feyerabend's *Against Method* is that its author insistently wants us to take him *very* seriously indeed, particularly when he impugns 'fixed' ideas, while at the same time he claims to be a happy-go-lucky bon vivant in the realm of ideas. Feyerabend, in effect, wants to have his cake and eat it too. His criticisms of 'method' are very challenging indeed – and if they are found to be flawed, their author cannot be permitted to saucily hide behind a Dadaesque veil to avoid the challenges they are obliged to confront.

Yet, surprisingly, almost everything in *Against Method* that has historical importance was explored more significantly by Kuhn, such as the problems of how and why Ptolemaic cosmology gave way to Copernican cosmology and Aristotelian mechanics to Galilean mechanics. Feyerabend is at pains to advise us, as Kuhn, Latour and their confrères have done, that scientists use every 'trick' they can to advance our knowledge of the world, in contrast to conventional claims that they are 'systematic' in their formulations of hypotheses.

Moreover, Feyerabend, no less than Kuhn, is oriented toward psychology. His emendations of Kuhn tend to be more dizzying in their details than enlightening in their substance. His knowledge of science is so highly selective and esoteric that he seems to know a great deal about details, but surprisingly little about the overall picture which they yield when viewed together and coherently.

But the 'Copernican revolution' and its spinoffs are not reducible to matters of psychology nor do they allow for Dadaesque pirouettes. Galileo's defense of the Copernican world view occurred at a time when astronomy was still embattled with the Church and trying to establish itself against theological dogma. Far from involving a mere difference in 'perspectives', the conflict opposed radically different approaches to *facts* about the nature of reality as well as the means for ascertaining them.

Similarly, when Darwin advanced his theory of evolution based on natural selection, science was still embattled with religion and superstition. The storm that followed the publication of *The Origin of Species,* and later, *The Descent of Man,* pitted rationality against faith, fact against illusion, and above all, conflicting ways of determining truth – in short, objective investigation and verification against mere tradition. By the time science came into its own at the end of the last century, Kuhn's revolutionary 'paradigm shifts' were less stormy; indeed, they were extraordinarily placid compared with those times when science had yet to establish itself as truth rather than the work of Lucifer.

Generally, the emergence of science as a basic form of ascertaining truth in contrast to the claims of religion can be slighted only by risking a regression into superstition and cultural barbarism. What Feyerabend has to explain is the historical unevenness of these advances, not examine them as though they are intellectual artifacts that have no social context or history. Thus, to place the problems that confronted Galileo and those that confronted Einstein on a 'level playing field', as though scientific criteria that had yet to be accepted four centuries ago were confronted with the same problems they encounter today, is to parody history and battles long overcome. If anything, there are 'paradigm shifts' that happen so rapidly today that scientists scarcely have the time to assimilate a new one before anomalies have accumulated to produce the need for another one, as witness recent developments in cosmology.

As a historian, Feyerabend is essentially a postmodernist. He is no different in his treatment of data than Theodore Zelden is in his treatment of history, which presumably attempts to liberate the past from such annoying constraints as dates, causal accounts of events, discussions of class, and even the confines of nationality. In a somewhat similar vein, Hayden White turns history into an atemporal aesthetic that views conventional events in the past as mere 'texts' in the present.

Feyerabend's other complaints against 'methodologists' are trite. Thus: '[s]cientific investigation, says [Karl] Popper, *starts* with a problem and proceeds by *solving* it,' we are told solemnly. One need not be an admirer of Karl Popper to see that this statement is a cliché. But for Feyerabend, Popper's 'characterization does not consider that problems may be wrongly formulated' – how, if 'anything goes,' can he know this? – 'that one may inquire about properties of things and processes which later views declare to be non-existent' – again, how can he be *sure* of this? 'Problems of this kind are not *solved*,' he adds, 'they are *dissolved* and removed from the domain of legitimate inquiry'[34] – which provides us with more wordplay than insight.

In fact, there is a certain measure of intellectual demagoguery, here, which not even a claimed affinity for the disordering strategy of Dadaism excuses. I have no doubt that Popper understood only too well that problems must be correctly formulated before they can be solved; indeed, that problems raised by the notion of the Earth's absolute velocity were 'dissolved' by relativity theory, an example that in no way challenges how Popper or any rational person views the 'problem'.

It is hardly stunning to learn that 'changes of ontology … are often accompanied by *conceptual changes*', as Feyerabend thumpingly declares.[35] Such clichés, often elaborated with references to both known and virtually unknown figures in the history of science, abound throughout Feyerabend's works and are woven into badly written, *very* serious, esoteric, and intramural arguments that are annoyingly at odds with his pretensions to be a flippant, light-hearted, and ever-charming Dadaist.

Nor does the sound and fury generated by Feyerabend justify seeing science as a parochial dogma that somehow oppresses us all. In fact, science demands very much of itself – factual verifiability and rational speculation – to ever become dogmatized, however much its results are misused. For Feyerabend to tremble before the prospect of scientific abuses without telling us that scientific results are grossly misused in the modern world, most particularly by the corporate and political powers that control it, is to raise a problem that is as feckless as his asocial interpretations of scientific history. Nor is it news to learn, as Feyerabend tells us, that endless frauds have been perpetrated in the name of science. Stalin's Trofim Lysenko is no more evidence of the failings of genetics, as Feyerabend suggests, than Himmler's Josef Mengele is evidence of the failings of modern medicine.

Indeed, science is today more democratic in its tolerance of heterodoxy and more naturalistic in its criteria for proof than any other body of ideas around. For all the antihumanist complaints that science exercises too much power over the human mind, it stands almost alone in its commitment to an ingrained naturalism and free exchange of ideas. It was one of the earliest modern exemplars of the democratic spirit in the modern world. The scientific societies that emerged in England in the seventeenth century, followed rapidly by others on the Continent and in America, were generally open to anyone of any social class, based on the merit of their work and the extent of their achievements. Van Leeuwenhoek, for example, who as a mere lensmaker would hardly qualify for an appearance at the British court, was more than welcome in the British Royal Society, as were men of comparable stature. Debate was more open and free, fact was more earnestly accepted over opinion, than in any other institutions in the European world. The 'commoner' Benjamin Franklin was respected both for his scientific studies and for his social ideas, and he was greeted with no condescension by his scientific peers, whatever their social class and political beliefs. That this democracy and naturalism ultimately rest on stern evidence rather than hazy sentiment − 'cold' as science may seem in its claims to objectivity − is nonetheless a primary bulwark against superstition, ideological tyranny, and mysticism today. Its edifice, for all its social difficulties, should not be challenged on ideologically tendentious and 'methodologically' flippant grounds − least of all by injunctions like 'anything goes'.

All of this brings us to what seems to be Feyerabend's basic complaint: the ills of Western reason. The rationalist claim that 'human beings are rational animals', he reminds us, is merely 'one view among many'. There is also, we are told,

> the view that humans are misfits in the material world, unable to understand their position and their purpose and 'with a distinctive need' for salvation; there is the view, closely related to the one just mentioned, that humans consist of a divine spark enclosed in an earthen vessel, a 'trace of gold embedded in dirt' as the Gnostics were in the habit of saying, 'with the distinctive need' for liberation by faith. And these are not just abstract and 'capricious' views − they have been, and still are, part of the lives of millions of people.[36]

In the Feyerabendian world, these views are all equally valid, including Don Juan's alleged visions and Rabbi Akiba's ecstatic experiences. Reason, in Feyerabend's view, is merely one tradition among many to which he extends an earnest farewell.

Indeed: '[b]eing a tradition, [reason] is neither good nor bad, it simply *is*,' Feyerabend observes in *Science and a Free Society*, a summing-up that expresses all that is repellent about postmodernism. 'The same applies to *all* traditions – they are neither good nor bad, they simply are. They become good or bad (rational/irrational; pious/impious; advanced/"primitive"; humanitarian/vicious; etc.) only when looked at from the point of view of some other tradition.'[37]

From this expression of amoral subjectivity, Feyerabend goes on to declare:

> *'Objectively' there is not much to choose between anti-semitism and humanitarianism. But racism will appear vicious to a humanitarian while humanitarianism will appear vapid to a racist. Relativism (in the old and simple sense of Protagoras) gives an adequate account of the situation which thus emerges. Powerful traditions that have means of forcing others to adopt their ways have of course little use for the relational character of value judgements (and the philosophers who defend them are helped by some rather elementary logical mistakes) and they can make their victims forget it as well (this is called 'education'). But let the victims get more power, let them revive their own traditions and the apparent superiority will disappear like a (good or bad – depending on the tradition) dream.*[38]

Let me note that these remarks, which reduce ethical issues to a power game between equally subjective 'traditions' that merely 'are', can no longer be regarded as a product of a naive relativism. Despite Feyerabend's denunciations of the inhumanities of our time, they provide the groundwork for a cynicism that reduces every ethical outlook to a matter of taste. The 'prevalence' of one ethical judgment over another depends upon the power it can exercise – socially as well as intellectually. Like Jean Baudrillard's capitulation to social and cultural conditions as they are, Feyerabend, with his anarchistic epistemology, leaves his readers to an amoral vacuum in which 'anything goes' – including, by his own admission, anti-Semitism and racism. And if 'anything goes' in this battle between racism and humanitarianism, Feyerabend's ethically neutral maxim supports the side that wins.

It is not the enlightened Protagoras who is speaking through Feyerabend's mouth, but rather Plato's caricature of the crude sophist in the First Book of *The Republic,* notably Thrasymachus – whose view was that 'might is right'.

Notes

1 Hence I do not use the words *sociology* or *psychology* as more than theoretical speculations. Like philosophy, they clearly have a place in the development of knowledge, but sciences they definitely are not. My respect for theoretical speculation, which also occurs in the 'hard sciences', is immense and I would not want to deflate its importance. What is disquieting, however, is the pretension that social theorizing can produce the kind of compelling laws that physicists and chemists formulate. Doubtless sociometrics, like Emile Durkheim's study of suicide, closely resembles a scientific endeavor and occupies a gray zone between the natural sciences and social theories. But the more sweeping claims to certainty made by so-called 'social scientists', such as Karl Mannheim or Talcott Parsons, are actually a form of speculative theoretics that cannot claim to have the kind of rigor demanded of a physicist.

2 Thomas S. Kuhn, *The Structure of Scientific Revolutions* (Chicago: University of Chicago Press, 1962; enlarged 1970).

3 Paul Hoyningen-Huene, *Reconstructing Scientific Revolutions: Thomas S. Kuhn's Philosophy of Science*, trans. Alexander T. Levine (Chicago and London: University of Chicago Press, 1993), p. xv.

4 Kuhn, *Structure,* p. viii.

5 *Ibid.*, p. vi.

6 Bruno Latour and Steve Woolgar, *Laboratory Life: The Construction of Scientific Facts,* 2nd ed. (Princeton: Princeton University Press, 1986); originally published in 1979.

7 *Ibid.*, p. 27.

8 *Ibid.*, p. 28, emphasis added.

9 *Ibid.*, p. 243, emphasis added.

10 *Ibid.*, p. 257.

11 *Ibid.*, p. 284.

12 *Ibid.*, p. 285.

13 Bruno Latour, *Science in Action: How to Follow Scientists and Engineers Through Society* (Cambridge, Mass.: Harvard University Press, 1985), p. 258.

14 Paul R. Gross and Norman Levitt, *Higher Superstition: The Academic Left and Its Quarrels with Science* (Baltimore and London: Johns Hopkins University Press, 1994), p. 58. The word *academic* should be emphasized in the title of this book; neither of the authors, a biologist and a mathematician respectively, seems to be launching yet another wearisome attack upon the left as such but basically its well-heeled, postmodernist mutation of the 1990s. However, they do tend to drift toward conservative positions, even singing the praise of Martin Lewis – a former radical ecologist who is now an apologist for capitalism – in reaction to the idiocies of the pseudo-'leftist' postmodernists in the American academy.

15 Mary Anne Campbell and Randall K. Campbell-Wright: 'Toward A Feminist Algebra', paper presented to the Mathematical Association of America (n.d.); cited in Gross and Levitt, *Higher Superstition,* p. 120.

16 *Ibid.*, p. 120.

17 Carolyn Merchant, *The Death of Nature: Women, Ecology and the Scientific Revolution* (San Francisco: Harper & Row, 1980).

18 *Ibid.*, p. 295.

19 Fritjof Capra, *The Tao of Physics: An Exploration of the Parallels Between Modern Physics and Eastern Mysticism* (Berkeley: Shambhala, 1975).

20 *Ibid.*, pp. 18–19.

21 *Ibid.*, p. 51.

22 *Ibid.*, p. 81.

23 *Ibid.*, p. 289.

24 James W. Jones, *The Redemption of Matter: Toward the Rapprochement of Science and Religion* (Lanham, MD, and London: University Press of America, 1984), pp. 131–2.

25 Philip Sherrard, *The Rape of Man and Nature: An Enquiry into the Origins and Consequences of Modern Science* (Ipswich, Suffolk: Golgonooza Press, 1987), p. 53.

26 *Ibid.*, pp. 63–4.

27 Paul Feyerabend, *Against Method: Outline of an Anarchistic Theory of Knowledge* (London: New Left Books, 1975).

28 E. A. Burtt, *The Metaphysical Foundations of Modern Science* (New York: Doubleday Anchor Books, 1923).

29 Feyerabend, *Against Method*, p. 190.

30 Paul Feyerabend, *Farewell to Reason* (London: Verso, 1987), p. 296.

31 Feyerabend, *Against Method*, pp. 27–8, emphasis added.

32 *Ibid.*, p. 21, note 12.

33 *Ibid.*

34 *Ibid.*, p. 274.

35 *Ibid.*, p. 275.

36 Feyerabend, *Farewell to Reason*, pp. 301–2.

37 Paul K. Feyerabend, *Science in a Free Society* (London: New Left Books, 1978), p. 8, emphasis added.

38 *Ibid.*, pp. 8–9.

CHAPTER 9

Re-enchanting humanity

To the extent that space and possibly the patience of the reader allow, I have tried to critically examine an historic shift away from the Enlightenment to an antihumanist outlook that incorporates a postmodernist celebration of mysticism and anti-rationalism, and very significantly, a subsuming of any social issues, intellectual critique, and moral criteria by a crude biologism of one kind or another.

By no means is my account of this shift complete; there are far too many antihumanisms abroad for me to include them all. Nor is it clear what forms this shift will take in the years ahead. As we have seen, major antihumanist tendencies seek in varying degrees to reduce human behavior to the morality of the gene, and human beings to intelligent fleas that feed on a mystified Gaia, or to fruit flies competing with each other in a mindless biological struggle over limited means of life in the macabre play of Malthusian demographics.

I have tried to give the reader a critical view of the explicitly antihumanistic notions of mystical ecology that abound today, and of a regressive primitivism predicated on a hatred of civilization as such and of science and technology in particular, both of which are commonly regarded as the principal causal factors in producing the pathologies of what antihumanists and postmodernists dismiss as modernity.

There is, to be sure, nothing new about a rise of interest in religion during times of crisis and personal disempowerment: it is the perennial palliative of a society in decline. Hence it is not surprising that one of the fastest-growing products on the market today, possibly second only to television sets and VCRs, is religion. What is dizzying is the rapidity with which this vast ideological counterrevolution has occurred. Within a span of less than twenty-five years, I have seen (as have many older readers of this book) a militant if theatrical social radicalism, influenced by anarchic and cultural socialists, give way to a political quietism that is almost unprecedented in this century. A new wisdom of passively dwelling and 'be-ing' on Gaia has defused social protest and revolutionary visions. The cry 'the personal is the political' has been reversed to read 'the political is the personal'. Where the former once linked the fate of the individual to the broader society and called for social intervention as a form of personal realization, the latter has displaced the social by the personal and calls for social withdrawal as a form of personal redemption.

What do nostrums that draw from an ostensibly scientific field like sociobiology have in common with postmodernism, whose adherents often exhibit an aversion for reason? Indeed, in what way can seemingly science-based nostrums with roots in genetics and demographics be linked to mythic if not religious cults like angelology?

However different they may be in specific respects, the one feature that these antihumanisms share is what developmentally oriented philosophers would call their lack of mediations. By mediations, I mean that their thinking lacks the *phased* and *articulated* unfoldings that reflect and articulate developmental processes in the real world. From the very outset, antihumanists think, feel, and sense phenomena immediately, directly, intuitively – and reductively. Whereas the immediate is elemental, simple, initial, and given, the mediated is the result of a *development,* the ascertainable phase of a continuum. Yet mediations are also distinctive, delineable, and 'determinate', to use philosophical language – phases that lend themselves to conceptual clarity and rational interpretation. To antihumanists, reflection, ideation, and the processual determinations that enter into the apprehension of a phenomenon pollute its 'authenticity'. However much antihumanists may disagree with one another on a variety of issues, in varying degrees they try to grasp phenomena in their 'pure' and reductively primal 'be-ing', free from the 'imposition' of rational categories – all of which, to one degree or another, stand in the way of grasping the 'authenticity' of phenomena. I am not using terms like 'being' and 'authenticity', so basic to Heidegger's philosophical vocabulary, in a Heideggerian sense here; the truth is that I have no choice but to use this language, since there are no satisfactory synonyms for these words.

Thus, fundamental to the morality of the gene, the dynamics of populations, the cybernetics of the Gaia hypothesis, the allegedly unspoiled attributes of primitive society, the fear of technology and science as such, and the rejection of reason is a devotion to *primality*. It is upon genes, populations dynamics, the primitive, and an uncomplicated technics that any discussion of philosophical, ecological, and social issues is anchored.

Their unmediated primality does not prevent antihumanists from exploding with wild speculations about the present and the future, but they are dismally minimalist. For antihumanists, the origins or substrate of things, from genes to the 'Big Bang', from reproductive behavior to a primal 'Cosmic Self' often radically determines what those things are. Results are confused with their origins. A minimalism of the thinnest kind is the surest way to 'get in touch' with one's 'feelings' and with the world, particularly a natural world conceived as virginal and unspoiled.

If genes determine many, perhaps most of our actions and values, culture is merely an artificial impediment that improperly redirects our 'inner self' away from doing what our molecular fundaments demand. In the face of Gaia's cosmic dictates, moreover, we wane into biological insignificance. Indeed, we taint our own capacity for self-realization if we intervene beyond the imperatives of meeting our simplest needs, in the larger Self of which we are mere constituents. Inasmuch as we are no more than animals, we can increase our numbers geometrically like fruit flies, but our means of life increase arithmetically, which presumably explains why we have the ecological and social dislocations that plague us. Worse still, technologies have an 'imperative' of their own. One technological innovation blindly leads to another until an industrial revolution emerges to befoul streams, oceans, and air, deforesting the planet, desiccating the soil, and warming the globe.

Having shed our primal 'Paleolithic sensibility', we are degraded creatures, intervening as we do in a once-pristine Nature. The gaps we have opened between our 'natural' past and our 'industrial' civilization must be closed by returning to the same primal harmony that shaped the behavior of our remote ancestors. How far back we have to go – whether to the dictates of our 'moral' or 'wise' genes, to the impulses of our hominid animality, to the foraging psyche of Paleolithic hunters, to the presumed pacifism of rustic Neolithic matriarchies, or to the various behavioral patterns of a simple preindustrial and prescientific past – is negotiable.

Like it or not, Heidegger has done more than any thinker in this century, however indirectly, to provide us with the vocabulary, prelapsarian mentality, and spirituality for this unmediated orientation toward reality. In large measure, the imagery of an unmediated world in which we are 'One' with first nature and with each other in 'interconnections' that dissolve our individuality, selfhood, and rationality in a black hole of antimodernism can be attributed to him, however unfamiliar many contemporary antihumanists are with his writings.

This antihumanist outlook is by no means as harmless as it may seem. In fact, disturbing consequences follow from any philosophy of immediacy.

The first one is the abolition of *history* – the denial of history's reality, importance, unity, and meaning. Our evolution out of first nature and beyond primal forms of association is viewed as a 'Fall': a steady loss of our pristine animality (including our responsiveness to genetic and demographic imperatives), a corruption of our hominid sensibilities (which, we are repeatedly advised, were shaped over two or three million years by a Paleolithic 'hunting' way of life), a descent from our 'direct' communication with first nature into (variously) agriculture, urbanity, advanced technology, and science, and finally our objectification and massification by quasi-mystical technological 'imperatives'. Thus was the edenic Golden Age of the Paleolithic superseded by the Silver Age of the Neolithic, the Bronze Age of fortress cities, and the Iron Age of industrial civilization.

This succession of ages represents not history in the sense of a progressive development away from primality but an atrophying, a steady erosion, a regressive undoing of our 'inner nature'. Civilization raises ever more mediations – impediments to our genetic, demographic, ecological, 'presencing', and intuitive awareness of our 'Oneness' with the animal world, first nature, Gaia, or the cosmos. True self-fulfilment lies in plumbing the bosom of our origins – whatever their depths – in a preconceived harmony that constitutes our 'authentic' destiny. History is merely a series of 'narratives' at best, each of which has no meaning, or a fall at worst, one that portends the apocalyptic destruction of the biosphere and ourselves.

I do not claim that all antihumanists hold this precise constellation of beliefs. Many would hesitate to condemn civilization or even science and technology as such; still others would not want to sacrifice the benefits they enjoy as a result of technological innovation, such as their computers, cameras, binoculars, and fax machines. But a growing number of antihumanists do hold all the views I have described and, in fact, are more consistent in following the logic of their beliefs than their half-hearted colleagues.

On social issues, moreover, antihumanists share commonalities that cannot be ignored. If there is no 'unitary' history, there can be no *progress*. This denial of progress does not prevent antihumanists from insisting that history has directionality – that is, a vast *regress* in human affairs. The notion that a rational infrastructure, so to speak, can be discerned in history (despite the terrible failings, even horrors, that mark its course) in which human intellectuality *does* become more sophisticated, ethics *does* become more responsive to protesting oppressions and social afflictions, art *does* become more sensitive to the human condition, society *does* become more secular, and knowledge *is* increasingly guided by thoughtful reflection and the criteria of proof – all of these developments are denied by antihumanists or fractured into episodic narratives, each of which is dealt with relativistically, as though it had a life of its own apart from the whole.

The very concept of advances in ideas, values, political ideals, social systems, productive power, and insights is eschewed for episodic events, for constellations of 'local' or 'discontinuous' phenomena, to use Foucauldian terms. The notion of a meaningful history of humanity that includes an ascent from primality to complexity, indeed from animality to increasing humanity, is displaced by mere *chronicles* that consist mainly of anecdotal events and particularistic cultural phenomena.

Having dispensed with the very idea of progress – even with criteria for judging what is and is not progressive – antihumanism leaves us at sea, bereft of any notion of civilization. Inasmuch as the fall of humanity refers more often to these chronicles than to any progressive ascent, human beings are little more than alienated beings who are the makers as well as the victims of a technocratic world, the product of their own hubris, rationality, and innate greediness or aggressiveness rooted in their genetic makeup, according to sociobiologists, or in their technically oriented culture, according to most postmodernists.

However distant many of the authors I have discussed may be from popular culture, Nietzsche, Heidegger, Foucault, and Derrida speak to millions of people today through the impresarios of widely viewed television documentaries, such as Bill Moyers, David Suzuki, and Desmond Morris. These impresarios themselves may have very little acquaintance with antihumanist philosophers, but in an era of dark pessimism, the public appetite for antihumanistic messages is growing rapidly. The close proximity, indeed, the conflation, of antihumanist campus thinkers with Yuppie-type New Age ideologies is remarkable. Shoddy antihumanistic or antimodernist journalists who may never have read a line of Nietzsche, Heidegger, Foucault, or Derrida regale us with books that define human beings as mere 'dwellers' on the planet who must recover their primal 'authenticity' by 'deconstructing' civilization, denying putative 'myths' of progress, and 'decentering' human claims to uniqueness. We are derided for our 'logocentry', 'ethnocentricity', 'anthropocentricity', 'Eurocentricity', or – for white males – 'phallocentricity'.

In calling for the 're-enchanting' of humanity, I refer – playfully – to the importance of recognizing humanity's *potentiality* for creating a rational, ecologically oriented, aesthetically exciting, and deeply humane world based on an ethics of complementarity and a society of sharing.

I use the word *potentiality* advisedly. The conventional way of exploring phenomena – through what I call conventional reason or conventional logic – is to intellectually carve out a realm of experience and subject it to close analysis. Given a particular object, we take it apart, so to speak, and explore its components and their interrelationships, then reconstruct it, all with a view toward understanding how it functions. This way of thinking is appropriate for making a watch or constructing a bridge, and even for determining how a living organism maintains itself. Without the rules of conventional logic, which are rigorously analytical and date back in the history of logic to Aristotle's syllogisms in his *Prior Analytics,* we could not engage in the multitude of activities that make up our everyday lives. A syllogism (Aristotle uses the word *deduction*) is 'a discourse in which, certain things being stated, something other than what is stated follows of necessity from their being so' (23b18). Most famously in elementary philosophy courses, syllogistic logic is illustrated by the propositions: 'All men are mortal / Socrates is a man / Therefore Socrates is mortal.'[1]

But such a deductive system of propositions does not adequately encompass *processes, developments,* and the *unfolding* of phenomena in which potentialities, like seeds, initiate the *becoming* of a given thing or condition. It cannot provide us with an adequate way of thinking out the evolution or history of an ever-differentiating potentiality and grasp its phases in a rational, eductive manner – indeed, of situating mind and body, the natural and the social, the individual and the collective, necessity and freedom in formative dualities that are not petrified 'dualisms', but rather new and complementary modes of emergent phenomena that enrich an unfolding continuum. Hence the tendency of so many people today to adhere to a simplistic reductionism that subsumes all differentiation or else to adopt a view of diversity in which utterly unrelated phenomena – a mere plurality of beings – are promiscuously united into a specious 'Oneness' like so many multicolored billiard balls contained in a wrack.

No – to understand evolution, to think historically, requires more than conventional logic. We have to ascertain the immanent drives that impel undifferentiated potentialities into ever-greater differentiation, complexity, and wholeness. We are obliged to ascertain the great parallels in history that unify humanity – the many similarities among independently developing cultures, the common issues that human beings confront throughout history, and the common solutions they so often devise.

It is not my intention to discuss dialectical logic, as it is usually called in contrast to conventional logic, except to emphasize that we cannot understand humanity, society, and their emergence out of first nature without recognizing humanity's potentiality to *become* more than a product of biological laws, however useful biology may be as a source of insight into the animalistic attributes of human beings.[2] Like all phenomena, humans are always undergoing transformation. They can no more be viewed with fixity than first nature can be reduced to a scenic view on a picture postcard.

As I have emphasized, human biology is rooted in an evolutionary elaboration of a specialized physical system – the nervous system – as well as a variety of anatomical attributes (stereoscopic vision, free forearms, opposable thumbs, and an oral flexibility in producing complex sounds) that have made it possible for our species to advance from adaptive behavior to innovative behavior. The unfolding of this potentiality marked a decisive breach with first nature that yielded the creation of a predominantly cultural evolution, or second nature. This breach, far from being a malevolent and aberrant creation of 'man the destroyer' is, above all, the consequence of potentialities that are latent in the evolution of life itself and that can very well yield the image of 'man the creator'.

To object that human beings might never have evolved but for chance occurrences over the course of organic evolution ignores the compelling fact that humanity *does* exist, and that it did not emerge *ab novo*. In varying degrees, humanity's emergence followed from developmental potentialities and a clearly discernible logic with a surprising degree of evolutionary autogeny. We are products of a self-developmental tendency in natural evolution, not only chance events and conjunctions of them.

Nor is it necessary to invoke supernatural agents to account for humanity's appearance. But by the same token, this species could not have emerged unless there were potentialities in first nature to account for human evolution.

I have also addressed the emergence of culture or second nature in earlier chapters, emphasizing its institutional roots in biological facts such as age groups, gender differences, and kinship ties. It is with the development of society – of history and more precisely with the appearance of civilization – that we are obliged to ask if humanity has indeed progressed or, if not, whether it *can* progress.

If many antihumanists see humanity's redemption in the form of a retreat to a non-interventionist, passive relationship with the natural world, I wish to contend, by contrast, that a crucial function of culture is to render it possible for humanity to *rationally* and *creatively* intervene in the world and improve upon existing conditions, be they the product of natural evolution or social development.

More specifically, the monumental work of social evolution or second nature is to innovatively *transcend* the narrow cultural horizons of early humanity, however beneficent many of them may be; to go beyond the early biologically conditioned social world, based on age cohorts, gender differences, and kinship ties, into an increasingly universalistic, secular, and hopefully rational world. The function of second nature has been to transform the parochial domain of ethnic communities, in which people were fragmented into kin groups based on a common ancestry, into a universal *humanitas* in which people recognize themselves as a species: indeed, to transform tribalized people into urbanized citizens, to exorcise superstition through the insights of reason, and – by no means a trifling task – to endow human beings with the material security to free their bodies and minds from economic uncertainty, the drudgery of toil, and craven submission to the seemingly overwhelming forces of first nature.

In short, insofar as humanity has ascended from a domain of passive animality guided by genetic makeup, myths, and material insecurities, into a more creative, civilized, and free second nature, the function of social evolution in the view of an enlightened humanism is the creation of a society guided by reason. It is in such a rational society that we can be truly human, according to norms worthy of being called ethical.

In a very real sense, then, we are still unfinished as human beings because we have not as yet fulfilled our potentiality for cooperation, understanding, and rational behavior. An enlightened humanism calls on us to be rational as well as imaginative, socially committed as well as highly individuated, and publicly involved as well as personally rounded. This enlightened humanism may sound to antihumanists like the rabid anthropocentrism of an unreconstructed humanist. But in my view humanity is faced with immense social and ecological dislocations not because there is too much civilization but rather because we are *not civilized enough*. I make no claim that social evolution has unilinearly and merrily unfolded toward civilization or that it will necessarily do so. Nor is there any guarantee that we will fulfill our potentialities to achieve a free, rational, and self-conscious society. Even so starkly teleological a philosopher as Hegel viewed 'History' as a 'slaughterbench', however much he regarded social development as the unfolding of reason toward complete human enlightenment.

Indeed, Hegel was hardly unique in his harsh judgment of history. Many of the eighteenth-century French Enlighteners advanced images of history even more critical than his. Opponents of the Enlightenment have mainly caricatured its thinkers and simplified its message, exaggerating its humanist outlook as a crude anthropocentrism if only to highlight their own antihumanist outlook.

But merely to agree that history has been a bloody slaughterbench, in which people commonly acted with terrible brutality, *presupposes* the existence of standards of humaneness, rationality, and virtue that provide the basis for defining that brutality. Without such standards, firmly grounded in reality as well as in philosophical thought, we are lost in a sea of meaningless adjectives and a relativism in which what is humane, rational, and virtuous is merely a matter of personal opinion and individual taste. This personalistic and relativistic approach divests us of the norms by which we may define what it means to be human – and hence our unique potentiality as social as well as individual beings.

In a very broad sense, our potentiality for achieving a rational society consists in the attainment of *freedom*. Freedom consists of a multitude of interrelated attainments: the opportunity to choose between various courses of action, to shape our personal and social lives creatively, to deal with each other and the natural world humanely, to be guided by an ethics of complementarity, to create communal forms of social organization, and to use reason in all our affairs. Hence rationally guided choice, certain basic virtues, and radically democratic institutions, constitute the partly realized potentialities for attaining humanness and achieving a free *humanitas*.

Freedom in this substantial sense is not attainable by animals. Guided by genetic imperatives, the immediate needs of survival and reproduction, and instinct, and distinctly limited in learning ability, animals generally make adaptive adjustments to environmental circumstances. Normally, an animal does not 'make' its world; it exists within a world in which it finds itself. Indeed, the survival of many species is highly vulnerable even to slight changes in habitat. The primitivist identification of 'wildness' or 'wilderness' with freedom in any human sense of multitudinous choices and innovations is grossly misplaced: the behavior of creatures that exist 'in the wild' is greatly restricted by imperatives beyond their understanding and control. No lion is born free, unless by freedom we simply mean the absence of physical confinement. An animal's existence is significantly determined by its inborn behavioral equipment, its fairly circumscribed learning capacity, and its inherited physical ability to sustain itself in a highly precarious world.

To be sure, a relatively intelligent animal will try to find tree cover or a den, say, to avoid the chilling effects of rain; but unless it is imprinted genetically to do so or has learned to build a very crude shelter against inclement weather, it is very much on its own in meeting climatic changes and similar environmental problems.

By contrast, human beings (and to a limited degree, certain non-human primates) can literally *create* choices which do not exist in their natural habitats. They can imagine a great variety of alternatives from which to choose, constructing them in forms that do not exist in first nature. With extraordinary flexibility, they can remake their immediate environments to suit clearly understood or anticipated needs. And very significantly, they can articulate through speech, writing, cooperation, and by other expressive representations, such as pictures, specific aims that go far beyond mere survival, comfort, and self-defense. Reasoning by analogy or by inference and deduction, they can create increasingly complex and effective institutions, customs, and methods of systematic learning, normally developing appropriate ways to guarantee the satisfaction of their emotional as well as their material needs.

In short, human beings can begin, however limited their consciousness at first, to discover that they have the potentiality to go well beyond the existing circumstances of their lives and, with the passing of generations, develop – conceptually as well as materially – new needs and expanding ideas about their own cultural domain. They can establish definable systems of rights and duties; they can rationally explain – even in mythic form – their place in the world as well as in their communities; and they can create mutable bands, tribes, villages, cities, and other elaborate forms of social organization. Not only can they create cultures, but depending upon time, place, and circumstances, they can *expand* their cultures and social ideas. These can be structured and embodied in a variety of ways by creating new methods of working together, distributing the products of their work, formulating belief systems, establishing institutions, and thinking out richer or more complex ideas about life and its meaning, including broad notions of justice and freedom.

To understand the vast historical movement of culture requires dialectical thinking beyond conventional logic, with its basis in the 'law of identity'. For it obliges us to deal with a dialectic of *becoming,* of educing *new* phases out of the seemingly fixed, easily analyzable static facts. It obliges us to address a seemingly antithetical 'other' that always represents what is new and often alien to what is old, even as the new incorporates and modifies older realities.

Yet innovative as we may be as human beings, we nevertheless retain strong animalistic desires to adapt to what exists unless it is difficult, if not impossible, for us to continue. Our animal heritage thus lives on in us as a stultifying conservatism that we may not shake off unless the imperative to change a given state of affairs and beliefs systems emerges as a compelling need or desire. The 'other' or antithesis of what exists is, by virtue of its uncertainty, often very fearsome; it threatens to disestablish deeply entrenched ways of life and belief systems. Indeed, there is no way of knowing how far an antithesis may unsettle stable, time-honored institutions, beliefs, reciprocities, social and personal habits.

It is out of this crucible of choices – whether presented to us by new circumstances or created by human consciousness – that the events that form humanity's chronicles emerge. Events and chronicles are merely changes understood without regard for their meaning, developmental context, or connections to one another – in short, as mere *displacements* in social affairs, like the movement of balls over a billiard table. However carefully reported they may be by chroniclers such as Herodotus or Froissart, such events do not have to be situated in a broad continuum of time. They are mere *events* in the simple sense that they are indistinguishable from episodes, however significant they may be for the people who are involved in them.

It makes little difference over the long term if events and episodes are remembered or forgotten, retained or dispensed with, celebrated or ignored. If remembered, they are usually more entertaining than instructive. As animalistic phenomena, they are not the consequences of a rational development that enlarges overall human experience. They are important to those who have been affected by them, but they are limited to specific times and places.

The *Odyssey,* which recapitulates important aspects of human history in mythic form, tells us of the island 'of the Lotus-eaters, who feast on fruit' that deprives men 'of any desire' and renders them 'forgetful of home', indeed of recollection of the past or concern for the future.[3] They live in an eternal present in which the immediacy of existence is perpetual. They live on the bounty of Nature in bliss and meaninglessness. In fact, they do not exist in time conceived as a flow of changing phenomena, still less as part of an expansive development. The Lotus-eaters exist on the level of animals, for whom existence is always fixed in the present and the immediately given – a condition, I should add, that some primitivists regard as the edenic condition of humanity, to which it should now return, having been afflicted by the 'nightmare' of history and civilization.

Such episodes are not what I mean by history. Events may be compiled as chronicles, unmediated by any association beyond sequential dates; history, by contrast, is an account of a *development* that unfolds as a consequence of the rational elaboration of humanity's potentiality for freedom and self-consciousness. History is in great measure the development of humanity *away* from the Island of the Lotus Eaters into the innovative fullness of freedom and self-consciousness. It consists of the mediations or 'steps' by which human beings have raised themselves out of a cultural void into a cultural development that has a complex past, a conflicted present, and the prospect of an emancipatory future.

History, then, is not what Foucault calls a 'genealogy', by which he means 'local, discontinuous, disqualified, illegitimate knowledges', and which he contrasts with history and its 'claims of a unitary body of theory which would filter, hierarchise and order [those knowledges] in the name of some true knowledge and some arbitrary idea of what constitutes a science and its objects.'[4] Given Foucault's proclivity for arbitrary, 'illegitimate' assortments of facts and events that constitute his own 'encapsulation' of various tortures, oppressions, and hells, he caricatures any endeavor to unearth a developmental meaning even in 'local' and 'discontinuous illegitimate knowledges'. Foucault's 'genealogies' order events through 'filters' of his own that are all the more dogmatic because his premises remain unstated, in contrast to many 'unitary' histories he arrogantly rejects.

Indeed, if it 'hierarchises' human development to assert that one era is more expansive in its concept of freedom, humaneness, rationality, and values than an earlier one, then historians can cheerfully acknowledge the accusation that they are hierarchical. But so much the worse, then, for the 'genealogist', who would dissolve the unfolding of human potentiality or fragment it into scattered 'discontinuous, illegitimate knowledges' that provide us with nothing from which we can develop any perspective beyond the local – and that limit us to celebrating the episodic, the riotous, and the 'ecstatic' as acts of 'resistance' to hierarchy.

On the other hand, to recognize a rational thread of development and rationally educible advances – yes, progress – in human affairs does not mean that there have not been discontinuities, regressions, diversions, and blind alleys. There has been no unilinear and undeviating advance in human affairs. History would indeed be mysterious if it consisted of an unbroken and predestined march toward an idyllic world, unsullied by brutalities and horrors.

But it is far too easy and perverse to make the breaches in second nature into a focal theme. No view is cheaper and more noxious than Theodor Adorno's dictum, 'No universal history leads from savagery to humanitarianism, but there is one leading from the slingshot to the megaton bomb.'[5] Whatever Adorno meant by *universal,* there is a massive history of humanity that consists of growing sensibilities, material achievements, culture, and, let it not be forgotten, great movements guided by high ideals to achieve a free society.

In fact, antihumanists and their 'genealogists' have an advantage over any endeavor to insightfully explore history: they can count on a general ignorance of extraordinary parallels over the course of humanity's development – parallels that reveal a remarkable 'unitary' cultural dimension to our species's history. They can also count on the laziness of thought that is easily wearied by nuances, explanations, and the painstaking effort to determine 'what went wrong' in history and why certain events have warped historical development, particularly during this century.

Given the current popularity of Foucauldian 'discontinuities', what is surprising when we consult history is how unitary it actually has been in areas of the world that did not have contact with each other for immensely long periods of time – indeed, for 10,000 years and possibly more – when enormous changes occurred in the human condition. In many regions of the globe a distinct social evolution occurred that brought growing populations out of small bands into tribal, feudal, and even imperial forms of organization, with almost identical material advances from foraging to large-scale agriculture. What is striking is the incredible similarity of progression in the belief systems and cultural features these regions shared over the course of their developments, from a simplistic belief in spirits probably derived from dreams to spiritual cosmologies and priestly guilds of imposing proportions.

Arguably, the often minute cultural features these historical civilizations shared may have been derivative, carried by traders or diffused by a multitude of possible contacts across land masses – or they might have developed independently. However unlikely it may be, the ancient Near East, for example, may have inspired the agricultural developments, city-states, and kingships in India and the Far East by diffusing agriculture and certain political institutions across Asia.

But it is as certain as any archaeological facts can be that major cultural and material traits arose quite independently in Mesoamerica, a region that could not have had contact with the Near East after the late Paleolithic. What is surprising when Mesopotamia and Mesoamerica are compared is not the fairly secondary differences that divide them but the enormous similarities that unite them. These similarities – not only their shared economic and cultural traits but their shared evolution from bands to large city-states – reveal a stunning unity in human history, from tribal life to fairly advanced civilizations.

The Paleoindians who crossed the large land bridge from Asia to America were undoubtedly late Paleolithic hunter-gatherers with a tool-kit that could not have been more advanced than, say, that of the hunting people who painted caves in the Pyrenees region some 30,000 to 15,000 years ago. With the retreat of the glaciers about 10,000 years ago, Paleoindians left Asia and continued to develop socially in the Americas, with only tentative contacts from Viking seafarers and stray mariners. It is now generally accepted that they learned very little, indeed probably nothing of any importance, from Europeans and Asians for thousands of years.

Yet archaeologists can trace an independent development in Mesoamerican inhabitants from nomadic foragers organized in fairly egalitarian and simple bands into increasingly hierarchical tribes, village gardening communities, feudal agricultural systems, warring kingly city states, and finally in the case of central Mexico, monarchical empires. All exhibit extraordinary parallels with the development of social life elsewhere in the world.

By the same token, in the Near East, late Paleolithic hunting bands and tribes underwent a transition to gardening villages at least 10,000 years ago and thence on to temple and kingly city-states based on the large-scale cultivation of grains (wheat and barley) about 6,000 years ago. Remarkably, in Mesoamerica there is evidence of grain (maize) cultivation and village gardening around 6,000 years ago, followed by a shift from nomadic foraging to a relatively settled village life.

Both regions went on to master pictographic writing, pottery, metallurgy, irrigation, and large-scale agriculture; and a highly functional calendar and mathematics (the Maya even discovered the zero). Both domesticated animals and plants. Both developed priestly, warrior, noble, and royal castes, together with temples, palaces, monumental architecture, and city-states – entirely independently of each other. Eventually, in both regions, some cities expanded to an immense size, supporting ever more craftspeople, merchants, and bureaucrats. Finally, the Aztecs developed an empire comparable in territory, population, and administrative techniques to some of the centralized states in the early Near East. In Mesoamerica as in Mesopotamia, cities engaged in the mass manufacture and trade over wide areas, making it possible for their populations to expand far beyond their agricultural base.

The extent to which status groups, quasi-feudal ties, religious practices, building techniques, and building materials resembled each other in both regions is almost uncanny. Complex status and class systems emerged, along with religious belief systems, deified kings and priestly corporations. Architectural styles were normally geometrical, indicating not only a similarity of style but a command of shared mathematical and structural strategies. Commonalities appear even in such seemingly trivial facts as the use of straw to make clay bricks.

In both regions these city-states became involved more and more in internecine warfare over control of trade routes and land. Systematic warfare was conducted to take captives for large-scale human sacrifices, as was the case not only among the Aztecs but among the Chinese of Anyang during the Shang dynasty some 3,300 years ago. It would be preposterous to ignore this shared evolution in Mesopotamia and Mesoamerica by emphasizing their local differences.

241

My account of these extraordinary similarities – and many more could be cited – is not designed to support the notion of an unwavering unilinear history that all civilizations had to follow. Indeed, for millennia, many people did not develop beyond the band and tribal level of social organization and foraging or horticultural techniques. Nor, where civilizations developed, did every one of them follow a path that corresponds to that of Mesoamerican and Mesopotamian civilizations. Peru's highly totalitarian Inca empire certainly followed a significantly different trajectory. Moreover, the furious warfare in the Mesoamerican 'classic era', some 1,700 to 1,000 years ago, led to the widespread mutual destruction of city-states, for reasons that are still unclear. So destructive was this warfare that many once well-cultivated, irrigated, and densely inhabited areas reverted to tropical jungles. Warfare seems to have become a culturally hypertrophic feature, wherein an increasingly warrior-oriented society developed such exaggerated forms and functions, beyond any service they provided for the cities, that they became ends in themselves and tore down an entire centuries-old society.[6]

Here, to be sure, the parallels diverge. In both cases Mesopotamia and Mesoamerica independently laid the bases – more precisely, created the potentiality – for parallel civilizations. But Mesoamerica saw the destruction of city-states by cultural hypertrophy that led to social stagnation, while Mesopotamian cultural achievements were picked up by Greece, later Rome, and Europe, and advanced to a more rational vision of a future that no tribal society could have developed.

However varied in details, even if warfare was endemic and shamans or priests conjured up terrifying 'imaginaries' (to use Cornelius Castoriadis's expression) that legitimate ongoing bloody sacrifices, these societies followed a unifying logic once they developed agrarian cultures and learned to vastly increase their food supply. Food cultivation makes possible large populations, often followed by an increasing division of labor. When powerful status groups, formed by alliances between chiefs, elders, and shamans, evolved, they all gained prestige, power, and material advantages by their collaboration. Normally, if not invariably, such societies followed a remarkably common path toward state formation, a warrior caste, and economic exploitation that either gave rise to cosmopolitan empires – or led to the ruin of a regional civilization. Indeed, what is surprising, then, are the *shared* stages of development – different in time, to be sure, but almost identical in trajectory – that unite Mesoamerican and Mesopotamian development, commonalities that flatly contradict the Foucauldian notion that a 'unitary' history of humanity is a dogma imposed upon social reality by historians with a 'totalitarian' predisposition for historical directivity and coherence.

The reasons a culture area undergoes a general breakdown rather than advance toward a greater degree of freedom and self-consciousness requires more of a nuanced analysis of history than flippant, selective Foucauldian assertions about the microscopic 'institutionalization' of power. Admirable as Foucault's concern for the mistreatment of imprisoned people may be, his account of the 'birth of the prison' in *Discipline and Punish* is often misleading owing precisely to its limited range of narrative material. The institutionalization of punishment, in fact, was quite as extensive and regimented in the Roman world, for example, as it was in the nineteenth century, and the 'alert gaze' that figures in Foucault's account of Jeremy Bentham's proposed 'panoptic' design for surveillance over prisoners was beggared by various all-encompassing surveillance techniques that were employed throughout history, particularly in ancient latifundia and in modern plantations worked by slave labor.

Foucault's 'genealogical' strategy emphasizes selective secondary, tertiary, and even hypothetical events – a strategy that grossly enlarges their meaning and implications at the expense of larger forces, patterns, and sequences that are found in broad historical accounts. Every bureaucracy and system of coercive power tends to expand and increase its power if it can – and such was the case historically, as legal and disciplinary systems became more entrenched at various times, no less in ancient Rome than in modern Europe. Little in Foucault's work on the institutionalization of power demonstrates that the modern world has been more coercive and punitive than earlier periods of history.

Indeed, antihumanist and postmodernist emphases on the minutiae of experience – valuable as their data may be in sensitizing us to authoritarian institutions and attitudes – often miss the forest for the trees. They are no substitute for broader historical accounts that reveal great cultural evolutionary processes that enlarge the promise for human emancipation. An able archaeologist like V. Gordon Childe, for example – however limited his detailed knowledge of the past may have been, two generations ago – still deserves respectful reading because he had a stronger grasp of macroscopic changes in history than the largely empirical and postmodernist monographers of recent times, whose dogmatic denial of a 'unitary' development of humanity abandons us to a warehouse of factual debris.[7] Contrary to what Foucault suggests, the institutionalization of punishment (and the reduction or elimination of earlier forms of physical punishment like the removal of hands, limbs, and finally death by quartering) was more the product of a specific society than it was a causal factor in shaping that society.

'The urban revolution', as Childe called it, beginning some 7,000 years ago, marked a vast turning point in social evolution, as did the consolidation of city-states into empires and later nations, the transition from Neolithic to the Bronze and Iron Ages, the accumulation of food surpluses and the stability these eras provided in human affairs, as well as the development of leisured elites, and finally the emergence of mass production. Indeed, rudimentary mass production based on assembly-line techniques dates back to the late Paleolithic and to Mesoamerican cities, as well as to Athens, Rome, Alexandria, and Sidon, and to medieval towns in northern Italy and Flanders, finally exploding with the Industrial Revolution in nineteenth-century England.

Thus, to dismiss Gerhard Lenski's fact-laden sequence of hunting-gathering, horticultural, agrarian, and industrial phases of social evolution – to which one can add innumerable intermediate phases – for a fashion-able concern for empirical albeit tendentiously selective minutiae, for example, would shroud over the rich body of history and trivialize human development.[8] Having developed away from the parochial bio-logical facts on which tribal society was based, humanity clearly followed a development that logically led it to construct cities, form complex civ-ilizations, create the fact of citizenship, and achieve ever-broader actual-izations of its potentiality for freedom and self-consciousness. That this development was arrested at certain levels of social evolution here and there or even regressed to earlier social forms does not alter the fact that its civic and economic forms of consociation, and its concepts of selfhood and personal freedom, of broad concepts of justice, responsibility, and empathy for its own kind – even for non-human beings – generally expanded to a point where differences in opinion over the progressive nature of evolution subtly attest to a radically new sensibility about what the human condition *should* be.

Put more concretely: terrible cruelties that were once taken for granted a few thousand years ago, indeed, only a few centuries ago, such as the extermination of entire cities in invasions and wars, now evoke shock where they once did not, even if they have not abated in practice. Today we no longer regard war as such as glorious or heroic. Torture, mental as well as physical, is regarded as shameful, however much it is practiced today – a view that only became widespread with the English, American, and French Revolutions. Elitism itself, once honored and mystified by religion, art, and poetry, is now viewed with suspicion, however much it is a reality of contemporary social life. Nearly every nation-state today tries to depict itself as a democracy, even as it dishon-ors the label in practice.

The prevalence of this higher ethical sensibility, in conjunction with the immense potentiality for providing for the basic material needs of everyone on the planet, due to technological advances and the secularization of knowledge, cannot be dismissed because of Stalin's gulags and Hitler's death camps. At the height of the Greek democracy and the Roman republic, it was conventional wisdom that an entire people could be 'put to the sword' and/or enslaved. Nor could the ancient world have had any thought of abandoning slavery for moral reasons, even after Christianity became ascendant and heightened society's sensitivity to individual uniqueness – indeed, the sanctity of the human soul. Despite terrible wars, the sophistication of military technology, and the ruthlessness of military conflicts, concurrent advances took place in human sensibility, expanding notions of freedom and a greatly expanding ethical awareness of virtue and evil. The mass murder of a people, whether systematically or sporadically, would not have been regarded as unacceptable in premodern times; today it is regarded as heinous and gives rise to widespread moral outrage.

It is easy to render history completely 'discontinuous' and flippantly deny the fact of progress, directivity, and sophistication in human development, wallowing in pessimism and dwelling on the dark side of human behavior. But aside from the incompleteness of such a view, it ignores the long, costly, and often unavoidable maturation process – material as well as cultural – that humanity underwent in emerging from the parochialism of a restricted and mystical world, developing and enlarging its ideals of humaneness and freedom. To fall back on conventional reason's faculty for decontextualizing social behavior would be to dissolve a broad view of history and to reduce our approach to tallying up its assorted virtues and vices. It would reduce us to mechanically classifying advances and retreats in the sophistication of human behavior, and to cultivating a tunnel vision focused exclusively on the horrors that humans have inflicted on each other. It would give precedence to eventful waves, over the sweeping movement of great historical tides.

Yet antihumanists refuse to acknowledge the extent to which our sensibilities have advanced markedly beyond those of 'dwellers' on the Pleistocene savannah and the Paleolithic tundras, beyond a shared fear of demonic spirits that inhabit animistic belief systems, and beyond a view of slavery as a normal condition of life. Having already cleared the way for the replacement of science with magic, they ignore the very real progress from stone tools to cybernetic devices – a history of technology that can rid us of onerous toil and provide us with the free time to manage a rational society. Ultimately they convey the regressive message that human beings are little more than brutes, and highly perverted ones at that.

The existence of a 'unitary' history is attested to not only by shared sequence of many social forms, each emerging out of an earlier one as part of a logic of continuous development; it is also attested to by the emergence of shared and abiding *issues* that are latent in humanity as a uniquely innovative species.

I refer to the conscious imperatives that drive people to insightfully change their environment and render it more secure, safe, abundant, and comfortable with minimal toil. This issue has always shadowed human behavior and thought. Unremittingly, it has demanded resolution, given the technological possibilities and social relations established at any given time.

Indeed, human beings are generally future-oriented. At one time, they may have accepted cyclical rather than linear concepts of time, and the rotation of seasons rather than the flow of history; but even within cyclical notions of time, they have tried to anticipate the problems that await them as one season passes into another. Indeed, the cyclical time within which certain 'primitive' and agrarian peoples lived was not always fatalistic. As Linda Schele and David Freidel put it in their account of the Maya:

> The Maya conception of time ... was very different from our own. Our old adage 'He who does not know history is doomed to repeat it' might have been expressed by the Maya as 'He who does know history cannot predict his own destiny.' The Maya believed in a past which always returned, in historical symmetries – endless cycles repeating patterns already set into the fabric of time and space.

But this does not mean that they were quietistic or passive about the future. Schele and Freidel go on to tell us that 'by understanding and *manipulating* this eternal, cyclic framework of *possibility*, divine rulers hoped to create a favorable destiny for their people.'[9] Hence, not even human beings rooted in cyclical temporal concepts like the Maya were necessarily at the mercy of inexorable changes of seasons. They could intervene in recurring events and alter them – a view that enhanced the function of their divine kings, who supposedly could manipulate the cycle in their own behalf and authority.

Ritual, too, was apparently regarded as a form of intervention, not merely the propitiation of the deities. 'Like the great metaphor of Maya life – the life cycle of maize – the continued well-being of the universe required the *active participation* of the human community through ritual,' Schele and Freidel tell us. 'As maize cannot seed itself without the intervention of human beings, so the cosmos required sacrificial blood to maintain life'[10] – and one may add, a panoply of ritualistic acts that involved the intervention of people into the functions of first nature. Rituals, like the stylized forms of human representation in Paleolithic cave paintings and sculpture, were probably not simply acts of propitiation but acts of human intervention – and eminently manipulative ones at that.

With any given set of conditions, there remains a 'beyond' that is latent with new possibilities for a better way of life, however fixed a people may seem in time and space. History, in fact, is a selective process in which a culture that is not driven to go 'beyond' the cultural confines that circumscribe its development risks the possibility of being overtaken and superseded by one that is more future-oriented. This probably accounts for why one Maya city-state staked out regional 'empires', subjugating others – possibly fairly static ones – or why the Aztecs and Incas established fairly large empires in a selective process that gave them ascendancy over more passive cultures.

We are considering the dynamics of societies that had barely advanced beyond middle or late Neolithic tool-kits, and whose well-being was overwhelmingly dependent upon natural vicissitudes. These vicissitudes significantly affected the well-being of huge populations up to the nineteenth-century revolutions in agricultural and industrial technology, as well as in means of transportation that could end the famines commonly caused not only by climatic vicissitudes but by poor communication between well-stocked regions and famine-stricken ones in the same country. Hence for thousands of years, as far back as the archaeological evidence allows us to judge, humankind was indeed 'united' by shared *concerns* and hence by elemental forces that made its overall evolution anything but 'local' and 'discontinuous', however numerous were the individual cultures that stagnated or even regressed to earlier levels of development, isolated as many of them were by physical features or by plundering invaders.

Thus we can say that a 'unitary' history, broadly speaking, existed that has been driven toward greater complexity, sophistication, and sensibility by the abiding demands that often compelled human beings to become part of a developing cultural continuum. However quietistically oppressed people have accepted their lot in the world, they seldom accepted their degradation without resentment toward materially privileged elites, which often broke out in revolutions as far back as ancient Sumerian and Egyptian times. Recent research suggests that in pre-Columbian America, popular uprisings did away with the centralized or feudal Mississippian mound culture in the midwestern United States, as well as with like societies in Asia, and in Europe during the Middle Ages. We have no way of knowing, due to the destruction of Maya records by their Spanish conquerors, whether or how frequently such revolts by lower classes exploded in Mesoamerica, but it is reasonable to suppose that they occurred.

I have emphasized the continuities and shared problems that exist in human history, the remarkable sequences in periods of social development that parallel each other among cultures that could not have had any contact with each other, and the common problems that faced humanity (the innovative species *par excellence*) because human development constitutes a very new kind of evolutionary process.

We can speak not only of a 'unitary' history – with due allowance for countless variations, degrees of advance, and even fairly static or regressive social conditions – but also of a *universalizing* history.

The word *universalizing,* rather than *universal,* is meant to emphasize the direction in which this overall history tended to unfold: notably, a drift away from the tribal parochialism defined by kinship ties toward an increasingly citified social domain that allowed for strangers to intermingle with each other. Human beings were steadily united by social facts like common vocational, intellectual, and class interests rather than biological facts like common ancestry, gender, and age cohorts.

The most important medium for establishing social commonalities between people of different ancestral lines was the *city* – an increasingly cosmopolitan urban terrain wherein people from different blood lines were able to commingle with each other and develop common interests as craftspeople, merchants, and administrators of various sorts. They often formed mutually protective guilds, embracing civic as well as occupational filiations that were stronger than the blood ties that traditionally cemented tribal forms of organization.

This movement of human beings from folk to citizens, from a life structured around biological facts to one structured around civic (more broadly, social) facts forms the subtly mediated evolution of people into second nature, which in turn constitutes a vast realm of social evolution beyond animal evolution. We can find its occurrence in what archaeologists call 'pristine cities', such as those that arose in Mesoamerica and Mesopotamia. Here the sharing of goods increasingly gave way to bartering and even the use of money-like tokens for the exchange of commodities. Commerce increasingly became an extensive and vital part of ordinary life. Indeed, cities emerged that depended more on their commercial connections with one another than on any shared ethnic ties.

The leveling by commerce of traditional distinctions based on inherited status positions and kinship ties occurred, to be sure, very slowly and irregularly over the course of human history. But its role in replacing folk with citizens was almost unrelenting. Initially, towns and cities were rarely completely civic in the sense of being free of real or fictitious hereditary elites. Nor were they, with rare exceptions, completely secular, in the sense of being dissociated from religious ties. Even classical

Athens, perhaps the most civic and secular of ancient cities, was named after a goddess, and the agendas of its citizens' assemblies were divided into sacred and profane items. The city's festivals intermingled secular with religious themes, just as trade fairs in Mayan city-states accompanied religious fairs, attracting people over wide regions of Mesoamerica. Such admixtures of the religious with the secular, indeed of the holy with the profane, persisted well into the Middle Ages. Only later, with the great democratic revolutions of the eighteenth century were Church and State definitively separated from each other, as was the religious from the secular. Civic life thereupon assumed a totally secular character, untainted by differences in religious creeds, ethnicity, and archaic traditions.

Thus a universalizing history – which we can interpret as a 'unitary' phenomenon only if we do not to lose sight of its immense implications – established the groundwork for a generalized *humanitas*. At various times in history this eminently humanistic goal of universality was raised and supported by radical movements, albeit ideologically, as a spiritual desideratum. Christianity conferred an egalitarian status on all human beings, in which everyone could hope for the salvation of their soul after death, and quasi-religious utopians tried to translate such egalitarianism into calls for freedom from oppression and happiness, which could be attained in an admittedly ideal society, commonly fashioned along monastic lines.

This account would be incomplete, however, if I failed to emphasize that it was primarily in Europe that a remarkable constellation of historical and ideological factors converged to produce a common emphasis on reason, the importance of the individual, and a healthy naturalism – unequaled in so fecund a combination by other cultures. The reasons for this unusual constellation are not difficult to explain. The combination of Germanic with Roman law, which together gave a common emphasis to the interests of the community as well as the individual; the growing sense of personal worth and uniqueness that Christianity conferred on the individual soul; the rational criteria in which European theology, particularly that of Thomas Aquinas, was rooted; and very significantly, the mixed economy of free peasants, yeoman farmers, urban craftspeople, a fairly independent commercial bourgeoisie, and relatively weak feudal lords – all, from the fourteenth century onward, produced a variegated, rounded, and innovative civilization whose diversity of forces, spiritual as well as natural, played against each other in a creative unity in diversity. While non-European civilizations fell into cultural torpor, Europe gathered considerable momentum from the interplay of its constituents, giving it a dynamism unequaled anywhere else in the world.[11]

The religious and quasi-religious patina that clung to egalitarian aspirations was not removed from history until the eighteenth century – notably, with the emergence of the Euro-American Enlightenment. For the first time on a significant scale, a new and powerful movement to secularize knowledge and foster rational canons of thought swept up the educated strata of Europe and English-speaking America, creating a sense of 'world citizenship' based on reason, naturalism, and science rather than faith, supernaturalism, and metaphysics.

Although by no means a homogeneous phenomenon – profound differences in outlook, for example, separate a Deist like Voltaire from an atheist like Diderot or a mechanist like La Mettrie from a dialectician like Hegel – all of these thinkers shared a common belief in a society guided by reason. They held that the natural world could best be understood by science, and to one degree or another they believed in the scientific view of the natural world, and in the malleability – and educability – of people. And notoriously these days, they believed in the possibility of human progress – not as a linear advance toward a glowing future but as a prospect, indeed a hope, that the future would be better, freer, and more rational than the present. As I indicated in an earlier chapter, it would be simplistic, as I have already noted, to insist that the author of *Candide* (Voltaire) held a conviction that the world is necessarily beneficent, or that the author of 'Old Man's Tale' in *The Supplement to Bougainville's Journey* (Diderot) regarded European civilization as an unrelieved blessing. The author of *Man the Machine* (La Mettrie) would have had nothing in common with the author of *The Science of Logic* (Hegel) in their definitions of reason.

But the Enlightenment was both an idea and an *ideal:* it advanced a vision, often quite spiritually charged, of the aborning of a new time in which the world would be guided by reason and freed of superstition, despotic rule, and hereditary privilege. It militantly demanded freedom of expression, the unimpaired exchange of ideas, and a deep concern for human material well-being.

The Enlightenment in all its forms never advanced beyond an ideal – more precisely, a program for intellectual reformation – but it was forward-looking in its hopes, progressive in its ideas, and deeply humanistic in its concern for human welfare. Translated into action, it nourished the ideas of the American revolutionaries – those avowed 'citizens of the world' such as the Virginia aristocrat Thomas Jefferson and the great plebeian Tom Paine. It reached one of its highest peaks in the Declaration of Independence in the United States and the Declaration of the Rights of Man in France, both legitimating revolution as great moral and political acts in the onward march of humanity away from tyranny of the mind as well as government.

But the fact that humanity that could not be free without the free time to *practice* freedom led, by the next century, to those great socialist movements that demanded not only political democracy but economic democracy – the public ownership of the means of production and the distributions of goods according to need. The Enlightenment quest for a political community comprehended by reason was rounded out by the socialist quest for an economic community comprehended by reason. Unless the basic means of life were placed at the service of human needs, argued socialists of all kinds, it meant little if political institutions, ostensibly democratic, were achieved. The use of these institutions would remain the privilege of those who had the material means and the free time to engage in public administration, thereby mystifying social problems by reducing them merely to legislative problems to be resolved between contending parties and parliamentarians.

It would not be sentimental to say that in that era, when socialism was fully wedded to democracy in material and political terms and further was equipped with concrete strategies for sweeping social change, humanity reached its most inspired, promising, and 'enchanted' moment. The disillusionment that directly preceded the outbreak of the First World War among European intellectuals – a disillusionment that Nietzsche articulated more clearly than he knew – reflected a climate of growing fear within the middle classes of Europe. It was not simply the growth of a 'technological society' divested of romantic heroics that frightened them but a seemingly revolutionary workers' movement – the stirring of the despised 'herd' – that seemed on the point of mastering the social issues that had haunted human history for millennia. Large socialist and syndicalist workers' movements seemed poised to seize power, while the governing classes were completely unnerved, as Bismarck's reforms to head off socialism in Germany reveal. It now seemed that the stirring of the 'herd' had opened the *practical* possibility of bringing humanity's potentialities for freedom to fruition in all aspects of reality. Among Marxists at least, no belief seemed more certain than the inevitability of socialism as an irresistible consequence of social laws.

Much as the horrors of the First World War dimmed this certainty with its revelation that civilization was more tenuous than the Western society had once believed, the Bolshevik Revolution lifted the sense of popular despair created by the war, redeeming for a time the promise of the Enlightenment and earlier European socialisms. Despite the failure of various continental socialist uprisings between 1919 and 1921, the 'enchanted' moment did not disappear. Indeed, it retained an extraordinary degree of life even as Stalin was engaged in tainting and finally bringing these hopes to grief. What cannot be recovered easily by the present generation of antihumanists and postmodernists is the sense of crisis, *yet one still pregnant with hope,* that existed during the interwar period between 1918 and 1939. Indeed, as late as the 1930s people had few sides to choose from, given the extremes of economic collapse, fascism, a still-powerful Left, the Spanish Civil War, and finally the imminence of a war that many expected would either mark the end of civilization or produce worldwide revolution.

The crisis that produced socialist movements in the last century has not disappeared. What has changed is the nature of the crisis and the way in which increasing numbers of people are responding to it.

Auschwitz has become for the present era what the slaughter of an entire generation of young men on the Western and Eastern fronts was for the interwar generation – the source of doubts about the West's claim to a humane civilization. But the interwar generation refused to reject entirely the Enlightenment and its promise of progress, as long as the *idea* of revolution – which the Russian Revolution of 1917 and the Spanish Revolution of 1936, seemed to legitimate – persisted. If humanity had indeed advanced, despite its regressions at various times, there was no reason to feel that the universalizing of the human condition would come to an end. Humanity was indeed an 'enchanting' phenomenon.

But more than at any time in the twentieth century, the *hope* that the interwar generation retained is now being subverted, for reasons that lie partly in the way the crisis is being interpreted. The classical era of social-ism, more precisely the era of *rational* rather than 'scientific' socialism, insightfully regarded the leveling and universalizing role of commerce as a means for transforming human beings in all their parochial mutations into a *humanitas,* united by its unique commonalities. Commerce – more specifically the commercial economy in its most advanced capitalistic form, based on commodity production – would (it was hoped) advance technology to the point where production for use rather than for exchange (or profit) would cease to be a chimerical ideal.

Our own era after the Second World War, however, no longer sees the reaction to the ills of capitalism as *social* problems to be solved by *social* means. Modern social pathologies are now attributed to effects rather than causes: the growth of technology, population, personal atti-tudes, even civilization itself – in short, to humanism, anthropocentrism, reason, science, and the like. Even though market competition and the global concentration of capital stare us in the face as the direct sources of social and ecological dislocations, these forces are currently being mysti-fied by antihumanism and renamed 'consumerism', 'anthropocentricity', loss of 'identity', and an 'absence of the sacred'.

The need to form social movements – so clear in the classical era of radical social thought – has been supplanted by the need to form encounter groups or ashrams for attaining Buddhist 'enlightenment'. If all else does not fully satisfy – and satisfaction is typically what contemporary mysticism is in the business of supplying – one may always take the voyage backward to the 'primitive' or to a recovery of ancestral 'origins' to immunize oneself against a turbulent social reality. Much of this flight to origins, to the unmediated world of instant experience, and to a divesture of reason, subjectivity, and intellectuality is legitimated by various postmodern 'immediatisms' that plead the case for instant and intuitive experience.

This 'decentering' of the social in favor of the personal, of intellectual analysis in favor of intuition, of reason in favor of feeling, and of a public life in favor of personal 'authenticity' – all, taken together as a cultural, even an aesthetic agenda for the turn of this century, constitute a major ideological subversion of any endeavor to achieve a rational society.

For what is ultimately at issue in this mutation of the social into the personal, indeed, this regression into the biological, the mystical, and an unmediated primality, is the *nature of humanity* itself. Either humanity is merely an animal species, perhaps more destructive than most, subject to blind and overwhelming 'forces of Nature', and as dispensable as a mosquito that exists on the mantle of Gaia; or it is a remarkable *transformative* agent that has produced a richly mediated history and a radically new evolutionary pathway of unequaled creativity and promise in giving meaning to the planet.

Given humanity's increasingly expansive knowledge of the world around it, its ability to remake that world (including the social world) along rational lines, and its innovation of values and institutions in an evolving, albeit very incomplete second nature, serious people are obliged to take a radically humanistic stand in upholding the 'enchanted' qualities of our species. A humanistic stand does not deny in any way that human beings can behave barbarously and with terrifying cruelty toward each other and toward non-human life-forms. Nor does it deny the need, already given immense weight in the New Age, mystical, and anti-humanistic literature of our time, for a new sensibility – one that highly values animals, forests, and ecological diversity – as *only* human beings can.

My call for the re-enchantment of humanity is meant not simply to reiterate, as I have for decades, the need for an ecological sensibility. Rather, it is to emphasize what is *not* being said today in this time of crisis – indeed, what by its very absence is producing a major lacuna in the causes of this crisis. In a society riddled by hierarchy and classes, human beings are too divided by conflicting class interests, ethnic distinctions, gender differences, and disparities in wealth to be regarded as a culpable species. Beneath the so-called 'population bomb', the deforestation of the planet, the diminution of biotic diversity, and the pollution of Gaia are the same underlying causes: an increasingly competitive marketplace, which leads to the unending growth of production so that one corporate entity can gain a competitive edge over its rivals. This competitive drive forces capital to pursue sources of cheap 'raw materials' in the farthermost recesses of the world's land masses and even its oceanic depths, irrespective of its impact on the well-being of humanity and the future of the biosphere.

To obscure this social cause of nearly all our basic problems today – economic as well as ecological, cultural as well as institutional, and personal as well as political; worse still, to conceal it, however inadvertently and clumsily, by blaming this devastation on 'our' malfeasances in reproducing, consuming, and seeking a materially rewarding life – this obfuscation fosters misanthropy, mystical quietism, and the withdrawal of an incalculable number of people from the public sphere into private life.

The need to address very real problems is replaced by an ambience of etherealization, 'spiritualization', and a new religiosity. New masks are added to a society that already thrives on its concealment from critical insight. The mask of exploitation that capital created, in Marx's view, by 'mysteriously' appropriating the surplus labor of its working class and the fetishistic quality of the commodity has produced the commodification of humanity's own 'fetishes' – its various belief systems, values, and symbols, which are now systematically marketed as cultural snake oil for remedying our grim social and personal pathologies.

Thus we seem to be captive to things of our own making, whether they be deities, ideologies, mystical forces, 'angels', myths, magical practices, misanthropies, transcendental value systems, institutions, social relationships, technologies, laboratories – and mundane commodities. Although all are humanly created phenomena, they have been woven around us like a cocoon by shamans and shamanesses, not to speak of mystical or theological evangelists. The antihumanist culture has itself become a commodity to be marketed, like television sets and VCRs, in spiritual boutiques and department stores.

Either the commodification of the 'fetishes' will be brought to an end, or our most cherished humanistic values and goals will yield to cultural kitsch for titillating weary bourgeois. Worse, the thanatology that surfaces from time to time among acolytes of the Gaia Hypothesis, deep ecology, and various antihumanist sects is cheapening the value of human life. If human beings are nothing but proliferating fleas on the body of Gaia, there is no reason in principle to single them out as personalities that deserve respect. Such attitudes are the raw material that could allow us to consider famines, epidemics, and worse as purely biological in origin, letting the hungry, homeless, and even whole peoples perish.

The re-enchantment of humanity begins with the disenchantment of archaic ghosts: the spirits derived from the world of incomprehensible dreams; the hidden realm of the sacred and its deities – which, as cynically formulated by shamans and priests, are simply anthropomorphic projections of human beings themselves; the mystical search for an unmediated or, equivalently, 'immediate' primality that effaces history and its wealth of experience; the edenic myth of original sin, secularized into a view of human nature as tainted by civilization; the hypostasization of the irrational and intuitive as the most 'authentic' means of 'disclosing' reality or 'Being'; and not least, the class and status interests that have perpetuated domination over thousands of years, including the idea of the 'domination of nature'.

To denounce technology and science in particular because their emancipatory promise has been brought to the service of domination and destruction is like denouncing a concern with public affairs because attempts to achieve the public good may benefit evil people as well as virtuous ones. If freedom is to be equated with mere survival in a world infused with myth and magic, then the less developed an aboriginal culture is, the freer it is – which is to say, the less burdened by writing, literature, adequate shelter, a secure food supply, and medical practices that preserve life. If this state of 'innocence' be freedom, then hyenas and zebras are freer than any 'primal' human beings who are obliged to live with social obligations and customs, not to speak of endless nightmarish fears.

Nor can human beings be free in a society, however pristine, if much of their lives is guided by the need to meet the material requirements for existence. That technology and science have been used for terribly oppressive ends does mean that they must invariably or inevitably be used in such a manner. Without technology and science, everyday life descends to one degree or another to the mere maintenance of one's own existence, and no rituals, magical practices, or myths can supplant the need to continually focus on survival. To attack technology and science as such is to recreate a mythic patina for the social order that misuses them and to exculpate the real culprits – those who use knowledge exclusively to accumulate wealth and power. Indeed, those who, with preposterous demands to return to the Paleolithic, denounce civilization, rationality, technology, and science as such, are merely apologists for the *status quo*.

Only by removing the fetishes that are obscuring our capacity to see reality as it is and as it *should* be, can we re-enchant humanity as a creative and innovative agent in the world and the living potentiality for self-realization as rational beings. Such rational beings can be expected to have an ethical responsibility for the welfare of non-human life *precisely* because they are sensible to the pain, suffering, and death of all living beings. If it is true that first nature, like Lovelock's Gaia, is 'blind' to the reality of needless misery – then only the human mind, freed of its mystical and exploitative trammels, can really know what is actually needless and what cannot be avoided. Only that mind, in fact, can become a presence in dealing consciously not only with its own affairs but with those of the natural world. In short, only human beings can, for better or worse, possess an eminently sophisticated form of knowledge, the product of reason, science, and experience, and only they are, potentially at least, that most marvelous or 'enchanted' of all beings: knowing beings for whom a sense of place, responsibility, care, and futurity is possible.

Notes

1 *The Complete Works of Aristotle*, vol. 1, ed. Jonathan Barnes (Princeton: Princeton University Press, 1984), p. 40.

2 To gain an appreciation of this developmental logic or form of reasoning, the interested reader can turn to G. W. F. Hegel's *Science of Logic*, which assembles all the logical categories known to the eighteenth century in an eductive continuum of truly magnificent proportions. The work has haunted – and perturbed – philosophy for nearly two centuries. See also Murray Bookchin, *The Philosophy of Social Ecology: Essays in Dialectical Naturalism*, rev. ed. (Montreal: Black Rose Books, 1995).

3 *The Odyssey of Homer*, trans. Ennis Rees (New York: Modern Library, 1960), p. 139.

4 Michel Foucault, *Power/Knowledge*, ed. Colin Gordon (New York: Pantheon Books, 1980), p. 83.

5 Theodor Adorno, *Negative Dialectics* (New York: Seabury Press, 1973), p. 320.

6 Cultural or institutional hypertrophy is by no means unique to Mesoamerica or any single region of the world. It occurred throughout ancient, medieval, and clearly modern history where capital accumulation is completely out of control and threatens not only to tear down social life as such but the natural world as we know it today.

7 V. Gordon Childe, *What Happened in History* (Harmondsworth, Middlesex: Pelican Books, 1942).

8 See Gerhard Lenski, Jean Lenski, and Patrick Nolan, *Human Societies: An Introduction to Macrosociology*, 6th ed. (New York: McGraw-Hill, 1970). Where Foucault's 'genealogies' are structured around stories, Lenski and his colleagues face the more demanding challenge of generalizing great quantities of data into a meaningful sequence.

9 Linda Schele and David Freidel, *A Forest of Kings: The Untold Story of the Ancient Maya* (New York: William Morrow, 1990), p. 18, emphasis added.

10 *Ibid.*, p. 19, emphasis added.

11 If these remarks seem Eurocentric, so be it. I have an immense respect for cultural creativity wherever it exists – whether in Asia, Africa, Polynesia, or Australia. But the fatalistic religion of the East is not on a level comparable to revolutionary Puritanism, nor are Taoism and Buddhism – particularly as filtered through California's Mystical Zone – comparable to the Renaissance, the Enlightenment, and socialism in its various forms, let alone to such great social eruptions as the English, American, and French revolutions.

Epilogue

What alternatives do we have to the antihumanistic moods percolating through Euro-American culture today?

To exude nothing but optimism would be as simplistic as the pessimism I have criticized in this book. Whether a rational choice is possible before the present market society exhausts itself in a frenzy of destruction is certainly debatable; capitalism – whose corrosive workings are abetted, not determined, by an ever more powerful technology – is spreading into the remotest areas of the planet. Europe and North America are not alone in being shaken to their foundations by the system they spawned less than two centuries ago. Today, large parts of Asia, Africa and Latin America have also been swept into its fold. Capital has become as 'rhizomatic' as anything treasured by Gilles Deleuze and Félix Guattari, whose concepts play neatly into the imagery of global capitalism.

But whatever may be the possibilities for a rational society in reality, a serious question still arises: is the existing reality *rational*? Thought too must develop its agenda, so to speak. It must always project ideas and their logic beyond what is given to us as the irrational 'real'. The serious thinker must look beyond the 'real' to speculate *what should be* rather than validate *what is*. By *what should be,* I mean the very real but latent possibility of an unfolding freedom and self-consciousness so treasured over centuries of thought and social action. As Marx so pithily put it: 'Not only must the idea follow the real, but the real must follow the idea.' Indeed, I would argue that the idea, conceived as the rational, must guide the 'real'; that is to say, it must seek the rational actualization of human potentiality and always preserve its ethical role of criticizing an irrational or 'untruthful reality'.

This is the function I have assigned to this book: a critique of the false existents of our time and the ideologies that reinforce them, particularly antihumanism. Thought can suggest rational alternatives to *what is,* and I have propounded those that I hold to be rational under the rubric of social ecology in a dozen books. Without pretending to be sanguine, a few guidelines for a rational future may be useful.

First, we must recover the social core that explains our present ecological crisis, a recovery that includes the need for an ecological sensibility. This core constitutes the heart of an enlightened humanism that is both critical and reconstructive, thoughtful and practical, speculative and interventionist. These views sharply break with antihumanistic myths of 'the primitive', 'immediatism', 'deep ecology', and the tendency to reduce humanity to one species among many, equatable to the others in 'intrinsic worth'. This view of humanity is fodder for the growing misanthropy, failure of nerve, indifference to human suffering, and denigration of reason and individuality in our time. For if human beings are nothing more than two-legged creatures who are subject to the same unfeeling and mindless 'laws of nature' celebrated by Gaians, Malthusians, microcosmologists, sociobiologists, and the like, then another Auschwitz is more than possible.

Second, we must reinforce the powers of reason to radically project the vision of a new society that would completely replace the present one. Tragically, we already presuppose the existence of commodity production, the marketplace, and capitalism as though they were God-given, beyond the pale of history and other forms of human relationships. A new society, I have contended for decades, must be a libertarian 'Commune of communes', a confederal network of balanced, directly democratic, and decentralized communities united administratively by councils on a regional and interregional level, constituting a counterpower against the centralized nation-state that prevails today. By 'direct democracy', I mean face-to-face assemblies of free *citizens,* as distinguished from folk, ethnic, or gender groups guided by their own special interests. A community that is not united by a general human interest, however riven it may be by disagreements over issues, is structured to tear itself apart over tangible privileges and particularistic concerns. Such particularistic groups with their own socioeconomic interests render citizenship impossible because they place their own concerns above the general welfare.

Third, we must advance technology and science along lines that will diminish work time (the realm of necessity) and enlarge free time (the realm of freedom). No people can be truly free if the needs of all are not satisfied and if the time needed to exercise the administration of public affairs is not available to all. That our needs should be rational and that we must value quality over quantity as well as aesthetics over gross appetites hardly requires emphasis. But people should be free to *choose* the life-style they want. Lacking the right to do so, they will remain with a sense of enforced privation that makes irrational choices seem desirable.

Fourth, we must totally reconceptualize our ideas of justice and freedom. No one is 'equal' to everyone else in *any* society, whether it be in terms of our personal diminishing powers in the life-cycle or the different capacities, experiences, and knowledge that distinguish one person from another (such as physical strength, certain abilities, and the like). A new society will want to be guided by an ethics of complementarity, as I have called it, that tries to *equalize* the differences within and between people – in short, that will be guided by an 'equality of unequals' – rather than retain the pretensions of justice that regard 'all people' as equal, notably as an 'inequality of equals'. Unlike justice, which works with the pretension that all are equal in theory, despite their many differences in fact, freedom makes no pretense that all are equal but tries to compensate for the inequalities that occur with age, physical infirmity, and different abilities.

It remains to be seen if the market society that prevails today will eventually so devitalize public life that an enlightened humanism will be untenable in the coming decades. Indeed, the human enterprise may end in wars, demoralization, instability, and an authoritarian society. Nor can we exclude the possibility that advances in technology and science will create new sources of non-polluting energy, genetically engineered foods, forests, and food animals that will largely absorb the biosphere by a technologically contrived sociosphere. In which case, Gaia will be turned into a plaything of corporate giants, to be manipulated freely for the benefit of profit and capital expansion.

If this should happen at some time in the future, antihumanists will have contributed to this dismal alternative because they perpetuate a grossly alienating atmosphere of indifference to humanity's social plight. The logic of their premises is a misanthropic view of humanity's most remarkable qualities: its rationality and capacity to act upon the world. It is not quietism and Asian resignation, so widely propagated by antihumanists of all kinds, that can save us from so dark a fate but activism and militancy. We live in a time when the free and rational society humanists have sought to achieve is barely a stone's throw away. But perhaps because of that fact, it will require a great *ethical* effort to cross the threshold from the old to the new. The achievement of freedom must be a free act on the highest level of intellectual and moral probity, for if we cannot act vigorously to free ourselves, we will not deserve to be free.

Index

75; Hardin on 78; heredity and 78; Malthus on 70
Popper, Karl 207–8, 223
population: deep ecology and 107–9; early views on 36; ecology movement and 83; Ehrlich on *see Population Bomb*; fertility rates and 80–2; food surpluses and 64–5; growth of *see* population growth; *see also Population Bomb*
Population Bomb (Ehrlich) 84n; biological reductionism in 65–6; on capitalist growth 65; Cold War and 63–4; on compulsory regulation 62; on compulsory sterilization 62, 65; for Department of Population and Environment 62; erroneous predictions in 64–5; on family planning 61–2; on financial controls 62; impact of 36, 59–60; misanthropy in 60–1; precursors of 76; on sex selection 63; social myopia of 65–6; on triage 63–4
Population Council 81
population growth: declines in 80–2; early 242; employment and 80; food surpluses and 64–5; lifeboat ethic and 79; statistics on 80–3; 'Tragedy of the Commons' thesis and 78–9; urbanization and 82; women and 82; *see also* Malthus, Thomas; *Population Bomb*
Postmodern Condition (Lyotard) 204n
postmodernism: antihumanism and 176–7; antirationalism of 176; background of 172–5; Baudrillard and 200–201; capitalism and 176–7; civilization and 176; commonalities in 175–7; Deleuze-Guattari and 198–9; Derrida and 192, 195–6; disenchantment and 172; Enlightenment and 172–3; Feyerabend and 222–3; Foucault and 180–6; Heidegger and 191–2, 194–5; Latour and 212; logocentricity and 232; Lyotard and 200; Nietzsche and 177–80; nihilism and 201; relativism of 176; science and 176;

social function of 175; socialism's failures and 172–3; truth and 176
Post-Scarcity Anarchism (Bookchin) 117n
potentiality: humanity's 232–4; in logic 232–3
power: early 242; Feyerabend on 225; Foucault on 181; science as source of 214
Power/Knowledge (Foucault) 202n, 256n
prehistoric peoples: aesthetic sentiments of 131; animal extinctions caused by 140–2; animism of 134–5; art of 28–9, 128–9, 131–2, 145, 247; civilization and 120–1; counterculture and 137; dream world of 133; environmental changes by 130–40; feminism and 126–9; fertility techniques of 130; figurines of 127–9; hierarchies among 134; 'Human Revolution' of 139; ignorance of 133, 134; industrial techniques of 134; lifespan of 31; misconceptions about 126–30, 133; modern aborigines and 126; Nature and 123–4, 127, 132; sacred among 130–1; scavenging by 138–9; social development of 240–1; spiritism among 132–3, 135; sympathetic magic of 132–3; technological advances of 139–40; unnatural features of 124–5; varieties of 24, 26
'Prehistoric Overkill' (Martin) 147n
prelapsarian outlook: Ellul's 167; Heidegger's 168, 170; Mander's 163, 165; postmodernist 176
priests, early 240
primality: antihumanism in 229; cultic 114; minimalism and 229–30; reason and 229
Primitive Culture (Tylor) 147n
primitive peoples *see* aboriginal peoples, modern; prehistoric peoples
primitivism vii, 259; cultural hypertrophy and 137; culture and 123–5; deep ecology and 89–90, 136; influence of 228; New Age and 125; primality of 229

primitivists 120–46: Ellul and 167; irresponsibility of 122–3; Mander and 165; myths of 123; prehistoric sensibilities and 122, 124–30; romanticism of 145; technology and 156, 165
privatism, growth of 114
production, increases in 65–6
profit 165; *see also* capitalism
progress: antihumanism and 231–2; artistic 231; denial of 228; Enlightenment and 148–50; evidence for 231–2, 239, 240–5; Foucault's denial of 184; postmodernist critique of 173; history and 239; Nietzsche and 179; technological 245; *see also* civilization
proletariat, Ellul on 168
Prometheus 149
Protagoras 225
Protestant Reformation 1, 257n
psychological issues: contemporary centrality of 113, 114; in science 207
Psychology Today Omnibook (Matson) 113, 119n
punishment: early 243; Foucault on 243
Puritanism, revolutionary 257n
Pygmies, Ituri forest 136, 142, 144
Pyne, Stephen J. 140, 147n

'Question Concerning Technology' (Heidegger) 171n
quietism: in antihumanism 260; Heidegger's 169–70
Quine, W. V. O. 216

Rabinow, Paul 202n
racism: Malthusianism and 70; in United States 75, 76
Ramer, Andrew 119n
Rape of Man and Nature (Sherrard) 226n
rational society 5; problems of 33, 133; prospects for 232–6; technology for 162–3
reason: advances in 231, 238–9; anti-science and 212; Christianity and 1–2; conventional 232–3; Deleuze and Guattari on